The Question of David

The Question of David

A Disabled Mother's Journey Through Adoption, Family, and Life

Denise Sherer Jacobson

CREATIVE ARTS BOOK COMPANY

Berkeley •1999

Front cover and back cover illustrations by
David Jacob Jacobson, author's son, first grade

Denise Sherer Jacobson photo by Doyle Saylor

Cover and book layout by
Wayne Pope, Pope Graphic Arts Center

For information contact:
Creative Arts Book Company
833 Bancroft Way
Berkeley, California 94710

EIN SOF Communications
6380 Wilshire Boulevard, Suite # 125
Los Angles, California 90048
(310) 578-5955

ISBN 0-88739-201-6 Paper
0-88739-145-1 Hard Cover
Library of Congress Catalog Number 97-68993

Printed in the United States of America

Dedication

In memory of my loving mother,
Lillian Blauschild Sherer,
who always knew.

Acknowledgements

In writing this book, THE QUESTION OF DAVID, I've felt as if I've been on a long journey. Many times I wasn't even sure where my path was going or how my trip would end. Fortunately, I met people along the way who guided me over the rockiest roads and befriended me along the loneliest stretches.

First, I would not have even gotten on the highway if not for my mother, Lillian Sherer, who had decided I would be a writer after hearing my first poem when I was seven. It wasn't until twenty-five years later when Edwin Gordon, a distant cousin with a long, successful career as a writer, boldly gave me a much needed push onto the on-ramp. After grumbling for a few months, I stepped on the gas and joined a writing workshop taught by feminist writer, Sandy Boucher. With Sandy's guidance, and enough patience for both of us, I began learning the craft of writing.

Four years later, a story unfolded involving a six-week-old baby, who might be disabled, in need of a family. An unconventional plan to find a home for him had been hatched by two ingenious women I had yet to meet, Kathleen Duckett and Colleen Starkloff. In their vigilant search, Colleen put out a call to a mutual friend, one of the foremost leaders in the disability community, Judy Heumann. Judy led her to Neil and me. Thanks to them, my life has never been the same.

I had no idea when I began writing about the adoption of our son David, that the story would grow into this book. The writing itself has, at times, been incredibly satisfying, and at other times, extremely difficult. Since this book is about family, I drew upon the rich context of the families I've been and still am a part of, the Sherers, Spiegels, and Jacobsons. Delving into my own history with my sister Shelley, my parents, and my in-laws challenged me to not only tell my story, but gave me an opportunity to appreciate theirs.

I'm astounded when I think of all the people who've had connections to the development of this book. My gratitude extends to the following individuals for believing in my work and encouraging me through their words and efforts: Marcy Allencraig, Gabrielle Kelley, and Allan Goldstein (for wanting more of the story), John Raeside, Martha Casselman, Candice Fuhrman, Mimi Roth, and Adair Lara.

I've also been fortunate in being surrounded by a community of family and friends, who, in one way or another, have supported and nurtured me in this ten-year endeavor: Norma Gordon, Janet Kaplan, Barbara Reiner, Ann Cupolo Freeman, Joni Breves, Nancy Bailey, Ched Myers, Freida Engel, Jan Santos, Valerie Vivona (for lending me THE COLOR PURPLE), Corbett O'Toole (for dragging me to John Raeside's class), Judi Rogers, Marge Madigan, and Elaine Pomerantz. My special thanks goes again to Sandy Boucher, and to Doyle Saylor and Susan Driscoll for being almost at my beck and call during the final stages of manuscript editing, proofreading, and packaging.

I am extremely grateful to the staff at Creative Arts Books, and especially, Don Ellis, for having the vision and wisdom to take a chance, and his assistant editor, Jenny Malnick, for following through. My gratitude extends to copy editor Nancy Riddiough, for patiently marking my many ellipses.

My acknowledgement also goes to my friend and publicist, Tari Susan Hartman, for realizing endless possibilities.

I saved mention of the two people most dear to me for last, my husband Neil and my son David. Without them I could never have written this book, for without them there would be no story.

Foreword

Ever wonder what your mother thinks are the most challenging parts of the career of motherhood? Or how every tiny detail of her day of on-the-job mothering influenced the way you grew up? Denise Sherer Jacobson's "The Question of David" reveals a first-time mother's most intimate emotions, fears, and uncertainties about being a competent mother. These are the universal truths all first-time mothers have, with one added dimension--she's a mother with a significant disability. Yet, in this rich tapestry of Sherer Jacobson's truth telling, her disability is but one strong thread woven into a textured fabric of motherhood. "Her" mothering faces the most critical challenge that most mother's don't--society's age old skepticism and prejudice.

That's the importance of "The Question of David." While the premise of the book begins with a disability focus, the subjects that move us from page to page are universal to women, wives, new mothers, and caregivers in every life category. Denise Sherer Jacobson takes us inside her head, her heart, even her bedroom in exploring the landscape of every woman's most intense experience, the transition from womanhood to motherhood. Though her narrative eye is constantly peeled for the differences that most illuminate her experience, what emerges for the reader is a touching statement on how much we all have in common.

As a working mother and television news anchor, I found a kindred spirit in Denise Sherer Jacobson. My own physical deformity is constantly visible, both in daily life and on camera. I am practiced in the art of pretending that my disability blends into the image others might choose to have of me. But my viewers, my friends, and even my family would find some of my deepest thoughts and fears and joys revealed in this raw, edgy, audacious journal.

Sherer Jacobson's book is a stunning wake-up call as we enter the 21st century; that disability rights must continue to emerge as our last great civil rights frontier. In the United States, this century brought unprecedented social advancement for women and racial minorities. But 54 million Americans with disabilities still struggle to evade the pernicious label "handicapped," the disability equivalent of "colored." Society most often perceives, defines, and categorizes us by our "conditions," not grasping that, for the majority of us, we have already incorporated them into our makeup. Our disabilities are integral components of our identity and pride. We are not defined by them, rather they have enriched us.

Ten years ago, when my daughter, Andrea, was born, I could hardly have been more visible. As anchor of two daily newscasts on the CBS-owned television station in New York, I was already seen as a symbol of acceptance, because my inherited hand and foot anomaly, ectrodactyly, was noticeable to millions of viewers every day. My "on camera" pregnancy drew both widespread unsolicited criticism and celebration. I knew that some of the people who admired me for my public professional accomplishment felt completely the opposite about my reproductive rights. Many of them didn't hesitate to tell me so.

Three years later, when my son, Aaron, was born under similar circumstances in Los Angeles, the feedback was more intense. Without permission, or warning, a nationally syndicated radio talk show host placed on the table the question of whether it was morally wrong for me to reproduce. That's when I fully understood how paternalistic attitudes and deep rooted prejudice create "permission" for public intrusion into our private lives - our births, reproductive choices, and even our rights to live and die. We need greater unity, more cooperation among all our disparate segments, and stronger voices.

Denise Sherer Jacobson is one of those stronger voices! There's a considerable difference between the daily inconveniences of being physically different and the greater complexities of living with cerebral palsy. Each of us, with and without disabilities, has unique parenting challenges that are the basis of our shared experiences. In the bigger picture of simply facing the world as an unconventional mother, Denise and I are sisters. And along with us, every mother who is a wheelchair user, deaf, hard-of-hearing, blind, has low vision, a developmental or speech disability, uses crutches, braces or assistive technology. In other words, all of us who must find different and creative ways of fulfilling the most timeless of dreams--that our children's lives will be better than ours, and that our life experiences will, in turn, enrich theirs.

"The Question of David" will get in your face and make you squirm. But it will also make you laugh and cry and celebrate every detail of the time-honored vocation of motherhood.

This is not just a book about parenting, not just a book about disability. It is a book about universal challenge and universal courage to demand and gain the rights that are entitled to all human beings. "The Question of David" is the kind of literary milestone we need as all of us who are members of the human race search for bonds with one another to map out the unified pathway toward a more inclusive future for everyone -- now, and for generations to come.

– Bree Walker Lampley

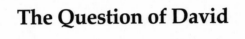
The Question of David

Chapter One
The Question of David
January, 1987

The phone rang.

With the folds of my jeans still gathered between my ankles and knees, I flicked on the switch of my motorized wheelchair, placed my palm on the joystick, and whizzed across the bedroom floor. I reached the phone on the third ring. "Hello."

"Oh, hello," the female voice responded with a hint of surprise. "Is Neil Jacobson there?"

"He's at work."

"Ah, I must have his work and home number mixed up," she explained in a slightly raspy, deep voice. I was about to say goodbye so she could call my husband at his office (and I could finish dressing), when she asked, "Are you Denise?"

"Yes."

She introduced herself as Colleen Somebody-or-other, a friend of a friend of mine. She was calling from St. Louis, almost 2,000 miles away from Oakland. "Didn't Judy tell you I'd be calling?"

"No," I replied, swallowing my sarcastic 'of course not.' Judy was a networker, putting people in touch with each other regardless of whether or not they wanted to be networked. I was wary of calls that began this way, and if she had told this woman to ask for Neil first, I already supposed it was something I would need to be talked into.

"Well . . . er," Colleen paused as if gearing up for a dive into a cold pool. A moment later, she took the plunge. "There's a baby boy, almost six weeks old, up for adoption, we just found out he may have cerebral palsy. . . . Judy said that you and Neil might be interested."

Her surprising words echoed in my head: *A baby, . . . up for adoption, . . . with CP.*

1

Years ago, unless the signs were really obvious, no one even suspected cerebral palsy until a baby started to develop voluntary muscle coordination, at least that was when my mother had begun to notice something was hindering my developmental progress; I wasn't turning over or crawling as my sister had done during her first nine months. Neil, on the other hand, had difficulty sucking and swallowing in early infancy (though he certainly has no trouble now!) Had this baby been born with the umbilical cord tangled around his neck, as Neil and I had been, which temporarily cut off the flow of oxygen to his brain, consequently causing permanent damage? Or had something else happened to lead the doctors to consider CP? Were his physical symptoms *that* apparent? Did he have seizures? Was he unable to drink from a bottle?

"How could they tell he might have CP so early?" I asked.

"Evan was born with a pronounced torticollis; he holds his head to one side," she said, using his name for the first time. "He also has increased muscle tone, more so than other newborns."

Colleen continued on with more background details. The baby's birth mother had fallen and hemorrhaged internally during her eighth month of pregnancy. Those series of facts raised some real concerns. Since his adoption had been arranged before he'd been born, the doctors had ordered a CAT scan and an EEG to find out more. The tests showed slight swelling in the frontal lobe of the brain. No one could be sure what it meant, if it meant anything at all.

"The prospective parents are having doubts about adopting him. They don't know anything about cerebral palsy. We've been trying to educate them. I've told them it's not a progressive or life-threatening disability," Colleen said. "And since I work at an independent living center, I've been able to put them in touch with other parents who have kids with CP, but at this point, they're really scared. . . . Sooo, we're trying to line up another couple just in case."

She rattled on without taking a breath, telling me that there seemed to be no other outward signs or symptoms of any disability. Evan had no trouble breathing or swallowing.

As I listened to her, the chilly winter dampness in the room raised goosebumps on my bare thighs. I clutched at the waistband of my jeans with the fingers of my less coordinated right hand. Managing to grab a wad of the material, I pulled them up over my purplish knees.

"He's so alert and responsive. Has the sweetest smile," she added, before she finally paused. It wasn't a long enough one, though, for me to get a word in—even if I could think of anything to say.

Colleen said that the doctor and therapist had already started this infant on physical therapy. "His foster mother and I stretch his neck and limbs three times a day to help relax his tight muscles."

I caught my grimace in the mirror as she described the exercises. I could feel a lump of bile rise from my stomach to my throat; the therapists in St. Louis were still using the same grueling, at times, painful method of physical therapy that Neil and I had been subjected to when we were children. It might have stretched the muscles but it also stressed and strained them; the whole ordeal wasn't relaxing at all. I didn't think anyone practiced that type of therapy anymore after research had proven a gentler approach more successful for children with cerebral palsy.

"It seems to have helped, too," Colleen remarked innocently. "His torticollis is hardly noticeable, anymore."

Lucky his neck didn't break, I thought.

"But Denise, this baby is so gorgeous!" she said, as if trying to convince me.

I glanced at the clock; I had an appointment in half an hour with a possible buyer for the out of tune player-piano I had inherited from Neil's first marriage. I needed to get dressed. *How do I get rid of this woman?*

"Oh, I almost forgot," she added. "I should tell you the baby's birth date. It's December nineteenth."

Was it the winter's coldness seeping into my bedroom, or phantom fingers chilling my spine? The baby and Neil had the same birthday!

"I'll talk to Neil," I heard myself saying. "We'll call you back." I took her number.

It was 12:15. Neil would be at lunch. The best thing to do was not think about the phone call. My pants and the piano came first. St. Louis was too far away, and besides, Neil had waited twenty-nine years for a chance to adopt so two more hours wouldn't make much of a difference.

"A baby?" I mused at my face in the mirror after I hung up the phone.

"From St. Louis?" It wrinkled back.

"Ridiculous!" I shook my head and returned to the task of pulling up my jeans.

The first time Neil and I had discussed adoption was on our first date. It wasn't a typical "getting-to-know-you" conversation. We didn't warm up with small talk. Instead, I listened to Neil's experiences of childhood—growing up with parents who were Holocaust survivors, who spoke little English, and who were frightened by a medical profession that had a very pessimistic view of children with cerebral palsy.

"When I was five, a doctor recommended my parents put me in an institution," he explained as he slouched casually in his wheelchair. "So I went with my father to see what it was like." He shook his head. "There were kids there, sitting on the cold floor—half-naked—just rocking back and forth. It was horrible. My father actually got sick to his stomach. Afterward, my parents got so frightened I might be taken away, my mom took all three of us kids to live with relatives in Florida for a year."

A knot tightened in my stomach. We all had our "war stories," but this seemed so incredible! To think that this man sitting across the restaurant table from me, a man who was now an esteemed computer scientist in the corporate world, had nearly ended up in a state institution, filled me with outrage. Yet he spoke about it so matter-of-factly.

"Doesn't it make you angry?"

"Naw," he said simply. "What would be the point? It happened a long time ago."

The waiter removed our barely touched, colder-than-room-temperature chicken Kiev. He came back momentarily with two cups of black coffee. We each asked him for a straw and to pour the cream. When we were alone again, I watched Neil uncover the glass lid of the sugar bowl and place it on the white tablecloth. Then, in a slow, rhythmic ritual, he carefully grasped the unwrapped cubes of sugar between the tips of his thumb and middle finger and, one by one, plop them into his coffee—eleven times! I tried not to cringe.

"Now you know why we came here," he grinned at me, as his sparkling brownish green eyes indicated the half-empty bowl. "Otherwise, people groan when they put the sugar in for me. The trouble with Berkeley—everyone's so healthy. . . .

"Anyhow," Neil said after taking a sip, "I've wanted to adopt a disabled child ever since."

I blinked at him. I had just gotten over his eleven lumps of sugar. *"Why?"*

"There are so many older kids out there in institutions needing homes. And a disabled child needs a good home even more."

His zeal about it intimidated me. I admired people who could be so selfless, but I'm not Mother Theresa. I knew my own limits. "Don't you think it would be hard raising a disabled kid? Having to relive some of the same things you went through as a child?"

"But I survived!" He answered with undaunted enthusiasm. "And that's what I can give to a child. . . . I've given it a lot of thought—"

"At least twenty-four years," I teased.

"Yeah," he nodded with a smile that creased his finely chiseled nose. "And I'm realistic. I know I wouldn't be able to handle a kid who's very physically disabled. And I wouldn't be good with one who was mentally retarded—I'm too impatient. . . . Yeah, I've got to be practical."

Neil and I had known each other for years, though not well. Our paths had crossed when we were kids in New York—at camps and recreation centers. And now, living in the San Francisco Bay Area, we had mutual friends. We'd bumped into each other from time to time since his divorce, but I never thought about dating him. I suspected Neil felt the same way I did about dating someone with cerebral palsy. I only saw him with nondisabled women, anyway. It had been only a few weeks ago, at Judy's potluck Rosh Hashanah dinner, that I realized Neil was quite an attractive man.

Before that, I just saw him as a stereotype—someone with cerebral palsy: uncoordinated body movements, impaired speech, and motorized wheelchair—a mirror image of myself, with a beard. And whenever I'd looked in the mirror, all my features—my smooth oval face, my blue-green eyes and auburn hair, my body with its adequate curves—blurred into my cerebral palsy. It had taken a lot of years of work and pain before my cerebral palsy became part of me; I think I used to believe that I was more a part of it. Now that I had waded through some of the quicksand of my own prejudices, Neil was there. . . . *But adopting a disabled child?*

"I've never given much thought to adoption," I said, tightly clasping my hands under the table before admitting, "I've always wanted to have a baby."

"So would I!" Neil's whole face brightened. "That would be such a kick!"

That conversation was the first of many we had on having kids before and after we got married—while I kept track of my monthly cycle. Neil believed more in fate than science when it came to conception; he managed to bring a little levity to my dogmatic approach as we tried to conceive. Yet every month, at the first sign of my menstrual blood, I felt a pang of disappointment and ultimately, despair. At my urging, we eventually ended up at a Planned Parenthood clinic to find that there was no real medical reason for our infertility; we resorted to sperm counts, a dye X ray of my uterus, and four months of artificial insemination so Neil's sperm would have a shorter swim to my egg. Nothing happened! The next step would have been a "sperm wash" to purify Neil's sperm. All this just to get pregnant!

I began questioning the logic of it, finally deciding that maybe Neil did have the better idea. Adopting an older child—say, three or four years old—certainly made more and more sense: no hassling with bottles or diapers and, with a child that age, we would be more certain of what the disability was like. So five months ago, in September, I phoned the local chapter of AASK (Aid to Adoption of Special Kids), an agency working to find homes for "hard to place" children.

We went through endless interviews, reference checks, fingerprinting (it took several takes to get clear prints from my nervously moving CP fingers), and a doctor's exam. We were still waiting for all the paperwork to clear before final approval from AASK. Then there would be even more waiting: to match us up with a child that would be right for us—taking into account that we were both disabled.

"It could take anywhere from three months to a year," the child placement worker warned with a patronizing smile, "because of your `special' circumstances. And once we find a child, we may have to convince a social worker that you'll be good parents."

The other agency staff were much more encouraging, but I kept hearing those words over and over again. They deepened my fears. I knew that even after we contended with the prejudices of the child's social worker, we would have to deal with that child's initial reaction to having disabled parents.

A baby would be so much simpler. A baby would have no preconceived ideas of what parents should be like. . . . Yet, babies were in such demand to be adopted by nondisabled couples. For Neil and me, trying to adopt a baby seemed as silly and futile as a dog chasing its own tail.

It was a little after 2 P.M. when I dialed Neil's office.

"Hiya."

"Um . . . " Clenching the phone to my ear, I stumbled through the purpose of my call. "Neil . . . I got a call a couple of hours ago. A woman in St. Louis—a friend of Judy's. . . . There's a six-week-old baby up for adoption. He might have CP, and Colleen, the woman— whoever the hell she is—said the couple set to take him is having doubts about adopting him. So now this Colleen is looking for a backup and *your friend*, Judy, gave her our name. . . . Goddammit, why couldn't she have warned us! Neil, this woman talked ten thousand words a minute." Trying to quell my growing hysteria, I continued. "I didn't know what to ask. . . . I said we'd call her back, but *you* do it, Neil. You call her back. Judy told her to ask for you, anyway."

"Denise, calm down," Neil said, when I paused for a swallow. "I can't tell if you're happy or upset."

"I'm pissed," I replied, feeling welling tears. *Couldn't he hear it in my voice?*

"Why?"

I didn't really know why. A tear rolled down my cheek. I struggled to hold back the rest so I could give him some answer. "Because Judy should have asked us first."

"But she knows we're already in the process," Neil patiently reminded me.

"How could some stranger just call us and offer a baby?" I ranted on, ignoring his logic. "From what she told me, he doesn't even sound very disabled. I bet once the other couple calm down, they'll probably keep him."

How could I have even tried to tell him that it felt as if someone were playing a practical joke on me? After I had "reasoned" myself out of wanting a baby, there it was dangling before me.

"Why don't I give the woman a call?" Neil suggested, responding, as usual, so pragmatically to my emotional outbursts.

I sniffed and read off the number I had scribbled, adding, "By the way, Neil, the baby was born on your birthday."

Neil called me back twenty minutes later. He hadn't gotten any more information, but by the high-pitched sounds that escaped his larynx, I knew once again, my logical, systems-analyst husband had been overtaken by passion. It made me nervous.

I didn't want to even think about it the rest of the afternoon. After his call, I threw on my plastic rain poncho, grabbed an English mystery from the bookcase, and tore down the ramp. Maybe the rain and a mocha would melt away the knot in the pit of my stomach.

When Neil came home that night, his eyes sparkled and he wore a grin at least five inches wide.

"Let's eat first!" I stated firmly, finding it difficult, as usual, not to be swept up by his exuberance. Besides, I didn't want to talk about it until our "airy-fairy" housekeeper, Chavallah, had left for the day.

The pungent smell of sauteed green peppers and onion lingered as Neil and I sat at the oversized dining room table (another first marriage leftover) sipping our coffee. From the kitchen, Chavallah hummed some Israeli song as she rinsed the dirty dishes placing them in the dishwasher. Her voice rose above the wooshing water and the clattering plates and silverware. I avoided looking at Neil, afraid we'd both start giggling. Ten minutes later, after she sponged down the counters, she was off into the night. Neil squealed at the same moment the door slammed.

Still trying to maintain some control, I blurted, "I thought you didn't want to adopt an infant; you always said you wouldn't know what to do with it. You'd be afraid to touch it."

"But I'd figure it out." He gave me a cocky smile. "Remember the shirt?"

I bit the smile on my lips as I remembered how Neil's shirt had kept us apart when we first started to become intimate. He hadn't been able to spend the night during the week because neither of us could fasten his top button in the morning and he was required to wear a tie to work. At his house, one of Neil's roommates woke up at the crack of dawn to button it for him—half asleep. At my place, it was just the two of us and our not very dexterous fingers. We were not about to let one button cramp our sex life, however. We considered several alternatives. First I attempted to button it with my buttonhook but, not having such a steady hand, aiming the looped wire so close to his throat seemed a bit life-threatening. Velcro, another possibility, didn't do well in the washing machine (multi-colored lint clung to the little nubby strips like leeches). Then one evening Neil appeared at my door, beaming. His fingers pushed aside his tie to show me a zipper sewn underneath a flap of fake buttons. The perfect solution!

"Yeah, I remember. But Neil, *how can you compare a zipper to a baby?*"

He chuckled, then reminded me. "You're the one who always

said that if we really wanted a baby, we'd be able to do it."

"I know, I know," I grudgingly admitted. Suddenly, I wasn't so confident, anymore. What if I accidentally socked the poor kid in the jaw while I was changing his diaper? And what would happen when he got sick; how would I take his temperature, or pour the right dose of medicine? Babies didn't swallow pills. . . .

"We don't know much about his disability," I pointed out.

"Colleen's sending us the medical report."

"It's a private adoption," I pointed out. "Can we afford it?"

He stroked his brown beard. "Can we afford not to?"

"Neil!" Sometimes he just infuriated me. I decided I'd change my approach. "Do you really think some woman from a Christian adoption agency is going to give a baby to a couple of Jewish cripples?"

"We'll find out, won't we?"

Never a straight answer. I plowed on. "Well, you know Colleen said the baby might be mentally retarded. And *you're* the one who didn't want a retarded child. If he is developmentally disabled (the contemporary term for mentally retarded), it could involve his hearing, vision, and a slew of other complications. . . . Neil, what if his CP is more than we can physically handle? If he can't learn to dress himself or feed himself? How would we deal with that? There's no guarantee that he'll turn out to be as independent as either one of us."

I felt guilty saying all this, but one of us had to lay out the cards!

"All I know is, there's a baby out there who needs a home," Neil responded somewhat somberly.

I groaned. *Were we going to go through this for every baby who needed a home?*

"I just didn't think it would be this soon," I sighed with exasperation. "We haven't even sold the piano. There's no room for a crib. . . ."

"Look, let's just see what happens," Neil finally suggested.

I sprawled out on the couch to watch the Thursday night comedies while Neil did some work at his desk. Laughter loosened some of the tension in my neck and shoulders, and by the time we got ready for bed, my mood had lightened.

"Do we have to name him Evan?" Neil asked while he kicked off his shoes. (He stammered with names that began with vowels.)

"I don't know . . . "

I thought more about it as I hooked my index finger inside the collar of my turtleneck and stretched it up over my chin. I grabbed a handful of the knitted material from behind and yanked it over my head. The chill in the air touched the uncovered parts of my body; I gave an involuntary snort and clamped my upper arms to my sides, bringing my wrist up to my mouth so I could grasp the knitted cuff with my teeth. I slid out one arm, and then the other. I let the turtleneck drop to the floor. I was hard on clothes!

"We always said that if we had a baby we'd name it after your father, Jacob," I said to Neil as I shivered from the cold. (According to Jewish tradition, a baby is named after a deceased relative to carry on that person's memory.)

"But J's aren't great, either," he answered, before arching his flat rear end slightly off his wheelchair seat. His thick, long fingers clumped onto the unfastened waist of his slacks. He slid them off easily.

"Well, my nephew Larry's already named after my mother, so it would be nice to name the baby for someone else." I thought a few moments, while I slipped my arms out of my bra straps, twisted it around, and pinched open the hooks. After I wormed on my flannel-lined nightgown, I spoke again. "Hey, my great aunt Dinah never had any kids. She adored my sister and me."

Neil raised his eyebrows. *"You want to name him Dinah?"*

"No," I laughed. "But all we have to do is find a name with D. Maybe David. As long as the Hebrew meaning's the same—"

"David," Neil repeated without a stammer or a stutter. He grinned. "David. I like it."

"Me, too." I smiled while I stood up, balanced myself on my wobbly legs, and tugged my jeans over my much rounder rear end than my husband's. *Who knows, maybe this will work out . . .*

My sober thoughts returned as I sat back down and kicked off my pants the rest of the way. I bent forward and clutched our collection of dirty clothes from the carpet to throw in the nearby hamper. "So, who's going to call the adoption agency in St. Louis?"

Making telephone calls to strangers was never on our "most fun things to do" list. Neil and I spoke clearly enough in person though our words flowed just about half a beat slower than a southern drawl. We also used facial expressions and gestures to help communicate our meaning. Once people got to know us, they had very little difficulty understanding our speech even over the phone unless we were really tired and we didn't have the energy to pronounce our words with precision. We were even called upon, every now and then, to lecture on disability issues at colleges and medical schools.

But when it came to phoning places like Sears or the local gas company, we recruited a friend instead of chancing that we'd get an impatient operator or receptionist—or worse, risking our pride and being hung up on. And now we had to telephone a stranger and ask for a baby!

To my surprise and relief, Neil volunteered. "But Colleen said that I shouldn't contact the agency until the other couple decides not to adopt David."

I clamped my mouth shut. He was already calling this baby "David."

A few days later, the thick copy of a rather impersonal medical report on Baby Boy K (in boldface type) arrived, along with some Polaroids. I grabbed the report while Neil looked at the pictures. I frowned; he, of course, squealed.

"It doesn't say anything more than we already know except it uses bigger words. Gives him a fifty-fifty chance of having cerebral palsy and/or mental retardation."

"Look at the pictures," Neil squawked, shoving the Polaroids in front of me. Propped up on cushions, the red-headed, blue-eyed infant, with his head upright, smiled a toothless smile.

"He's cute, I guess." I shrugged, disappointed that I didn't feel the same excitement. "But Neil, his head looks big. I think the report mentioned hydrocephalus."

Neil rolled his eyes. "Denise!"

I re-read the report three times and couldn't find it. I smiled sheepishly, "Well, maybe I am being too critical."

I didn't know why I was being so hard. I just felt so confused. Was I ready for a baby . . . a disabled baby? Would I have to relive my own experience of childhood—the demanding therapy, the "special education," the loneliness of a child not being accepted by the nondisabled world? (I still dealt with that same loneliness in adulthood.) And what if he weren't disabled? Who would rescue him when he climbed the plum tree outside the kitchen window? And when he got older, would he be embarrassed to bring friends home? How would I handle that? Why should I have to?

Neil had already made up his mind. It was easy for him. He spent nearly twelve hours a day at the office. He wouldn't have to deal with the details of dependence on au pairs and housekeepers, like Chavallah, with strong or peculiar personalities, annoying habits, stupidity. I was a writer; I liked my privacy. I had struggled all of my life to be physically independent and had succeeded, except at tasks involving acute dexterity (clipping toenails or cutting food), careful steadiness (lighting *Shabbos* candles), and long periods of physical exertion (cleaning up a shattered thirty-two-ounce jar of apple sauce). After spending a good portion of my thirty-six years in self-absorption, could I suddenly become a devoted mother of an adopted child?

A week later, we got the news—the other couple had backed out.

We decided to put off telling our relatives, particularly Neil's mother, who hadn't been too pleased about Neil's marrying me, because I had CP. We told our friends; a few seemed skeptical but most of them were supportive. Some offered well-intentioned advice: "Get a lawyer," one friend told us. "His disability looks mild," another said. "But you'll probably be eligible for financial assistance from state disability services."

". . . And don't worry, Denise," my friend who had just become a mother tried reassuring. "When you see him, you'll know."

Sure, I humphed to myself, knowing that I'd always had trouble listening to my own instinct. Rationality, guilt, and fear seemed to constantly interfere when it came to my gut feelings.

Time wasn't even on my side. Neil gleefully informed me after he had spoken to the social worker at the adoption center in St. Louis that, if everything went smoothly, the baby could be in our home in four to six weeks!

"We haven't sold the piano; we have nowhere to put your desk or the computer," I ranted. "And where are we going to find an au pair?"

"Don't you want Chavallah—?"

"Chavallah," I resounded. "Chavallah! That woman hasn't listened to me for the past two weeks since she started working here! She does everything *her* way. Moved the furniture around *her* way. She put strange things into my mother's meatloaf; I specifically asked her to follow the recipe. God only knows what was in it!"

Neil grinned knowingly. His smile wrinkled his nose and put creases across his freckled cheeks.

"Don't!" I warned, struggling not to yield. "You didn't like it either. . . . You know, I had a feeling about her even when she called in response to the ad. She sounded pushy. . . . But you, you liked her, so I figured why not? But," I succumbed to an accusing grin, *"you like everybody."*

"Well, she makes good coffee."

I shot him a glance. He placed his strong, soothing hand on mine, which rested on the dining room table. "Don't worry, we'll get rid of her," Neil said.

I knew getting rid of Chavallah wasn't going to be easy. After all these years of hiring attendants, Neil and I still could have used assertiveness training as employers. And we not only had to fire Chavallah, we needed to evict her, since she was living in the little studio apartment in the back—the one we had built for the au pair.

"It's not fair! Most people have nine months to get ready." I shook my head. "Neil, where are we going to get a type of crib we can use? And what about baby clothes, diapers, bottles, . . . ?"

"Details, details, details," was my husband's classic reply.

Hunched over the table and in a state of frazzled fatigue, I managed to shoot him another sharp look before glancing at my wristwatch. Seven o'clock. Time for me to call the baby's foster mother, Kate—as I had dutifully done every other evening for the last two weeks—to check on the baby.

Kate, I had learned, was the one who had instigated this whole unusual production for getting the baby into a wanted home. When she realized that things might not go smoothly with his adoption, she had given Colleen a call. (Kate had cared for Colleen's youngest adopted child when he was first born.) Kate figured that Colleen would know what to do with a baby who might be disabled, since she worked in an independent living center (ILC).

"The baby's doing fine," Kate warmly assured me after our first hellos. Her voice was strong, with just a trace of an ancestral Irish brogue. I pictured her a large, rounded earth mother, having long reddish brown hair and wearing Birkenstocks; babies and toddlers crawling over her feet and clinging to her peasant skirt, some probably her own.

She sounded so comforting, too, as if she were an old friend. "You know, he's so alert. He smiles at you. Why, he was smiling when he was two weeks old." She bragged, "I told everybody and they said it was gas. But I've been taking care of babies long enough to know the difference—it definitely was a smile."

After our conversation, tears stung my eyes. He was so real, this negotiation, this baby; this baby I was so afraid of wanting. He did things babies do. He was soft and round, and he smiled.

I sat there in silence for a moment, remembering the story my mother had once told me about the time she took me to a clinic to find out why my development was delayed. The group of doctors surrounded me spewing out intimidating medical jargon, convincing one another that I had most of the signs of mental retardation (this was years before EEGs and CAT scans). Hearing their discussion, even my seemingly retiring mother decided they were crazy. She'd told me: "They didn't see the twinkle in your eyes."

"Neil, I need to go to St. Louis," I stated after swallowing the lump in my throat.

"Of course," he agreed eagerly. "One of us should go and check it out."

I gave him a sad smile; we were on such different wavelengths.

Neil drove me to the airport one week later, as the stars faded into the gray daylight. Unfortunately, it wasn't early enough to assure me a front seat in coach. I ended up in an aisle seat in the thirty-second row—a long way back and an even longer way out—without my chair.

When the plane landed in St. Louis three hours later I unbuckled my seatbelt and waited. The other passengers had to disembark first—those not going to New York, that is—before someone came to assist me. As usual, it was taking forever, and I just hoped that the plane didn't take off for its final destination with me still on board. Yet, somehow I didn't think Colleen, who had said she would meet me, would let them.

I swallowed, trying to pop my ears, and breathed in the thin, stale airplane air that hissed out of the small metal cones above my head. With cold, clammy hands, I stuffed my *GAMES* magazine and Cynthia Ozick's anthology into my backpack and placed it on the seat beside me. Then I put on my jacket; I wanted to be ready when the narrow aisle-chair (a dollylike conveyance) and the always impatient ground crew came to transport me to my wheelchair.

Twenty minutes later, my stomach rumbled and my fingers tugged at the neckline of my sweater. I squirmed under the incessant little light bulb staring down at me from between the air cones, while my other hand absently rummaged through my open-mouthed backpack. I first felt the sharp edges of the magazine before I brushed a furry snout. I snatched the softness.

Holding the brown teddy bear up with both hands, I inspected its friendly face. I had bought it just yesterday, with some reservation and ambivalence. I felt an empty, gnawing ache inside. *Did I come here to make sure I did or didn't want this baby?*

Finally, the aisle-chair appeared! I stuffed the teddy bear down into my pack. Not that I cared if anybody thought it was mine; I just didn't want it to fall out when the two, overdue crewmen assisted me. The men parked the chair alongside my seat and prepared to lift. I didn't bother trying to explain to them that I could transfer myself from the seat to the chair; from past experiences, I knew they'd rather lift than communicate.

"My bag," I uttered the simplest words to the man nervously buckling the crisscrossed straps over my chest.

He glanced to the seat where I'd been sitting and called over my head. "Better get her bag. She's worried about it." I watched my backpack being slung from the man behind to the man in front. "Ready?" he asked his peer as he stepped aside, without a word to me.

I was tilted back and wheeled through the cabin—their cargo. I detached myself, first looking to my left, through rows of windows framing the blue winter's sky, and then to my right at the passengers settling in for the last leg of the flight.

"Bye now," called the friendly gray haired man, who had smiled at me on my way in. *He must be from the Bay Area!*

We were in the first cabin now, when I was surprised by a strong, slightly broguish voice. "Denise?"

I turned my head to look straight ahead. I saw just enough of the small, neat, fiftyish looking woman to realize she wasn't the Kate that I had pictured. She stood in front of me, but my eyes instantly latched onto the bundle she held. He was just at my eye level.

"Oh, my God!" I gasped.

"Here's your son," she offered with outstretched arms.

His small, solid body sat snugly in my lap. My arm cradled him. I felt my eyes blazing as I stared at him with wonder. He tilted back his fuzzy golden head. Red "stork bites" peppered his forehead and eyelids, but his cheeks were round, as smooth and white as a spring lily. He smiled at me and his blue eyes, locking on to mine, seemed to whisper: "It's about time you got here."

"You were born so far away," I blinked back.

"I want to go home." His laughing eyes demanded.

In our silent dialogue, his bright, steady gaze bored like a steel lance into my heart, piercing my core with a deep, painful joy I had never known before—a feeling without word or thought. Tears streamed down my cheeks.

"My baby, my baby," I blubbered and pulled him close to me.

I could smell his sweet, gentle scent as my lips brushed his hair. A buzz of voices murmured above us. I didn't look up. I just held onto my precious David.

Chapter Two

Pampered in the Afternoon

"**Y**ou'll have to take the baby now," an airline employee directed Kate as we halted at the plane's exit.

"Why?" Kate inquired.

"She's not allowed to carry him on her lap while they're wheeling her on through the jetport."

"How come?" Kate persisted.

The employee shrugged. "Regulations."

Kate was about to protest, but I interrupted; I had been on that plane long enough.

"It's all right, Kate," I assured.

"I wonder when they made up *that* rule," she whispered to me as she bent over to take David from my arms.

Reluctantly, I relinquished him. Reluctantly, she took him.

Kate kept stride with the crewman as he wheeled me up the hollow corridor so that I could keep an eye on my son. Up ahead a tall, wiry, dark-haired woman shuffled from one foot to the other next to my empty wheelchair. As soon as I was on the level terminal carpet, she bent down to hug me. It was Colleen.

"We can take it from here," she said to the flock of airport personnel I had trailing behind. It took them a few seconds to disperse. Colleen helped me unbuckle the crisscrossed straps and asked, "Do you need help transferring into your wheelchair?"

I shook my head and smiled, impressed that this woman knew her protocol.

Grabbing onto the armrest of my E&J wheelchair, I pulled myself to my feet, pivoted, and sat down on my chair's brown vinyl seat. All the while, the two women bantered back and forth. Colleen ribbed Kate for sidestepping the rules and walking onto the plane with the baby.

"I must have looked like I was supposed to go on," Kate smugly defended. "I just couldn't help it. My feet just took off — one in front of the other — and before I knew it, I was there."

I scooted back in my seat and looked at the two women. Visually, they were a female version of Mutt and Jeff. Kate had to be at least an inch or two shorter than me (I'm a little over 5'2"), and Colleen had to be a good six inches taller than Kate. Like Mutt and Jeff, too, they seemed like a pair of characters.

They both turned to me just as I kicked down my footrests. Kate took a few steps toward me. "Here he is," she readily offered the baby.

I hesitated. I had to use my left hand, the more coordinated one, to power my wheelchair; I knew I wouldn't be able to cradle him with my right. I thought about my seatbelt, though I wasn't sure how comfortable it would be for a two-month-old infant. After a deep swallow, I made the suggestion. "Let's give it a try with my seatbelt."

Kate sat David in my lap and fastened the black strap, making sure the buckle didn't press into his chest. He sat in the curve of my body with amazing balance. I still used my right arm to brace him, just in case he flopped over when we rounded a corner or weaved in and out of pedestrians' paths on our way to baggage claim.

I drove slowly at first, quite aware of the precious cargo I held in my lap. My mind, however, raced. *This kid is gorgeous! The pictures didn't even come close. How could anyone wanting a child give him up — CP or no CP? And what CP? So he's stiff, maybe it's spasticity, so he'll have little leg movement but good use of his arms and hands, like Valerie (a friend of mine) — we'll be a three-wheelchair family. Or he'll be like Susan (a colleague) and have minor paralysis of one side of his body — walk with a limp and play piano with one hand (the piano we're selling, anyway).*

He sat so erect, even as we glided through the airport crowd. We jiggled a bit—my front wheel casters needed new bearings—but David just gurgled at every little jerk and jolt. I was surprised by his solidness; I thought two-month-old babies usually keeled over and had to be cradled. Yet his fuzzy reddish—blond head, resting on my chest, remained upright, and I savored his sweet, innocent scent as his head bobbed up and down under my chin.

At the same time I stopped, realizing I had no idea where I was going, I heard Kate and Colleen call from behind. I spun around. They were yards away. I waited while they jogged to catch up. "This is the way to baggage claim," Colleen panted as she pointed in the right direction.

"Oh, I thought we were going to the departure gate," I grinned. "After all, I got what I came for. Now I can go home. Right?"

"No-no-no-no-no," Kate shook her head as Colleen squeaked a giggle. "Do you know how much explaining we would have to do to Rita Sue?" (Rita Sue James was the head of the Christian Family Community Adoption Agency.) "She'd have a fit if she knew we took him to the airport. That woman gets so flustered over everything. . . . Not that your idea doesn't appeal to me," she added mischievously.

We collected my brown and tan suitcase and immediately pulled out the Polaroid camera — the camera Neil had bought on Saturday as a Valentine's Day gift for himself so I could take it on this trip. I hadn't been too thrilled when we purchased it, since all I got from him was an unwrapped stuffed Panda holding a heart. It had irked me even more when he pulled out his checkbook crammed with the loose pictures Colleen had sent us, leading the saleswoman to ask about "that cute baby." "He's my son!" Neil beamed. To which I lowly grumbled, "not yet." But now I was the one who beamed as Colleen snapped the first picture of me with my son, before we bundled up and headed for her van.

Colleen had an adapted van, equipped with a lift, like ours. Unlike ours, her van had a raised roof because Colleen's husband, Max, was quadriplegic from a motorcycle accident more than twenty years ago, and happened to be over six feet tall. A lift equipped van made this trip more inviting, for it meant that I could take my power (motorized) wheelchair—which doesn't fold to fit in a standard vehicle—with me instead of my push (manual) chair. My power chair not only is more comfortable to sit in but, as its appellation implies, I feel and am much more autonomous and independent using it.

I waited for Colleen to creak open the van doors and lower the grumbling wheelchair lift. The February air was crisp and cold. Looking down I saw patches of snow on the concrete; even covered with at least day-old soot, the whiteness shone through. I had forgotten about city winters.

Kate went in through the passenger door and settled David in an infant carseat. She cleared some of the debris of empty soda cans and toys away from the lift entrance. Before my fingers numbed, I boarded the lift. After it was raised, I maneuvered in to the tight spot beside the infant seat. I locked my brakes, carefully crept my arm over to the seat next to me, and wedged my forefinger into David's little pink palm. His warm fingers curled around my cold skin.

Kate and Colleen chattered as we drove along the highway. With the motor roaring and the van rattling, it would be almost impossible for me to take part in the conversation. My sinuses were still stuffy from the plane ride, anyway. So I just sat, leaning to my left, watching as we rolled by the outskirts of the St. Louis countryside while keeping a newly acquired mother's eye on my son, who had fallen into a gentle sleep.

I had never been to St. Louis, yet as we drove from the airport to Kate's house, the stretches of scattered bare trees, the patches of snow on the slightly sloped roadside, and the view of a few single-family brick houses sitting along the highway reminded me of the outskirts of New York: the city where I grew up and the place I still think of as home, even though I'm happily settled in the Bay Area. My sense of familiarity grew stronger when we entered the residential part of the city, where buildings got taller and streets widened. I felt as if our destination was going to be the second floor of a five-story, brown brick walk-up (an apartment building with no elevator) in the three-bedroom apartment where I had lived with my mother and father, my sister, and periodically an uncle (my mother's youngest brother) for the first eighteen years of my life. It had seemed like an eternity ago when I hobbled around on crutches, certain that I'd be spending the rest of my life in that same apartment.

St. Louis triggered a sense of awareness that both haunted and seduced me. Much of the time over the next four days, I felt as if I were back in the world I grew up in, both good and bad.

Kate's home was large, warm, and comfortable. Although it was much bigger than the apartment I grew up in, the smell and feel of it was very much the same. No hardwood floors or trim, sleek furniture to create that modern, stark, yuppie, transient look. Instead, a woolly, well-walked-on olive green carpet stretched through the downstairs rooms and wended its way upstairs to the second and perhaps third stories. The rooms generated warmth and permanence, graced with antique knickknacks resting on matching pieces of mahogany furniture—the kind that stood on intricately carved lion's paws and was crowned with regally crested swirls. So like my mother's furniture that had been passed down from her mother, but my sister and I had been too young to appreciate its somber dignity when my mother died; we had been only eighteen and fifteen years old, respectively, so we convinced our father to gold-leaf some of it and sell the rest.

I spent most of my four-day visit to St. Louis in Kate's den—a thick-curtained, cozy little room with a day crib, a card table stocked with all sorts of baby-powder-smelling paraphenalia, a remote-control TV, a loveseat, and an overstuffed sofa with pink flowered cushions that swallowed me up when I plopped down on it. As soon as I took my coat off and an unbundled David was propped up beside me, Colleen and Kate fired the same question. "What's his name?"

I hesitated. In the last two months, the baby had already been through two names—one by his birth mother and one by the other couple. I also had the feeling that if Colleen and Kate didn't like his new name, I'd have two disgruntled "aunts" to contend with. Finally, I blurted out, after eying both of them carefully, "David."

"I like it," Kate said. "It's good and solid."

I was drawn to Kate immediately, for, in a way, she reminded me of my mother—generous, compassionate, encouraging. But Kate seemed more sure of herself—a quality my mother might have acquired had she lived beyond fifty (though Kate was only fifty-two). My mother had a behind-the-scenes strength that my father, at heated times, characterized as stubbornness (he'd accuse me of being just like her, too, at other heated moments). Kate's strength was more feisty; she broke rules if she thought they were meant to be broken, and did it without guilt—like her little stunt to introduce me to my son at the airport.

After Colleen left to do some errands, Kate threw a diaper at me. "You might as well start now," she said, leaving the room before I could protest.

I clenched the diaper and my jaw. I had never diapered a baby. I knew how; I'd seen it done many times, but no one had ever asked me to do it—and I never thought they would, so of course, I never practiced or even visualized myself doing it. And here Kate was showing no qualms whatsoever about even leaving me alone to change this infant. I shook my head, thinking of all the years of occupational therapy I had had as a child to learn how to dress myself— practicing on button boards but never on dolls, as if my therapists feared I would get the lofty idea that one day I'd be dressing my own child. *What an absurd notion*—though it might have inspired me more. Come to think of it, those therapists were not the most creative bunch; why, if they had only told me that some of my exercises, including walking, would make having sex easier when I grew up, I might have been more motivated to stick with the grueling regimen. Then again, to them, sex was another *absurd notion*, too!

I unfolded the diaper and laid it on the nearby coffee table. Then I turned to David. "Are you ready for this?" I cooed, leaning down over him. Looking straight at me, he smiled. "I hope you know what you're in for, David."

As gently as I could, I slid him onto his back. He was a solid little baby, round and compact, and his increased muscle tone worked to my advantage—he didn't flip and flop all over. I wasn't as afraid of handling him as I might have been with a more fragile-looking infant.

I unsnapped David's white terry-cloth sleeper, knowing I'd probably not get it snapped again before his next diaper change. Grasping a smidgen of material from the toe between my teeth while slipping my left hand around his bare thigh, I pulled out a cooperative leg. I did the same with his other one.

Pillsbury's Poppin' Fresh Dough-Boy, I thought, when I saw the white softness of his partially uncovered body, and *he didn't feel stiff to me at all.*

Getting the diaper off was easy. Putting a new one on before David's baby bladder filled and fountained again took more speed and practice than I could exhibit for my first time. My sinking sitting position didn't help either. My body dampened with sweat, and the muscles from my neck to my toes ached with strain. I managed to get one corner loosely taped on the diaper so that it umbrellaed David's warm little shower (which had a toasty smell of almond extract) before it hit the floral design on the sofa.

Perhaps twenty minutes had passed; Kate returned.

I had wanted to show Kate that I could diaper David, even though the couch was too soft and I wasn't sitting in the best position. I feared Kate would just assume I couldn't do it; maybe she'd think I wasn't capable of being a mother.

"I could use some help," I said, heaving a sigh and falling back into the cushions.

"I imagine it's going to take some figuring out," she responded so matter-of-factly as she strode over to us.

My muscles suddenly relaxed from the mental pressure I had put myself under; Kate was on my side.

"I think I'd do better if we were on the floor," I said, uncertain of how she'd react to having a two-month-old lying on the carpet.

Kate immediately disappeared. She reappeared moments later carrying a bundle of blankets. She spread them out in front of the couch after moving the coffee table off to one side. Before I knew it I found myself on my knees on an old faded pastel quilt with David. We stayed there most of the afternoon, and once, I even diapered him, although it still took me longer to get the diaper on than David's next spurt.

I thought about the other couple. Looking at David, I had a hard time understanding how a couple who wanted a baby so much could decide not to keep him. He was, after all, the most beautiful baby I'd ever seen. I had already concluded, too, that if he had a disability at all, it would be relatively insignificant (to Neil and me, at least). If I was wrong and his disability turned out to be more involved, well... I'd deal with that too, even though I always told Neil I wouldn't have another wheelchair in the house. . . . But there are never any guarantees.

Kate had told me that the couple (Pete and Lisa, she called them) had a very hard time making their decision—Lisa especially.

"She came every day and held him," Kate said. "I think Pete knew long before she did. But Lisa agonized over it. She talked to people Colleen put her in contact with, but there was never that bond. She was too afraid."

Neil, the realist, had suspected that money had something to do with their decision, too. Only two months old, David had already incurred $8,000 worth of medical and related expenses. And the way it looked now, the amount would only go up throughout David's life. It costs money to be disabled—Neil and I spent more than $2,000 a year in wheelchair maintenance alone, and another $8,000 for home attendant assistance. That didn't even include our general and disability-related medical expenses (physical therapy for periodic back pain, physical checkups, etc.), and we were fairly healthy, self-reliant people.

Though Neil's reasoning may have been logical, I couldn't ignore the emotional side of it. The harsh fact was that they rejected David because he might have been disabled. For a long time I seethed at the thought of it; I took it very personally. Unlike Kate and Colleen, I had no room for compassion, particularly for Lisa, perhaps because it incensed me that she could reject him even after she spoke to someone as knowledgeable about disability as Colleen.

"She said she wanted to meet you," Colleen had mentioned during one of our phone conversations over the past week.

I didn't respond; it wasn't a question. What could I have possibly said to the woman, anyway? What could she have wanted from me? If she couldn't accept a beautiful-looking David, how repulsed would she be by the sight of me and my pronounced movements, which would become even more pronounced in my awkwardness with her? Or what if, after seeing me, she'd decide that David's potential disability, by comparison, wasn't so "bad" and she'd change her mind about giving him up? I wasn't ready to take that chance, even if it were an unlikely possibility.

Kate pampered me all afternoon with coffee, snacks, pillows, and talk. She would excuse herself now and then to check on her son, Donny, home with the flu, or another foster baby, who would be going home soon.

"I sure wish there would be some way for me to talk to your mother about what she experienced when you were an infant," she said on one of her returns.

"I wish you could," I answered, "but she died when I was fifteen. She had kidney disease."

"That must have been so hard for you."

I nodded. "It was. She did a lot for me—dressing, feeding, homework, taking me to doctors."

"You know," Kate said, "I've been surprised at myself; I find myself giving more attention to David than the other babies who've been here while he's been here. And he's not a fussy baby at all."

"That happens a lot in families where there's a disabled child," I responded. "My mother gave a lot of time and attention to me. At least, that's how my sister felt. . . . It's very sad when it happens."

"But understandable, all the same," she offered. "I know that I've wanted David to know that he's all right. That no matter what happens, he's loved and wanted. I know that's what your mother wanted for you."

I raised an eyebrow and quietly challenged, "How do you know?"

"Because of how you are," she answered simply.

Kate certainly had a way of expressing feelings as facts. And I believed her. After spending the afternoon with her, I began getting a different view of life, especially adoption.

I never knew many children or adults who were adopted, but I remember, growing up, that adoption, like sex, always seemed cloaked in secrecy. It was often whispered about among adults and teased about among kids. One couple, neighbors who lived in our apartment house when I was a little girl, adopted a baby and moved away shortly afterward. At the time I didn't realize there could be a connection, but in the 1950s (and perhaps even now), being adopted seemed to carry the stigma of "unwanted babies." During arguments with my sister, she and I would sometimes cruelly snap at each other, "You were adopted" or "They ought to send you back to the home."

Yet adopted babies are very much wanted. In one short afternoon, Kate introduced me to adoption as a way of life. "Half the kids around here," she said of her old, well-established neighborhood, "got their start as one of my foster babies. "David," she boasted, "is my fifty-ninth. Andrea, my youngest child, was my first."

I stared at Kate with awe as she told me the incredible story that began with the death of her oldest son from an auto accident eight years earlier.

"I was depressed for the whole following year," she said, after placing two coffee cups beside us on the coffee table as we sat on the floor. "Didn't know what to do with myself. Then, sometime in the fall, I dragged myself to this cocktail party, some kind of benefit, and this woman I knew started talking to me about how the Lutheran Church needed foster mothers, asked me if I was interested. I said I'd think about it, never dreaming she'd be at my door the next day ready to sign me up.

"After I took a three-month training, I had three-day-old Andrea—a biracial baby going to be adopted by a black professional couple. They took her home two days later; brought her back the next day—I think parenthood was too overwhelming for them. . . . But when she came back, I knew . . . ," Kate shook her head emphatically from side to side, "I wasn't gonna let her go again."

"I bet the social worker was in shock when you told her."

Kate laughed. "Oh, yes! The whole family was gathered around when she came. We sat her down and told her. Her eyes grew wide and she turned to me and said, `Kate, you're not supposed to keep 'em.' . . . My son, Donny, who was seven at the time, cried, `But we love her; doesn't *that* count for anything?'"

"Does Andrea ever bring it up that she's adopted?" I wondered shyly.

"Oh, yes. And when she's mad she'll start ranting and raving about being in the wrong family," Kate answered with a grin.

That afternoon I spent at Kate's, I got a bird's-eye view into a very intimately connected world of adoption: a network of people like Kate and Colleen who scurried around like busy bees making honey. I was lucky enough to realize that honey was sweet, no matter where it came from.

David dozed beside me on and off all afternoon. He never fell into a deep sleep. "He's usually a good napper," Kate remarked. It seemed, though, that every time Kate left the den, David would open his eyes and hold me in his gaze.

I have heard it said that babies are the most powerful creatures in the universe. It was hard to believe it possible, thinking of a helpless, dependent infant who needs total care for feeding, bathing, changing, moving. Yet when I spent those hours alone with David, I felt that power. His sparkling eyes searched my face with such purpose and depth, as if his soul were a thousand years old. His birth had caused an incredible set of circumstances to occur—quite an awesome phenomenon to consider—over such a long distance involving people who wouldn't have otherwise met.

I leaned down over him, my face inches away from his, while our eyes held each other's gaze as they did in those first moments. "This was all your doing," I murmured to him, feeling a frenetic type of energy buzzing around us. David smiled.

It was close to five o'clock when Kate switched on the lamp and announced it was time for David's exercises. She handed me Xeroxed instruction sheets with simple drawings. I looked them over while she cleared the coffee table and covered the hard surface with a soft pink blanket. She took off David's sleeper and laid him on the blanket wearing just his diaper and a white cotton undershirt. The warm room got warmer as I followed the instruction sheets with her.

All afternoon I was dreading this. I was hoping that Colleen would return and we'd leave before the session would begin, but Kate was eager for me to see how conscientiously she had been working with David, unaware of my own memories. So, silently I watched as she held one little leg down while pushing the other as high as it would go. Wearing an expressionless mask, I swallowed the lump in my throat.

"They tell me it doesn't hurt him," Kate said.

I couldn't respond.

"First I thought they told me that 'cause they knew I wouldn't do it otherwise," she continued. "But he doesn't seem to mind it. He doesn't cry."

David fidgeted. His fists jabbed the air. I brushed my lips against his head. My heart filled with pained frustration.

I remembered Jay Kobbeloff. We went to elementary school together; he was a few years older. Compared to Jay, I was a ballerina. Miss Roland, our physical therapist, could stretch my leg up to a 45 degree angle, without too much resistance, and hold for a count of ten. Jay's legs were more bent and rigid. Even with his braces locked at the knees, ten degrees was about the maximum elevation for one of his legs to go. Sometimes our therapy sessions would overlap. I'd be practicing "heel-toe" walking on the parallel bars while Miss Roland stretched Jay on the exercise table.

"Aiyee," Jay would shriek. "Goddammit!'

"Watch your language, Jay!" Miss Roland scolded. "It isn't that bad. Besides, if you relax those muscles, it won't hurt as much."

I always wondered how a taut rubber band relaxed. I knew that rubber never seemed to slacken or wear out like elastic. If a rubber band were stretched too far, it just snapped.

One day, Miss Roland pushed too far. She broke Jay's leg.

"She feels terrible," I overheard my mother tell another mother. My mother and Mrs. Kobbeloff were friends. "Miss Roland's taking it hard."

No one talked about how Jay was taking it. He wore a cast for a long time, but he used a wheelchair, anyway. Before the accident, though, he was able to walk a little bit with crutches. After the cast was off, he didn't need them anymore; he never even stood on his own again.

Kate believed she was doing the right thing. So did Colleen. I knew there were gentler methods of therapy, but I had no expertise, just intuition. I felt so alone. I missed Neil.

David's other exercises, for the most part, didn't seem as stressful to him: bicycling his legs, and sitting on Kate's lap while she raised and lowered his arms and bent and flexed his forearms. His coppery eyebrows raised with a curious expression as if he were trying to discern whether or not he liked what was being foisted upon him.

It was time for the last exercise. "This is his least favorite," Kate admitted.

It was the exercise to correct the torticollis in his neck, "hardly apparent at all, now." Placing firm hands on either side of his sweet round face, she slowly turned David's head from left to right and right to left. David grunted. I cringed.

"Don't tell Colleen," Kate confided secretively, "but I don't always do this one."

"Good!" I spurted with a knee-jerk reaction, yet I worried how Kate would take my response.

"I know Colleen is a physical therapist and knows more about CP than I do," Kate continued as though my interjection were just part of her thought, "but most babies are born with kinks in the neck. Just think, they're in cramped quarters for nine months. Marie, David's birth mother, is a little bit of thing; no taller than I am. If it weren't for the medical tests, I would never have suspected there was anything wrong other than the fact that a fairly good-sized seven-and-some-pound baby came out of a tiny woman. No wonder he's stiff!"

It would have been so easy to incite a revolt, but I wanted David so badly. I kept myself quiet.

"But I do the exercises," she assured me. "He seems to like the attention, too." She began dressing him and cooed, "You like 'em, don'tcha, li'l fella?"

I could see his face brighten. A deep gurgle escaped his throat, sounding like a belly laugh. I felt my heart rippling with delight.

The phone rang. She handed David over to me before she went to answer it. I cuddled him.

Moments later Kate reappeared with a cordless phone. "It's Neil."

I traded David for the receiver, trying not to press any buttons to disconnect the call. "Neil!"

"Hi, Bubbie."

It was so good to hear his rich, gravelly voice. "Whatever you have to do—beg, borrow, steal, sell your body—I don't care," I began immediately, "just do it. This is our kid. I don't care if Rita Sue James wants ten million dollars for him, you gotta get the money."

He laughed. "When do you meet her, anyway?" he asked about the woman from the Christian Family Community Adoption Agency.

"Tomorrow morning," I answered. "She's coming over to Colleen's because her office isn't wheelchair accessible."

"Do me a favor, Bubbie, don't offer the ten million right away."

"Okay," I agreed. We both knew I'd never make it in the world of high finance.

"How's it going?"

I told Neil I spent the afternoon with David at Kate's house. "She just finished exercising him."

"How was that?"

"Hard. It's the same stuff we had when we were kids," I replied, feeling my own sadness as I talked. "They told Kate it doesn't hurt him—to make sure she'd do it—and he doesn't cry, but, you know, when I watched her holding one leg down and pushing the other one straight up, I could feel the pain again. I know it hurts."

"Hang in there, Bubbie." His voice consoled me.

"I'm trying," I said, wishing he weren't so far away. There were too many memories in this new domain. Sights and sounds hurled me into childhood places and painful silences I thought I had finally left behind. Neil was my only link, at present, to the world I lived in now.

Colleen picked me up late in the afternoon. I left David in a deep sleep, snuggling in a warm blanket in the day crib with his brand new teddy bear. My heart ached a little when I whispered good-bye.

Chapter Three

A Matter of Perspective

Kate had wanted me to stay at her house. She was ready to drag down a mattress from one of the second floor-bedrooms so I could camp out in the den, but I thought it best for me to go to Colleen's. For one thing, Colleen's three-story house was equipped with an elevator and several accessible bathrooms. My other reason had to do with David's birth mother, Marie, who was still part of the picture.

Marie had decided to give up her baby shortly after she found out she was pregnant. At a young nineteen, in her first year of junior college, and a part-time salesperson, she wasn't ready to marry the baby's biological father (if that were ever a possibility), who was in pretty much the same position as she was, and raise a child. She contacted Rita Sue James, who arranged the adoption, making her only request that the baby be brought up in a Catholic home. Of course, that wouldn't have been a problem had Pete and Lisa decided to go through with the adoption. Her pregnancy was normal, too, until her eighth month when a fall off a ladder caused Marie to hemorrhage— and raised a red flag for possible injury to the fetus.

Marie had no second thoughts about the adoption and was ready to sign the necessary papers in her court appearance a month after she gave birth. The judge, however, decided to give her another two months to think it over because of the new developments. This meant she was allowed to visit the baby and, more crucially, she still had a choice of approving the baby's home.

No one thought it would be too good of an idea to tell her I was disabled. It was bad enough I was Jewish. At Rita Sue's suggestion I even wrote Marie a letter assuring that "Christopher" (Marie's birth name for David) "would be exposed to the teachings of Jesus." It was certainly true, I thought, easing my conscience when I wrote it—after all, in the Bay Area he'll have exposure to any kind of religion that exists. I also wrote that I had "a great deal of experience with disabled people," since I felt it might be a more persuasive factor than being Jewish.

Marie still had doubts, and Kate again came to the rescue. Marie agreed to talk with Kate's priest. That, however, wouldn't happen until Friday—two more days away. I was concerned about it just enough to maintain some distance between David and me. Staying at Colleen's served as my own little refuge.

Colleen's house was not nearly as serene as Kate's. Before I had even taken off my jacket, Colleen raced across the hardwood floors and up and down the stairs at least three times—two of them in pursuit of eleven-month-old Jefferson, who seemed to enjoy testing his mother's physical endurance. *(Perhaps David would be disabled just enough to slow him down so I'd be able to catch him.)* And though she cussed with mild exasperation, she eagerly met Jefferson's challenge. His deep sea blue eyes and her brown ones held the same ready-for-mischief look. They both seemed to have the same energetic nature, very different from the other two members of the family—Max, a big somber bear of a man, and seven-year-old, freckle-faced Maggie with pensive gray eyes.

"Now, Jefferson," she said, scooping him off the third step for the second time, "come sit in your high chair and eat Cheerios while I get dinner together."

She settled him in the wooden seat and scurried around the kitchen, piling what looked like last night's dirty dishes into an already overflowing sink. Simultaneously, she began answering my question about what Rita Sue James was like.

"The woman has to have some loose bolts," she said, "which has worked out to our advantage. She's let Kate and me interfere as much as we want. At one point she told me she thought she could get this born-again Christian family to adopt him, and I talked her out of it. I said that the baby should go to a home where he's really wanted."

I swallowed a little bit of guilt, for it wasn't until Kate plopped David in my lap on the airplane that I knew I really wanted him. I wasn't sure I wanted Colleen or Kate to know that.

Ten o'clock the next morning in Colleen's drafty yellow-walled dining room, I met Rita Sue.

"Oh, Denise, I'm so glad to meet you," she greeted as she clip-clopped in high-heeled black leather boots into the room. Her right hand jutted out toward me, unfortunately, leaving me with my often posed dilemma: am I going to self-consciously aim for it with my less coordinated right hand or should I grip it firmly and surely (and more easily) with my left? I decided the latter would display the most finesse.

She placed her gold-trimmed maroon folder and black leather purse on the white crocheted dining room tablecloth, untied the belt of her knee-length cream-colored cashmere coat and slipped it off, carefully folding it over the straight-back wooden chair.

I apologetically tugged at the creases in my sweater as she smoothed out her brown knitted dress and adjusted her cameo brooch. The drafty air that came from the kitchen suddenly filled with her expensive, faint-smelling perfume.

I should have worn a dress, earrings, the jade and pink quartz necklace my affluent sister-in-law had given me.

"Well, now, have you seen the baby?" she began as she took her ladylike seat. "Isn't he darling?"

I nodded and murmured a "yes" to both questions. She spoke with a smile and a singsong voice, one that exuded detached warmth.

The conversation lasted all of forty-five minutes. Surprisingly, she didn't ask me many questions. Perhaps she assumed everything was in order because our home study had been taken care of by AASK. Or perhaps she didn't relish the thought of dealing with me in too much detail. Or, as Colleen implied, she was almost ecstatic to have this baby taken off her hands. The businesswoman in her, however, was not ready to ignore mentioning her fee of $6,200, after graciously deducting the $500 for the home study, "since we don't have to worry about that."

Placing the figures off to the side—for me to take home—Rita Sue (carefully avoiding, I sensed, those `unpleasant' words like "pregnancy" and "abortion") gave her pitch. "We really perform such an important service, Denise. Those girls come to us caring so much about their babies. They have so much courage. They only want the best for their babies. . . . Poor Marie has been so upset about Christopher. She had her hopes set that everything would work out. I just encouraged her to keep praying," she smiled gloriously, "and now, you're here answering our prayers."

I managed a faint, bemused smile. I wondered if she would quote from the Scriptures soon. "How is Marie feeling about Neil's and my being Jewish?"

Rita Sue sighed wistfully, "Well, Denise, you know she had her heart set on Christopher being raised Catholic. But I've been talking to her. . . ."

I had no doubt about *that!* I leaned my elbow on the table and brought my hand up to cover my amusement and the urge to blurt out that his name was David.

". . . I told Marie that, well, you know, after all, Jesus was Jewish before he converted to Christianity," Rita Sue said with sincerity.

I didn't think he could have converted; I'd been under the impression Christianity didn't exist before Jesus. However, this wasn't the time for a theological discussion.

Checking her watch, Rita Sue announced she had to be going, but not before she had the chance to advise me on "just one more thing . . . I must tell you, Denise, about this program for children with all kinds of handicaps. In fact, the center is located in Palo Alto—not far from you. I brought you this article on it. They do such wonderful work there."

It was a program I was familiar with, having to do with a theory on re-education, or to be less euphemistic, sanctioned brainwashing. Its focus was on making the child as "normal" as possible. Rita Sue just "couldn't recommend it highly enough."

"We worked with someone from the center a few years ago when we discovered our son had a learning handicap. Denise, it did wonders for him. The program is so regimented and structured, and that's so important for a child. Stephen's just doing fine now . . ."

As an android, I added silently. "I'll look into it," I lied.

"Oh, Denise, I do hope so," she implored, slipping on her cashmere coat. "I sincerely believe they can help. And with faith and prayers, who knows what miracles can happen?"

"Who knows," I echoed complacently, wondering how in the world this woman could say that in the presence of someone with a disability. Besides, the miracle had already happened: David found his way into my arms.

I tend to bring out the patronizing side in many people. I know it isn't always because they assume I'm retarded; Rita Sue James knew I wasn't. I don't know if people think that my disability perpetuates a childlike innocence or whether it causes inhibition of my common sense. There are times, too, when people don't engage me in conversation because they may be uncomfortable listening to my slow, seemingly labored speech, or they're afraid they won't understand me and are too embarrassed to ask me to repeat myself.

Rita Sue's behavior toward me, however, struck me as having little to do with my disability; I imagined that she presented herself the same way with those "courageous young girls" and child-seeking couples. Kate and Colleen had been exposed to her not-so-gracious side of being furious with Pete and Lisa behind their backs while assuring them that they would have a chance to adopt another baby, without any intention of keeping her word, according to Colleen. Still, I felt my meeting with the woman was rather benign, at least compared to the next appointment I had to keep two days later.

The pediatric clinic was located in an urban hospital, one that dimly greets its visitors and patients with fluorescent lights and dark-squared vinyl floors and stuffs their noses with the oppressive sterile odor of ammonia. I had experienced these sights and smells so many times before as a child; now I faced them as a mother. No matter which role, it was still intimidating, bringing back memories I found myself unable to block out. Carrying David on my lap, I remembered another day at another clinic more than twenty years ago—the last time my mother was well enough to go with me. I had just turned fifteen.

My mother and I had sat along the cool, white-walled waiting area of the hospital corridor. Seeing a familiar white-haired, white-coated doctor doddering toward us, my mother nudged me to wipe the saliva from my lips and sit up straight. He stopped right in front of us.

"Well, Mother," he greeted her as he had done for probably the past twelve years without having our names before him on my chart. "And how is she doing?"

"Very well, Doctor," my mother replied, never missing the opportunity to embarrass me by bragging, "she's on the honor roll at school."

"That's nice." He flashed a fake smile at me. "But tell me, Mother, have you thought about what comes next?"

My mother's brow wrinkled. I recognized her "uneasy" voice when she answered him. "She'll probably go on to college."

He shook his head and smacked his lips as if she had given the wrong answer. "Why?" he rhetorically asked, wrinkling his forehead.

"These children only end up as vegetables; they won't get jobs. They'll just end up in institutions. . . ."

The voice over the loudspeaker cut him off by paging his name. He shuffled away without another word while my mother's all-year-round tanned face ashened. I played with the idea of sticking out my crutch to trip him, but my teenage rebelliousness was, unfortunately, not due to surface for another seven years. So, instead, I impotently tried to comfort my mother using the same words she used on me at previous clinic visits.

"Mommy, don't listen to him," I pleaded, tugging at her arm. "It isn't true. He's old. He doesn't know what he's saying. You said so yourself. That's why he's not head of the clinic no more."

She sat there as if she'd been zapped by a lightning bolt. She didn't even bother to correct my grammar. The wrinkles deepened in her long, thin face. Her green eyes lost their life. A few months afterward, the kidney disease she had been battling since I was born defeated her, and I always suspected that last clinic visit exacerbated her inevitably losing out to the illness. That day, I watched the fight go out of her and be replaced by despair. My mother had focused the past fifteen years on caring for me, encouraging me, prodding me on against the experts' so-called objective reality. She was tired. Those words spoken by that doddering old fool were part of her death sentence, even preventing her from dying in peace.

And now, I was the mother . . .

The four of us, Kate, Colleen, David, and myself, sat in a small narrow waiting room of cream-colored walls, bright orange molding and neat gray industrial carpet. It was in the pediatric physical therapy department; there were no toys.

When our turn came, I maneuvered around the sharp corners and followed Colleen into an empty room. There was a bookcase in one corner, a basket of toys, and a double-sized dull gray, plastic mat, the kind I learned how to fall on before I was taught how to walk.

Another five minutes passed before a curly, brown-haired woman entered the room. After Colleen introduced us, Diane took David from me and sat down with him on the mat. She undressed him down to his diaper for inspection.

"Well, let's see how that torticollis is," she began, firmly plying his head from side to side. "Mmm, his neck seems looser."

Kate and Colleen beamed as I silently looked on. Diane handled

David gently enough, and according to Colleen, she was quite taken with him, but the whole experience felt so . . . clinical. Methodically she went over every joint, bending his elbows, wrists, hips, knees, ankles and whatever else, like a machinist checking her equipment for creaks and flaws. She used words like retractors and flexors, instead of leg or arm muscles. (And we wondered growing up, my disabled friends and I, why we had such a hard time accepting our bodies as our bodies?) After finishing her examination, she looked at us.

"I'm still feeling spasticity in his arms and legs, maybe a little less than before, but still obvious," she said.

To whom? I wanted to defy.

"I'm going to give you a couple more exercises to do with -"

She was interrupted when one of the red rubber balls rolled off a shelf and bounced onto the mat. Its suddenness startled David.

"He's still exhibiting an overactive Moro reflex," Diane remarked.

I smiled knowingly at David. We had something in common! Quite a usual occurrence for those of us having CP, the reflex would too often cause me embarrassment in public places. Sitting alone enjoying a mocha in a cafe, lost in a book or in deep thought, I would jump at any sudden noise or sound—a clattering spoon, a friendly voice unexpectedly addressing me. My knees would hit the tabletop or my hand would send the glass flying over the table's edge.

"At this point, Diane, could you tell us anything about what might be in store?" Colleen asked.

"It's so hard to say," she replied as Kate got down on the mat and started dressing David. "He could be mildly disabled, he could be severely disabled . . ."

I cringed. *Severely disabled?* My stomach muscles tightened. How many disabled babies had this woman ever come across? Maybe in St. Louis they didn't have enough of a variety to compare and contrast. I've seen babies with cerebral palsy who couldn't hold their heads up or suck on a bottle. In fact, when Neil was an infant, his mother had to spoon milk into his mouth and massage it down his throat. I've seen babies that are so miserable with hunger and discomfort they cry all the time. *Severely disabled?* David? Alert, well-nourished, gurgling David?

For someone with cerebral palsy or mental retardation, the term *severely disabled* had somewhat different implications than for individuals having polio and spinal cord injuries. When applied to the latter, *severely disabled* described a physical set of circumstances that then established a set of needs in a service delivery system: personal assistance, mobility, health care, adaptive technology—those things that would help the most physically disabled people lead independent lives. In recent years, the label had become popular for political expediency. Yet I silently winced every time I heard it used in reference to me; it categorized me, and those like me, according to a medical and social system that had a dim view of children and adults with CP and other developmental disabilities and our potential. And judging from how David's case had been managed, it still carried that stigma.

I wouldn't deny that my disability was significant, but being classified as severely disabled felt so inappropriate. It pigeonholed me based on the outward appearance of my cerebral palsy, not on my ability. It confused people and led them to assume that I shouldn't be expected to do all the things I can do: drag myself out of bed in the morning, make my own instant coffee, dustbust the cat litter that got on the floor when I cleaned out the poop from the cat box. I wondered, had I been given that label as a child, would the goals and expectations for me have been different? The label itself seemed arbitrarily dependent on how someone got around. When I hobbled at a sweaty, white-knuckled, slower-than-a-snail pace on my crutches, I was considered only moderately disabled. Now that I use a power chair, I'm called severely disabled, even though I'm much more "able" in my wheelchair than I ever was on crutches. I might not be able to get up a flight of stairs, but I can cross a floor in way less than ten minutes—with a baby on my lap, too!

I wanted to say something to Diane. But what? I had the feeling that nothing I would be able to articulate at the moment would have made any difference in her prognosis of David. Besides, I feared that it was not safe to express my dissenting opinion until David came home.

I kept excruciatingly silent while I watched Kate dress David and Diane left to get the new exercises. My thoughts went to Pete and Lisa with a somewhat clearer view: no wonder they reneged on the adoption.

Lisa had been through the very same experience with David that I was now going through. I was finding it difficult, even with everything I knew, to watch David's body being manipulated and to listen to Diane speculate on David's prognosis. There was a big discrepancy between Diane's projected image of David and the delightful baby I saw before me. I could imagine the impact it must have had on Lisa, who knew virtually nothing about the world of disability (like so many other new parents), unable to discern and question the validity of what the "experts" were saying. As hard as this was for me now, it would likely continue as the years rolled on. Perhaps Lisa, realizing her own limits, had sense enough to know she wouldn't be able to handle such emotionally draining experiences. . . . And, of course, she just wasn't meant to be his mother; I was!

We met Diane out in the waiting room. She gave Kate new Xeroxed sheets while Colleen strapped my seatbelt around David and me and then opened the heavy door. Without waiting for either of them, we burned rubber.

During my last two days in St. Louis, I spent as much time with David as I could, knowing that if everything worked out it would still be a month or longer before he could come home. Marie's court appearance to relinquish custody was set for March 19th. Anything could happen between now and then. I had heard so many dismal stories of birth mothers deciding at the last minute to keep their babies. Kate reassured me that everything was going smoothly— Marie had spoken to Kate's priest, who calmed her fears about the baby going to heaven and assured her that what was most important was that her baby would be loved and cared for. Marie, too, had figured out I was disabled; she had asked Kate during her final visit with the baby, when Marie, her mother, and Rita Sue held hands and prayed over him (Kate somehow managed to extricate herself from the scene). Marie didn't ask for details, though, and Kate thought it best not to offer any. But a month was so far away. Marie could change her mind. . . . She could have second thoughts about our religion, our disability . . . , and David was so beautiful . . .

"I was thinking," Colleen said, when we were all settled in Kate's den Friday afternoon. "D'you think it would be okay if David spent the night with Denise at my house?" There was that mischievous gleam in her eye again.

"I was thinking that myself," Kate excitedly responded, adding her impish warning, "but we can't let Rita Sue find out."

I chuckled. They were quite a pair. If these two ever got it in their heads to go on to bigger schemes, their adversaries wouldn't have a chance. In fact, they seemed so pleased with themselves with this latest scheme, I didn't know how to tell them that I was slightly petrified!

It's not that I wasn't enticed by the thought of being together with my son. I was just in a state of concealed panic at the idea of spending the whole dark night alone with a baby, even with Colleen only a wake-up-the-whole-house yell away. I would be feeding David his two o'clock bottle. I'd have to burp him, still nervous about slapping him too hard. I'd have to make sure that the pillows I used for propping him up when I fed him didn't smother him when he slept. And I'd have to make sure he slept on his right side—another therapeutic strategy to remedy his torticollis (he couldn't even sleep without therapeutic intervention!). . . . Finally, I'd have to make sure that in my sleep, I didn't roll over and crush him.

If Neil were here, I could do it. . . . We could do it! He was always so rational and confident, coming up with answers as his green-brown eyes would scan the data banks of his mind. I had missed him these last few days, feeling so alone as I relived memories and thoughts about growing up disabled and now living in a nondisabled world—feelings he and I often shared with just a smirk or a roll of our eyes, or a snide comment murmured so unclearly no one else could understand it. I missed his sweet, gentle scent, lying with him at night as his strong, smooth arm draped my waist and I'd intertwine my legs with his, carefully avoiding the sharpness of his bony knees and overgrown toenails. I felt safe with Neil. He knew how to handle situations—most situations, ones that didn't involve emotions (hurt and anger made him sulk). But he wasn't here and I felt so alone. . . . Yet Colleen and Kate seemed confident and I was hesitant to show my vulnerability so I went along.

To celebrate my last evening in St. Louis, Kate prepared a big dinner. Colleen, the kids, and even Colleen's husband, Max, joined us, since the portable ramps were already out for me (Kate's house had a few steps). Max was a homebody, and Kate was thrilled that he accepted her invitation. Colleen picked him up after work; He ran Paraquad, St. Louis's independent living center.

Max was a big, quiet man in his late forties. He sat regally in his wheelchair; broad shoulders, long face with dignified graying beard, and arched eyebrows. He presented himself with authority, partly because of his quadriplegic unmoving limbs, and partly because he said very little. I found it hard, due to my own shyness and his reticence, to get to know him during my short visit.

David sat next to me in his swing, looking about at the crowd that was seated around the long dining room table and up at the shining lights from the chandelier. I tried to pay attention to the different conversations going on, but my eyes always riveted back to David, knowing that after tomorrow morning I wouldn't see him again for a long time.

After dinner we gathered in front of the fireplace in the living room and took Polaroids. The pictures would help get me through the coming weeks and perhaps months. A short while later, we left; it was past Jefferson's bedtime.

"I'm going up to put the kids to bed," Colleen announced, settling David beside me on another flowery, brocaded, soft-cushioned loveseat. A moment later, she bounded up the stairs, leaving Max and me with David, who was slowly sliding off the pillows.

First I tried tugging him up. He started to fuss, even with the pacifier in his mouth. The more I jostled him the more agitated he became, until at last, he spit out the pacifier and went into a full-fledged wail. His face reddened and his little body quivered, including his tiny pink tongue. I desperately wanted to pick him up and hold him in my arms. He was on my wrong side. I was on the wrong couch. He was crying. I glanced up at Max, who could just look on. The only thing I could think of was to grab hold of his terry-cloth sleeper, but with David crying and Max watching I was too nervous to get a good grip. As I lifted David into the air, the cloth started slipping through my fingers. David landed on my knees just in time. After pulling him into the curve of my lap, I stuck the pacifier in his mouth. He sucked eagerly.

Sweat dripped down my back while my labored snorts eased into more natural breaths. I felt Max's eyes on me. He was probably thinking—echoing my own doubt—*how could this woman take care of a baby?*

I was the first to break the poignant silence. "Scared all of us there, didn't I?"

"For a minute," Max said simply, raising those arched eyebrows. I wondered just what he would tell Colleen in the privacy of their bedroom.

Later that evening, the soft light of the barely audible TV flickered on David as I crawled under the covers on the sofa bed. He slept soundly as I laid my head on the pillow and turned to look at him, my face inches away from his. I heard his shallow breath and felt it gently brush my finger. I smelled his warm almond scent mixed with A & D Ointment. I studied his face, letting my eyes savor the fuzz on his head, his fine eyebrows, his translucent eyelids fringed by blond lashes, his apple-round cheeks of Poppin' Fresh dough, the nostrils of his pug nose easily breathing the quiet night air, and his pale pink lips that every now and then would suckle an imaginary nipple. I put my arm around his soft, silent body. I was so in love with this baby. I would do anything for him. It surprised me; I never thought love could feel so unselfish.

Sleep passed over me like a thin blanket. The murmur of voices from the TV lulled me into a light snooze, though my mind remained conscious. I must have awakened the moment David stirred for his two o'clock bottle. I then proceeded to have the most physical exercise I had had in a long time. Without any inhibitions, I scooted around on the bed as I positioned and repositioned David, me, and the pillows to get us just right. After I fed him, burped him, and laid him back down, I fell into a deeper sleep. I opened my eyes as the dark sky faded into the grayness of early morning. I switched off the snowy TV screen.

It was an hour or so before I heard the old house creak with Colleen's footsteps and stir with Jefferson's yearning voice calling "Mama." She hushed him with a whisper right before she opened the guest room door. I gave her a thumbs-up sign and she grabbed the Polaroid, capturing a sleeping infant and his nothing-short-of-ecstatic, exhausted mother.

The pain of having to leave did not hit me until I was zipping through the crowded airport with Colleen. We arrived late, leaving Kate to unload Jefferson and David from the van and meet us at the departure gate while Colleen and I went ahead to make the seating arrangement. Maneuvering through the crowd, I was suddenly in tears. I didn't want to go. I felt as if I were a child again going off to summer camp and being torn from my mother, her warmth and comfort—a feeling I hadn't felt with such intensity in a long, long time.

In four days, I had found two women who cared and nurtured, understood and gave—the kind of women that I thought were lost to a generation who now struggled for their own "space." "Space"—a very modern cliché. Somehow I couldn't imagine either Colleen or Kate using such an esoteric phrase as "I need more space," except in reference to more room in their houses. Yet they seemed to be very much in control of their own lives—something that was a struggle for me. They were able to handle situations and people like Rita Sue James. I still had to learn—not just for my sake now, but for my child's. Colleen and Kate offered me a glimpse of what was possible. I wished I could take their "secret" back with me.

And I wished I could take David back with me.

I fought my sobs as Colleen and I arrived at the gate mobbed with people. Kate and the kids were nowhere in sight, and the crewman wanted me to board. I frantically looked at Colleen. I couldn't leave my baby without saying good-bye.

"They'll be here, don't worry," she tried assuring me, stretching on tiptoes to see over heads.

"We have to get her seated so we can get her wheelchair down to baggage," he said, grabbing my chair handles.

"No!" I shouted, applying reversed pressure on my joystick to thwart his slightest effort. He couldn't push that easily anyway—he didn't know he had to disengage the motors first by releasing two simple little levers. I wasn't about to offer that information, either; I wasn't going to be pushed around this time.

"Here they come, here they come!"

Moments later, David was on my lap and we headed down to the plane entrance. I parked my chair and, with Colleen's help, walked to the seat not far from the door—the flight attendant (with some common sense) assigned me an empty one in first class. I belted in and Kate, who had held David while I walked, gave him back to me until the other passengers were seated.

"I'll send pictures every week," Kate promised. "And he'll be home before you know it!"

I broke into sobs as we all hugged good-bye and posed for last-minute pictures. Tears streamed down my cheeks and wails escaped my opened mouth. In my hysteria my front tooth bumped David's head. He started to cry. "I hurt him, I hurt him," I sobbed even louder, but there was too much commotion for anyone to have understood me. I squeezed David to my breast, trying to ease both of our pain. Colleen snapped another Polaroid: David and I had the same miserable look—red noses and all.

Drained of tears and sleep, I settled back in my wide-bodied, nubby red and blue seat after they left. I dried my face on the worn-out Kleenex Kate had given me. There was a lot to think about, a lot to get done, but for now, I'd just rest. I had been through too much these last four days. I needed to rest—I'd just left a piece of my heart in St. Louis.

Chapter Four

The Patchwork Quilts of Children Grown

My wheelchair was waiting for me as soon as the other passengers deplaned in San Francisco. A flight attendant helped me walk to the exit and made sure I got comfortably settled in my chair. I wasted no time switching on the motor. I swirled around and sped up the tunneled jetport to the terminal where Neil waited. He beamed when he saw me and, as soon as I stopped, he gave me a warm, crushing hug.

"I missed you, Bubbie," he cried. "I'm glad you're home!"

"Me, too. Me, too," I repeated into his neck.

I loved Neil's hugs, even though they could be too enthusiastic, at times, and cut off oxygen or circulation to key organs of my body. His strong, sinewy arms around me made me feel wanted and safe. Yet he didn't put them around me all that often, even when he came home after a long day at work. Usually, I'd open the door to see him slumped in his chair with his bearded chin resting on his chest. His feet would drag on the hardwood floor as he slowly crossed over the threshold; even his power chair seemed tuckered out. He didn't have the energy to embrace me or to position himself so that I could get close enough to kiss him hello. Yet it wasn't just fatigue: he rolled his eyes almost every time I tried to snuggle up to him for no apparent reason. He just didn't see any point in demonstrating affection.

I came from an affectionate family. My paternal grandparents would sit side by side holding hands. My father and mother smooched right in front of us. My mother lavished me with loving words, hugs, and kisses at every opportunity. Even my father, who had very few child-rearing skills, fondly kissed us every morning when he left for work and every evening when he returned. There were times when my sister and I genuinely "kissed and made up," after hair-pulling, nail-scratching fights.

Neil didn't come from that kind of family. The Jacobsons never planted kisses, they brushed cheeks. Their phone conversations never ended with "I love you" or "I miss you" or, for that matter, even "Good-bye." Many times, I would hear Neil talking and then suddenly hanging up the phone because "they had to go."

Many of my arguments with Neil centered on my frustration with his reticence to communicate and show affection. Now that we were going to adopt David, I was very curious (and a bit concerned) to see what Neil would be like with his own baby.

"So, what's up?" he asked, as he separated from me.

I told him about my night with David, feeding him a bottle, burping him, my aerobics on the bed to rearrange pillows and blankets and the baby. "I didn't get much sleep." I saw his eyes brighten; I could guess what he was thinking, but I continued on with my next thought. "Anyway, what's been going on around here?"

"I spoke to my mother," he replied flatly.

My stomach sank onto my intestines. "How'd she take it?"

"Not too well," he groaned.

I should have asked for the details but I was a coward, certain that whatever his mother had said would ruin my homecoming and the euphoria I still felt from spending the night with my son. I tried swallowing the lump in my throat to find my voice.

"Anyhow . . . ," Neil saved me by using his favorite adverb to change the subject, "let's get your suitcase and go home."

We went to baggage claim and picked up my tan-and-brown suitcase without any further discussion of his mother's call. There would be plenty of time for that, since we probably wouldn't hear from her again until her usual wake-up call at eight-thirty next Saturday morning.

Neil filled me in on other news as we drove home. "I told my brother. He was okay about it."

"Did he say anything?"

"Not really. Just not to let my mother get to me," he shrugged. "She's giving him a hard time, too, because his girlfriend isn't Jewish."

"So what else is new?" I felt slightly irritated. "She's been doing that for years. Didn't he say *anything* about becoming an uncle?"

"We didn't talk that long," Neil defended.

I shook my head hopelessly. There was so much distance between him and his siblings, his younger brother, Stevie, and his older sister, Eta. Neil was so proud of them: Stevie was a virologist for the National Institute of Health in Washington, D.C., and Eta was an interior decorator with a half-million-dollar home in an exclusive Long Island neighborhood. But Neil's phone conversations with them (as infrequent as they were) never seemed to go beyond polite inquiry. He spoke with them as if he were speaking with new acquaintances, stammering through his questions and answers, leading the discussions away from himself. It was Neil's typical modus operandi with most people; it gave him time to get comfortable speaking and also to avoid sharing a lot about himself. I found it odd that he would be that way with his siblings.

"Stevie will probably let Eta know," Neil remarked.

I wondered what that conversation would be like.

"Shelley called, too," Neil said, as we finally pulled up in front of our brown shingled house. "She wants you to call her back."

Shelley, my older sister, was the only member of my small immediate or dwindling extended family whom I kept in regular contact with. We spoke over the phone once a week. Three thousand miles separated us, as it also separated me from most of my other relatives. Occasionally, I'd get a short note or call from my father and Aunt Rita, or I'd call them on holidays. I didn't write them many letters; after spending most of the day pecking out a couple of pages of prose, I was hardly in the mood to be a detailed correspondent. Through the years, both my father and my aunt's gradual hearing losses and infrequent verbal communication with me (so they weren't use to my speech pattern anymore) made it frustrating for all three of us to have lengthy discussions over the phone. But there wasn't much to tell my father and aunt that they wanted to hear: I had no steady job and I wasn't back in school. To them, writing was just a hobby. It didn't count, unless I made money. Sometimes I took part-time jobs teaching and counseling, I think, just so I wouldn't hear the disappointment in their voices.

Except for Shelley, I didn't feel much attachment to my family. I knew my father and my Aunt Rita were proud of me. I had exceeded their expectations—moving to California, living on my own, and marrying a computer scientist with a real job in a bank! *Can you imagine, a CP who made something of himself?* Yet I always felt a void when it came to family, the void my mother left when she died.

For the first thirteen years of my life, my mother took care of us. She kept house (a Kosher one, no less) for my father, who always complained that she spent too much money (the concept of inflation escaped him). She nudged my sister to finish her homework and nagged her to clean up the mess she made in our room. For me, well, she was always there, except on her weekly mah jongg night . . .

Every school day morning from the time I was four and a half, after she threw on a musty-smelling old housedress and breakfasted on a cup of coffee and a cigarette, she'd come sit at the edge of my bed.

"Come on, Puss," she coaxed, as she reached under my quilt to gently tug at my feet. "Neise, it's time to wake up."

I cooperated by letting her guide my feet into her lap. As my mother slipped on each cotton sock, she made sure that the seams coincided with my heels and toes, not an easy task to do in the early morning darkness with the soles of my feet turned up, while I caught a few more minutes of sleep on my stomach.

Even when I became older and could dress myself, she continued our morning ritual. She saw no point in waking me up an hour earlier just so I could begin my day struggling to put my socks on in the cold darkness of morning; the steam didn't even start hissing through the radiators until six-thirty and the chill made my muscles tighten up even more. I got plenty of practice dressing myself on weekends, she reasoned, and what the therapists didn't know wouldn't hurt them.

In the afternoon when I came home from school, I sat down at my corner of the rectangular kitchen table. I drank my two glasses of milk and gobbled up four Mallomar cookies while she took out my books and supplies from my bookbag. She set the books, my loose-leaf, and math instruments off to one side of the table and kept the pencils in her hand as she walked a few steps to the old crank-handled sharpener attached to the silverware counter. Vigorously she sharpened the worn lead ends of those No. 2 pencils into needle-fine points. The flesh of her upper arm would jiggle and her chin-length brunette flip would bob around her thin face. Her torso swayed with rhythmic motion. My mother was an average-sized woman with an amply shaped body, always conscious of her weight. She had lost sixty pounds in the last few years and boasted that she fit into a size ten. Yet I had never thought of her as fat or thin, as attractive or not.

She was my mother; very comfortable to be around.

Putting the newly sharpened pencils down beside my books, she cleared off my empty glass and the milk container and sponged down the plastic tablecloth. Then she'd sit down with me to do my homework. Under my dictation, she wrote answers to history questions and reading assignments, sentences for new vocabulary words, essays for English in her fine cursive handwriting. We developed a rhythm: I'd watch for her to finish writing one phrase before I'd say the next. She'd never rush me if I had to think awhile. Periodically, her soft hazel eyes would peer at me over the sparkle-rimmed glasses that sat on the bridge of her long nose. Her full lips puffed patiently on a cigarette. Sometimes, her wrinkled fingers would gently pull a loose strand of brown hair from my lips before it ended up in my mouth; she was careful not to interrupt my concentration. If I got stuck thinking up sentences or if I used incorrect grammar, she calmly prompted me. She helped my sister, too, who called out questions from the living room where she did her homework watching TV.

My mother liked doing my homework more than I did, especially when I entered high school. She regretted dropping out more than thirty years earlier, so she became a vicarious student. She caught on quickly in subjects like geometry and French—using rulers and compasses and protractors to draw isosceles triangles and parallelograms on graph paper, and writing headings and sentences in a foreign language she didn't understand, complete with cedillas and accent marks. My homework never had smudges.

On Saturday nights, she was my companion. My mother and I sat in the cozy smoke-draped living room watching *Saturday Night at the Movies,* reading, doing the crossword puzzle, or playing game after game of Scrabble, while my father dozed off in bed reading the sports page and my sister went out with her friends or on blind dates.

In the spring of my freshman year of high school, my mother had a heart attack at age forty-eight. I'd just turned fourteen. She had to take it easier. No longer did she wake me on school mornings by gently uncovering my feet to slip on my shoes and socks. My father, all dressed for work and smelling of Old Spice, woke me instead; the new demands on him disrupted his routine of leaving for work before anyone in the house even fluttered their eyelids.

"Neisie, wake up!" He flung the covers off my legs with his typical impatience. "You have to turn over. I can't put your socks on like this. You've gotta help me out here!"

He never knew how to be gentle, whether he was wiping chocolate off my face or cutting my toenails. In fact, whenever I complained that the scissors pinched some skin while he trimmed my nails, he chided me: "Don't worry, you've got nine others." Like my mother, he readily helped when he saw that I had difficulty with doing something physically, but he always had to remind me that he could do it "better" or "faster" or "easier" than I could.

His morning duty ended when he put me on the school bus, which would invariably be late. In the afternoons, my sister, a graduating senior in high school, would meet my bus and help me walk up the twenty-two stone steps of the courtyard and the one flight of marble steps inside to reach our apartment. My mother would be waiting in the kitchen to greet me with milk and Mallomars and we'd still tackle geometry and French, but the session drained her energy and enthusiasm too soon.

She became bedridden a little over a year later. Shelley and my father got stuck sitting with me at the table in the evenings, helping me do the homework that I couldn't get done in my free periods at school. They had no interest in trigonometry or economics, disappearing into another room whenever I took too long looking up answers I didn't remember from my reading hours earlier.

I was pushed farther and farther away from my mother, not understanding, not knowing how sick she was.

Every day, I hobbled into her room on my aluminum crutches and tried to cheer her up. She had always been my greatest fan, praising my juvenile attempts at poetry ("Did you ever see a dog with spots/It may look like the chicken pox") or laughing at my rendition of "I come for the rent, the rent, the rent," using a wrinkled napkin as mustache, hair bow, and bow tie.

"Oh, my man I love him so, he'll never know," I belted out as I leaned on one of the posts at the foot of my parents' four-poster bed. I had seen Barbra Streisand in a similar pose the previous night on Ed Sullivan and thought my mother would get a kick out of it.

"Neisie, stop shaking the bed!" she said harshly.

"But Mommy, I —"

"Neisie, don't lean on the bed!" Shelley snapped with sharper irritation. "Don't be a show-off!"

I bit my lip and held back my tears. Where was my mother who used to laugh at my antics, who used to hug me and kiss my *keppelah*? I couldn't even get close to her. It was almost impossible to climb on the four-poster; I jostled it too much. I was barely able to reach her to kiss her goodnight.

Right before the beginning of my junior year, when I was fifteen, the doctor admitted my mother into the hospital. No one told Shelley or me that she was dying from uremic poisoning, the end stage of kidney disease.

It had been almost eight weeks. "She's a little better today," or "It wasn't such a good day for her," or "Maybe she'll be home next week," the grown-ups would tell me after they'd visit her while they secretively whispered in another room.

I'd only get to see my mother on weekends, since it would complicate things if I went during the week. From week to week, her presence withered; her skin paled and shriveled as the poisons of her body's wastes swelled and discolored her legs.

When she'd first see me, a smile would brighten her drawn, thin face, but it faded all too quickly. My mother who had nurtured and comforted me all of my life had disappeared into this distant sick woman. I needed to know if she was ever coming back!

One evening when my father and Shelley left for the hospital, I reached over to the black rotary phone beside my bed and laboriously (and nervously) dialed the upstairs neighbor's number. Pearlie had been my mother's friend since high school.

"Hi, Pearlie," my breath caught in my chest. "Could you come down? I want to talk to you."

I hobbled through the living room and the foyer to the door. By the time I unlocked and cracked open the door, she was there. Moments later, I sat on the edge of the gold and orange flowered couch while Pearlie sat in the adjacent rust-colored armchair.

"What's going on, Pearlie?" I gathered up all my courage. *There were just some things one has to know.* "How sick is my mother?"

She adjusted her thick bifocals. "Very . . . Neisie, there's not much hope."

I swallowed, considering the fact without tears. Now I could prepare myself.

I never got to see my mother again. She died three days later on a miserably gray Friday, two days before Halloween. Pearlie met my bus that afternoon. I knew before she told me. I cried as Shelley sat beside me on the arm of the blue club chair with her arm around me. My Aunt Dinah hovered over us with tears of loss, sorrow, and pity in her large saucer eyes.

We wore black ribbons, covered the mirrors, and sat shivah after the funeral. People came to pay their respects; some I never even knew. Our house so full, I couldn't feel. They stayed late into the night talking grown-up talk.

I heard their low voices in the kitchen as I tossed and turned in my parents' bed with my sister sleeping beside me; my father and an uncle had taken over our twin beds for the week.

"Al, are you going to keep this apartment?" someone asked my father.

"Well, Shelley will probably meet someone and get married in a few years," he said. "Then it will be just Neisie and me, so what will I need this big apartment for?"

I imagined them all nodding in agreement. Poor Al, they were probably thinking, left alone with a handicapped child to raise. For who knows how long? Their silent pity hung within the apartment walls much more heavily than the linen draped across the mirrors.

Lying in the shadowy darkness, I wiped away my salty tears; each drop filled with anger, fear, and pain. The hopelessness in their voices frightened me. What if they were right? What if I ended up living with my father, doing nothing with my life? My mother was gone. She wasn't there to believe in me anymore. I had to do it myself. . . . But I was only fifteen. What on earth did I know? I just wanted much, much more of life than they expected me to have.

My sister Shelley and I became closer after my mother died. There was no one left to vie for attention from anymore. The wedge between us was gone.

Shelley, out of everyone in the family, always had a much more rounded view of me. I was always seen as sweet, angelic, and studious, having my nose buried in a book (there was nothing else to do: I couldn't run around and play with the other kids.) Shelley knew better. She never dashed my dreaming of getting married, though I rarely spoke of it in front of anyone else. When I finally did marry Neil, she could hardly wait to become an aunt. She was the only member of the family who knew about David before I went on my trip.

I called her as soon as I took off my jacket to gush about my baby. "Shelley, he's gorgeous! Absolutely gorgeous! I'll send you pictures, but they don't even do him justice."

Her voice was filled with excitement as she inundated me with advice on what I needed to buy, what books to read, and unsolicited details on how to breastfeed an adopted infant; her friend worked for the La Leche League. It was a bit too much. *Didn't she realize that reading books and breastfeeding didn't even make my priority list?*

"So, you told Daddy and Aunt Rita?" Mildly annoyed, I changed the subject. Shelley and I could never seem to outgrow our childhood pattern of antagonism. "What'd they say?"

"They're not too thrilled," she said, wasting no time to elaborate. "Aunt Rita thinks you don't know what you're doing. Daddy started yelling at me: `Why does she want to do a thing like that? Is she crazy? It's a cockamamie idea!'"

Their reactions didn't surprise me at all, but I still felt a pang of sadness. I sighed. "Well, I'll write them both a letter and put in a few pictures. Once they see him, they'll come around."

"Yeah," my sister agreed. "Give them a little time to get used to the idea."

At least I had my sister. "Shelley, you'll come out here when the baby comes, won't you?"

"Well, with the kids and work . . . I don't know—"

"Oh, Shelley, please," I pleaded before remembering I was a grown-up. Then I gulped down the desperation in my voice and said in a neutral tone, "It would really help us out if you came."

"Well, maybe I can work it out over Easter," she offered.

David would probably be here weeks before that, but I didn't dare say any more about it. She couldn't just leave everything to come out from New York. Yet there were times since my mother died more than twenty years ago when I felt so alone. I was fifteen years old again and I just wanted somebody on my side, somebody to come when I yelled for help—my mother. What irony: David had found a family when I was still looking for one to belong to.

As soon as I hung up, I heard Neil's voice call me. I found him sitting on our bed naked from his waist to his sweat socks.

"We have to go food shopping," I said, remaining in the doorway.

He gleamed at me. "We could go later."

"I really don't want to spend Saturday night at the supermarket," I groaned.

"I'll go by myself if you make up a list."

"All right," I conceded, turning the corner of my side of the bed. I wasn't really in the mood to go shopping, but I wasn't in the mood for sex, either. Still, in my state of excited exhaustion, getting out of my wheelchair and into a nice warm bed did appeal to me.

I discovered over the years, during my few adult sexual encounters, that I liked the idea of sex more than actually having sex. Although I never would have acknowledged it before Neil, my first consistent lover, I think I was much too "proper" to have a satisfying physical relationship without emotional intimacy. Besides, I wouldn't let myself trust my body or my mind, let alone someone I hardly even knew. After three-and-a-half years of marriage, I was still trying to figure out and communicate what I wanted and needed as a lover.

Romance was definitely something I wanted. However, Neil failed to see any connection between romance and sex.

Neil certainly had had more experience with sex than I did; he was even married before for four years. His first wife, he told me (while smiling impishly), had a similar complaint. I suspected that Neil's reluctance to be more amorous, apart from physically reserved upbringing, stemmed from both his attitude toward his own body and his avoidance of doing things that he didn't think he could do well. With respect to the first, Neil didn't have any particular interest in his own body beyond the practical neatness and cleanliness sorts of things. I'd catch his mocking grin whenever someone gave him a sincere compliment on his good looks or if I even made a flattering remark about his sexy arms. I don't know whether his reaction was due more to his disbelief of his own handsomeness, or that he thought such comments were superfluous.

As to the second, though Neil enjoyed having sex, he wasn't fond of kissing or fondling any not-too-subtly-placed erogenous zones, like the nape of my neck or behind my ears. True, it would take finer motor coordination, and his hands were big, my neck was small, but I would have appreciated even a few attempted caresses. I couldn't seem to get that across to him. . . . There was hope for him, though; after three-and-a-half years, I got him to French kiss (only in bed), and he even liked it, much to his surprise.

Neil was already lying down by the time I stripped off my clothes and got my shivering, naked body under the quilt. Anticipation replaced my reluctance as I moved closer to him. We had been apart for four days and nights. They were long nights without him, especially the last. At the moment, I could think of no better way to celebrate our reunion and the joy of becoming parents.

"How 'bout whispering sweet nothings in my ear?" I smiled at him coyly.

Neil draped his long, muscular arm over my bare waist. He pulled me close to the warmth of his body and he put his lips to my ear. In a half whisper, he mouthed each syllable distinctly. "Sweet nothings. Sweet nothings."

I laughed, of course, but he missed the point again: humor did *not* necessarily get me wet!

I turned my head to look at him. His laughing green eyes sparkled irresistibly. My fingers began stroking his bushy beard. I kissed his freckles.

He held me close. I pressed my cheek against his chest, avoiding getting my nose tickled by the small, coarse, diamond-shaped patch of hair between his nipples. I listened to his strong, steady heartbeat. Gentleness. There was a gentleness about Neil, though not necessarily in his movements; I would occasionally get jabbed in the neck by his pointed chin, dented in my side by a sharp elbow, or have my knees momentarily pinned under his spastic, bony legs as he maneuvered on top of me for intercourse (my favorite of the positions we could manage). Yet the gentleness existed in the faint, sweet smell of his body and the feel of his smooth, cool skin, so pale and almost translucent as it stretched across his hard chest. There was also the gentleness of his acceptance; he never showed any disappointment in our lovemaking.

I turned slightly to slip my right leg underneath his two pretzeled ones. His mouth went eagerly down to my breast while I stroked his back and rubbed my left foot up and down his silky-haired thigh.

He stopped momentarily and raised his head. "How about you? You wanna play solo a little?"

(Neil and I used masturbation commonly as part of our sex play. It didn't offend either of us, since we knew our own bodies better than each other's, and proved the surest way for me to reach orgasm.)

"No," I answered, having no desire to physically separate from him. It was sweet of him to ask, considering how horny he must have been, but, at the moment, feeling him inside me would be just as satisfying.

I reached up under the pillow for the lightly scented body lotion. Neil opened the spout and helped me pour a generous amount into my palm. My hand found its way under the covers, down between

Neil's legs. I began to stroke him. My stomach quivered as I felt my own tender longing for him growing stronger. He slowly slid inside me, as if into a soft leather glove.

"You feel so good," he murmured.

"So do you."

He shifted his torso, letting me wrap my legs around his gaunt lower body while he held himself up with steady, strong arms. I looked up at him. Our eyes held each other's gazes with more emotion than words or gestures could ever express. Little sounds escaped from deep within me as his rhythmic movements made me ache with pleasure. I didn't want him to stop; I never do.

"I think it's time," he whispered with some urgency.

His warning always gave me a chuckle; it sounded a little like he was asking permission.

Neil shuddered as he lowered himself to me.

"Are you okay?" He managed to groan.

"Yeah.".

I put my arm around him and drifted into a light sleep. Some time later, we moved into more comfortable positions. When I opened my eyes again, it was already dark.

I slipped on a floor-length muu-muu and went into the kitchen while Neil got fully dressed.

Dinner was simple. Chavallah, our soon-to-be-fired-if-we-ever-got-up-our-chutzpah housekeeper, had weekends off; it was nice having the house to ourselves. Thanks to modern technology, Neil used the electric can opener to open the baked beans while I cut some hot dogs with a not-too-lethal-looking hand chopper. I doctored up the casserole with barbecue sauce, brown sugar, and frozen diced onion. I transferred the dish from the counter to my lap to the oven, then took out the wilted salad from the fridge. When I guessed the casserole was hot, Neil removed it from the oven and brought it to the dining room table—he was calmer, and consequently steadier, than I was when it came to handling heated food.

Out of guilt for not facing the Saturday night supermarket crowd with him (though Neil thought of shopping as a fun thing to do), I cleaned up by myself (it helped digest the beans, too). Afterward, I settled on the couch with the Sunday crossword puzzle.

I was just starting to unwind when the phone rang. I dropped the pen (lead pencil points break under my hand pressure) into my lap as I reached for the yellow receiver nearby and put it to my ear. "Hello."

I heard a long pause over the long-distance static. My stomach rippled. I knew it was her, Neil's mother; she always paused when I picked up the phone, as if to swallow her disappointment that it wasn't Neil.

"Deneeze?"

I took a deep breath, and braced myself. "Hello, Guta. How are you?"

"Ah, not so good," she replied, stretching each accented monosyllable into one long moan. "I couldn't sleep."

I shut my eyes tightly and winced. "Why?"

"Why?" she repeated. "Why. I'm very, very upset . . . because now, you have a very good life. You have a nice home. You do what you want. So why do you need this? What do you want a sick baby for?"

I felt numbing pain inside. "He's not sick. He's disabled."

"Disabled," she reluctantly corrected herself. "You know, it's not so easy raising a child like that. I know. I did it. I did everything. I fed him, dressed him, took him to the hospital, did his exercise . . . I had a husband and two other children I neglected. Poor Stevie—a thirteen-year-old boy should be in the hospital with a bleeding ulcer?"

Poor Stevie. I always heard about Poor Stevie, Neil's younger brother, and that ulcer he had almost twenty years ago. Like Miss Roland and Jay Kobbeloff, everyone had sympathy for Poor Stevie and his pain. But what about Neil's? Medical procedures left Neil in casts from his toes to his waist: one immobilized him for a month to stretch his hamstrings (muscles in back of his knees)—Neil's legs remained as bent as ever, afterward—and another casting lasted six weeks following surgery for his dislocated hip, the same one that I can hear going in and out of its socket sometimes when we have intercourse. Orthopedists always welcomed the chance to practice and experiment on a live body, no matter how many scars they left, inside or out.

"Deneeze, you don't need this, believe me," Neil's mother droned.

Nausea rose in my throat as I tried to think of what to say. Again she repeated: "You don't need a sick baby."

I hung up.

A few moments later I heard Chavallah's distinctive titter-tat on the front door. My voice automatically responded. "Come in."

Her soft-soled sandals flip-flopped across the bare floor.

"Hi, Devorah," she greeted, using my Hebrew name. (She had asked if she could call me that when she first began working for us; I agreed—it sounded so pretty, especially with her Israeli accent. However, the more I grew to dislike the woman, the more I felt that calling me Devorah was just another one of her manipulative ploys.) "I came to find out how your trip went, and also I need to borrow the broom."

The broom — the real reason she showed up here on a Saturday night.

"My trip was wonderful," I said with contained emotion. I hesitated before my next sentence. "But I'm not doing too well right now."

She sat down on the edge of the rocker adjacent to the couch. "Why?"

I took a moment to chew my lips. Then I told her what just happened.

"But why did you hang up on her?" Chavallah countered with disdain in her voice.

I fought back tears of inadequacy. Yes, I hung up, like a willful, angry child. That's how it seemed to her. But how could I explain in words something that held such deep intensity; something that had never been in her realm of experience to even fathom? She was only viewing a patch of the quilt, not the pattern of squares that had been stitched together years before.

On our first date, Neil had described his mother as a "hard" woman. Unlike his father, who tried to put the Holocaust behind him, his mother carried the memories with her every day of her life. Neil grew up on stories of the Lodz ghetto and Auschwitz told by his mother, as other children grew up on lullabies and fairy tales. He had been her captive audience.

"She's the most powerful woman I know. . . . With my mother," he told me, "you have to be sure of what you want, because she looks for weakness," he made a gesture with his hand, "and then, sticks it to you."

It was difficult for me to imagine a mother like that. Surely Neil exaggerated; she couldn't be *that* hard. She sounded like she only wanted the best for her son. . . . And then she came out for a visit in December, three months after Neil and I started dating.

"There she is!" Neil indicated to me as we waited behind the stationary seats in the airport terminal.

Even if I hadn't seen her photograph, I would have spotted her easily in that moving line of passengers coming off the plane from Florida. Overshadowed by two taller people in front and back, she looked like a Miami matron (even if she did live in Fort Lauderdale) in her white linen pantsuit and champagne-colored hair teased in the latest bouffant style of the sixties.

When she saw Neil, she smiled immediately and began waving her arm, her oversized white pocketbook swinging back and forth like a pendulum. She carried a squared insulated bag in her other hand. Then suddenly, her waving hand stopped in midair and the rare (as I later discovered) smile vanished from her lips. Her bespectacled eyes, beneath the same arched eyebrows that Neil inherited, inspected me. Her reaction indicated surprise.

It's understandable that she might be a little taken aback, I thought. After all, the picture Neil had sent her—the one of me sitting in a romantic pose on the grass under an old oak tree—presented a different image than the one of me in person framed in my vinyl and chrome wheelchair without the stillness captured by the camera.

Her steps quickened as she neared us. *"Tottalah,"* she cried to Neil. "Is so good to see you."

Without asking, she rested the insulated bag on his lap, bent her short torso slightly forward, and put two thick hands on either side of Neil's face, oblivious that her swinging pocketbook came within range of my wheelchair's joystick. I switched off my motor, just in time, while she pressed Neil's forehead to her red lips and left him marked. He slumped back when she let go.

"I baked you cookies, *Tottalah,*" she told him, patting the case on his lap. "This bag, is a good idea, no? They should stay fresh."

"Ma, th-th-this is Denise," he stammered. Muscles twitching, he turned his body in my direction so she would look at me.

"Hello, Deneeze," she greeted with a polite smile and brushed my cheek with a kiss before she faced her son again. "Come Neily, let's go to the baggage! Which way?"

As she lifted the bag from his lap, Neil nodded toward baggage claim. Without waiting, his mother turned in her white flats and walked off. I glanced at Neil to see his eyes roll before we followed at her heels.

The next night Neil briefly stopped by my apartment. "She asked me why I couldn't have picked a polio," Neil told me. "I mean, she wanted you to be disabled so you wouldn't take advantage of me," he smirked, "but not *that* disabled."

I tried to keep my sense of humor, but after a few days I found nothing funny about that dreadful week. In her presence, I felt like a specimen under a microscope. Her watchful eyes scrutinized me for every cerebral palsied flaw. I became so self-conscious that I couldn't even place my lips on a straw without struggling against nervous incoordination.

Although Neil's mother had lived in the United States for more than thirty years, she preferred speaking to Neil in Yiddish or Polish, two of the seven foreign languages she spoke fluently that he could understand. I only knew a few words of Yiddish: my American-born father spoke it occasionally with his Russian-born parents, but my mother's American-born family had hardly used it around their house. Neil had to constantly remind his mother that English was my only fluent language.

"Your parents didn't speak it?" she questioned when he first told her, one of the few times that she initiated a brief dialogue with me.

"No," I answered uneasily, sensing the criticism of me in her tone because I didn't know the language of my ancestors.

She raised her eyebrows and nodded, but it would take only a sentence or two before she'd again lapse into her native tongues.

My speech impairment made matters worse; she had difficulty understanding me. The few times I spoke directly to her (other than saying one or two words), Neil had to translate. It gave her another reason not to talk to me, although I'd gotten the impression that she knew as much about me as she needed to know: I didn't speak Yiddish and, more significantly, my family hadn't been personally touched by the Holocaust.

Both sides of my family had escaped the horror of the Nazis, but the legacy of my family history had never been bestowed upon me in great detail. My mother's side of the family had emigrated from what they called "Deutschland" in the early 1800s and proudly referred to themselves as American Jews. My father's parents came from "the old country," fleeing the Eastern European pogroms at the turn of the century. I remember hearing stories of the existence of anti-Semitism in the distant places of the world. I knew about quotas and discrimination in the United States, but it seemed as if that only happened to other Jews who had ambitions to be doctors, or lawyers, or teachers. My relatives generally ended up in the densely Jewish-populated

garment industry and chicken farming or, from my maternal grandfather's side, questionable small-time politics and numbers running.
I heard racial slurs in school and camp referring to "kikes" and
"mockeys," and sometimes they even came from the lips of my own
mother's crude-mouthed father, but any anti-Semitism that my family might have experienced could never equal the terror of imprison-
ment in Auschwitz.

I don't know how much of Neil's mother's treatment of me was
due to my disability and how much was due to my heritage. She did-
n't even bother getting to know me well enough to dislike me; my
existence was irrelevant. The woman was insufferable!

During that week, I also saw another side of Neil. I found out
that while Neil had keenly perfected the art of persuasion, which he
used so skillfully with most people, when it came to his mother he
rarely offered a word on his or my own behalf. Whatever she said to
him when they were alone, he just took; his silence scared me.

"She doesn't have the right to make you miserable," I argued on
one of the evenings that week when he appeared at my door looking
as though he had been wrung through one of those old-fashioned
washing machine wringers. She kept harping to him that I was too
crippled!

"She's my mother," he replied with a helpless shrug.

"So?" I retorted. "Look, why don't you just tell her you're
happy?"

He looked at me as if I'd just grown another head and then
moaned, "It wouldn't make any difference. She is the way she is."

"But you'd feel better," I said adamantly.

I'd just grown a third head. In three months with Neil, our main
arguments always centered around feelings—anger and sadness. I
argued that it was unhealthy to hold them in. I pointed out that his
father, a man who rarely showed his anger, died of a heart attack at
the age of fifty-eight. Neil smugly responded that his father died just
when he was ready.

Before she left that week, I invited Neil and his mother over for
coffee and dessert. I naively thought that I could prove to her that
even though I had cerebral palsy, I was capable of being what she
thought would be a good wife. (Neil always said I was more domes-
tic than his first wife had ever been.) So what if I was only serving
instant coffee—his mother just drank Sanka, anyway—and my little
Sunbeam Hot Shot could boil only two cups of water at a time. I

thought she would at least give me some acknowledgment for my intentions.

To avoid making a spectacle out of the whole production, I made my coffee before they arrived and drank half of it so that I could transfer the cup from the inch-high wooden platform (attached to the Hot Shot) to the table without spilling it. Then while I waited for them, I poured all the ingredients into Neil's cup—the coffee, milk, and half the sugar dispenser. I figured Mrs. Jacobson would prefer measuring out her own Sanka.

As soon as I opened the door, she walked past me carrying a square bakery box with her pocketbook dangling from her arm. "We brought nice cake," she said. "Where should I put it?"

"Over there, please," I answered, pointing off to the simple wooden table in the small dinette while I eyed Neil, barely inside the threshold. His face looked pale and tired.

"You want I should cut some?" His mother asked, placing her pocketbook on the chair.

I should have had them bring cookies! I rolled over to her, clenching my teeth. "Yes, please. Everything you need is right on the table."

She dispensed the water for her Sanka in her cup, a little surprised (and maybe disappointed?) that Neil's coffee just had to be moved off the platform and not made. Leaving Neil with his coffee and cake at the table, I ushered her into the living room area.

She sat down with her coffee and cake on the green couch. I gathered up my courage and rolled closer to her.

"Nice apartment," she murmured.

"Thank you," I replied, skeptical of her sincerity. She was used to white carpeting and brand new furniture covered in plastic. My floors had easy-to-roll-on linoleum and I had inherited the second-hand (or third-hand) couch from my old roommate. I took a deep breath and blurted, "So, what do you think of Neil and me?"

She wiped the crumbs of the apple crumb cake from her wrinkled lips as Neil slowly strained his wheelchair over toward us. "Is good," she nodded slightly, "but don't get married. . . . This wouldn't be good."

"Why not?" I asked, eyeing the white knuckles of my clenched fist.

"It would only make things harder," she answered. "You know, being handicapped is not easy."

After thirty-three years of cerebral palsy, new information!

"Yes, but both Neil and I are very independent. We do very well on our own," I said. "I would think we'd do even better if we live together."

"Living together, that's okay. Marry, no."

Being `crippled,' were we beneath or beyond morality? Or maybe morality didn't even enter into it, since I doubted that she would ever see us as an independent adult couple?

She folded her napkin, picked up her cup from the little end table, stood up, flicked crumbs off her white sweater, and walked toward the kitchen—passing her silent, brooding son who was slumped in his wheelchair. The discussion was over.

I didn't say anything more to Chavallah after her disdainful response. I knew she wouldn't have understood how it just felt for me to have listened to my mother-in-law rave on and on about her suffering and misery raising a disabled child: Neil, the man I had married. Nor could Chavallah have known my pain at hearing Neil's mother call David, the most blissful infant I had ever seen, a "sick" baby, because, like Neil and me, he might be disabled—damaged goods. No matter what we did, his mother would always see us that way.

Besides, Chavallah seemed only interested in pointing out that nothing had been accomplished by hanging up. And after all, the moon-faced woman reminded me, "she *is* Neil's mother."

"You're probably right," I said, hoping to give Chavallah the illusion that she had "talked some sense" into me. Then I nodded her and the broom out the door.

A chill rushed in as the door slammed. There were goosebumps on my bare arms. The short-sleeved cotton dress that I had thrown on after my afternoon in bed didn't protect me from the cool, damp air that seeped through every crack of our corner house.

I pulled myself into my wheelchair. I went to the wall heater beside the couch and turned it on. It rattled and hissed with insufficiency while I went into the bedroom for a sweater.

I sighed. I wished that I'd been made of stone—hard rock and granite. Then I wouldn't be hurt by anyone's words or innuendos, or by bayonets of pitying stares, or by the barbed wire of prejudice that have assaulted me ever since I was a child.

I rolled over to my dresser. My hand reached down to grasp the brass handle of the second drawer, but my eyes rested on the pile of

Polaroid pictures from St. Louis on top of the dresser. I stared at the first one—the one Colleen took of David and me that morning when we woke up. Both our heads were on one pillow and my tousled brown hair spilled onto his reddish gold pate; I smiled with such joy as I snuggled close to him.

My eyes wandered to catch sight of another picture, oak framed, hanging on the wall in front of me. It was a picture of my childhood that I've long cherished: my sister and I posed on the mahogany coffee table. Perhaps I was just four or five, my hair still fine and blonde and outgrowing a permanent that didn't quite take. A photographer had come that day to take that treasured picture. It was on a weekend; I didn't have my braces on. Shelley and I wore our nicest dresses. Hers had a white skirt with tiny black flowers and a short-sleeved red top. Mine had tiny brown flowers on a white background, a big blue collar, and matching short-sleeved cuffs. I sat cross-legged with Shelley's arms around me—to keep me from falling off the narrow table—with a wistful look on my face.

At four years old I already knew what I looked like in other people's eyes: a pretty child who could hardly walk or talk, who had to be carried up and down stairs and fed, and schlepped to doctors and therapists. I was viewed as a tragedy by well-meaning family and friends who pitied my mother and admired her devotion to me. I also knew, at four years old, that I wasn't a tragedy at all.

I'm sure it would have surprised them to know that it never occurred to me to wish I weren't disabled, any more than I would have wished to have locomotive wheels when I pretended to be a choo-choo train. Oh, I may have wished I had polio—it was more acceptable to society—but polio had its drawbacks. It would have been harder to pretend to be a ballerina if I had had polio; I wouldn't have had the muscle strength in my legs to hold onto the bedpost and swirl myself around, enjoying the freedom of movement without my braces. But even if I might have wanted to become a ballerina when I grew up, as any other little girl might, I never thought my cerebral palsy would be solely responsible for whom or what I would become in life.

I looked down at the Polaroid again, smiled, and shook my head. Neil's mother wasn't trying to be mean or insensitive. She was a woman stuck in her own beliefs about disability. There was nothing I could say to change that, to help her understand that adopting David wouldn't be yet another tragedy in her life. I'm certain she saw it that way: first Auschwitz, then Neil, his marriage to me, and now an adopted CP grandchild . . . Tragedy. Neil's mother's life had been so hard and painful. The war had been over for forty years, but the memories remained, the tragedy remained. Her unyielding strength was admirable; it kept her alive and carried her through all of her life. It also made her a difficult person for me to deal with, but for Neil's sake, for my sake, and for David's sake, I knew I had to find my own strength to try.

I braced myself at the desk in what soon would be David's room and made the call.

"I'm sorry I hung up," I apologized as soon as I heard her voice.

"Deneeze," she responded in an almost pleading tone. "I didn't say this to hurt you or upset you. But what you and Neil want to do won't be easy. It wasn't easy for me. When Neil was young, he couldn't talk, he couldn't walk. I had to feed him, dress him. Every day, in the morning, after breakfast, I spread a blanket on the table and exercised his legs. I wanted he should be as independent as possible —"

"And he is. Look how he turned out because of your care," I praised, trying to keep my words simple so that she would understand me.

But she seemed not to hear; she continued, "I worked hard, believe me. I learned how to drive so I could schlep him to doctors and therapists. Agh, most of them didn't know what they were talking about! I knew what he needed. I made sure he was stimulated. Ah, such a bright boy he was."

"And see how he turned out," I said. "So, wasn't it worth it?"

"Sure," she concurred, sounding as if she surprised herself. "Tell me, you saw the baby?"

"Yes," I said.

"And how is he? I mean, is he alert?"

"Very," I quickly responded. I cringed a little when, for her benefit, I added, "In fact, the CP looks very mild. He's a beautiful looking baby, too."

"He eats and everything?"

"Well, he's still on formula."

"I mean, can he suck the bottle?"

"No problem," I answered with Neil's favorite response. "He weighs over twelve pounds."

"Oy, that's some baby!" she remarked with a little laugh in her voice.

I don't know if what I said made a difference, or if Neil's brother or sister, as distant but loyal siblings, kept her at bay, but after that night she never voiced any further disapproval about David—at least not to Neil or me. I didn't fool myself, either; she would never like the idea of us adopting a child, but as she did when Neil married me, she would accept it.

Chapter Five

A Few Details

Neil let me feel miserable about his mother's phone call for a full day. Then it was time to "get on with it!" He kindly informed me that he had decided that David would be home by March 20th, one day less than a month away!

I stared at him and protested. "We haven't even s—"

"Sold the piano yet," he finished my sentence, smiling deviously.

"Neil, how are we going to get everything done?"

"Details, details, details," he smugly retorted.

I eyed him sternly, envisioning myself getting stuck with most of those details.

A knock on the door interrupted our conversation. I sat in the dining room while Neil opened the door for Karen and John, and a box of Pampers. They were only the first of our friends to help welcome our baby.

Both Neil and I had trouble asking for help; we never want to impose. Since we had needed so much physical help as children, perhaps, we sensed the burden of resentment many members of our family felt toward us. No one talked about that resentment directly, but it always managed to seep through in deep sighs and verbal innuendos. It was enough to need to be dressed or fed; asking to be taken shopping was always "too much of a *schlep.*" For me, that phrase was one I always had to swallow, because the few times I had expressed my hurt, I would be scolded for being selfish and inconsiderate; my anger and pain was too much for them to bear. . . . If members of my family felt that way, what could I have dared to expect from friends?

I had spent most of my childhood around my mother and other adults. Although there were plenty of kids in the neighborhood, I couldn't run up and down stairs with them or race around the corner. On rainy days, when their mothers played mah-jongg in our apartment, the kids (Shelley included) were more or less coerced into letting me play board games like Monopoly, or "dress up and pretend." I was always cast as the wicked witch or evil stepmother. Invariably, on those days, I ended up with headaches.

Grown-ups liked me. I read books; I had a quick sense of humor and, for the most part, I never interrupted their conversations or mah-jongg games. In the fifties and sixties, it was admirable to be a child who was seen and not heard.

I had few friendships even in elementary school. In our segregated Health Class Unit (designated for disabled children), I stayed pretty much a loner, though not by choice. The kids my age were suspicious of me, labeling me "Know-it-all," and, when I advanced into the older class, most of the teenagers wanted nothing to do with an eleven-year-old who was smart for her age. Even so, the few peer relationships I had in P.S. 85 received no encouragement to develop outside of school. We made no play or movie dates after school or on weekends; we didn't live in each other's neighborhoods and we couldn't very well travel by ourselves. Yet, even if we could have spent time together, we all knew that the racial and social tolerance that existed in our "special" (*I hated that word*) school felt uncomfortable outside of it. I'd go to school with black and Spanish children, Catholic and Protestant, middle class and poor, but I'd hear racial, religious, and social epithets among "my own kind." I didn't seem to fit in anywhere.

My father had been surprised when I made nondisabled friends in high school and college, and at camp with counselors close to my age. Since he considered me a burden (although not completely without attributes), he thought of those friends as nothing less than saints. If I ever voiced a feeling about them to the contrary, he admonished me.

"Jean invited Paula and Alice to go with her down to The Village, but not me," I'd gripe.

"Neisie, they can't schlep you everywhere."

There was *that word* again.

"You're lucky you have friends like them," he'd remind me. "They take you places, don't they?"

According to my father, I never "went with" anyone, they always "took" me. They "took" me with them to the movies or out to dinner. They pushed me to class, catching rides on the back of my manual wheelchair as we coasted down hill. They carried my chair up and down steps and even on the New York City subway.

Because of the physical reality and my own inexperience with the give and take of relationships, I never felt trusting enough to assume I could go with them. I waited for them to include me. For me to ask would be too imposing. I guessed my father and other adults were right; I should have been grateful, accepting that sometimes I just didn't get to go. Yet I silently bore my own feeling that an injustice existed, that because I was disabled, friendship became a matter of convenience.

Even after living in California for more than five years, I was still getting used to having friendships. I had difficulty seeing myself as being an equal in a relationship, particularly with nondisabled people. But the impending arrival of a two-month-old infant, fortunately, gave Neil and me the chance to open ourselves to the idea of receiving assistance as a gift. And we discovered that our friends were eager to offer and give.

My friend Catherine found a buyer for the piano (so I had to find something else to obsess about). Karen and John offered to paint what would soon be David's bedroom. Judy, who had given Colleen our number to call in her quest to find a home for a then five-week-old baby, organized a baby shower.

"Are you sure about this?" I asked her skeptically.

"Why not?"

"Well, isn't a baby shower for a baby who's not born yet?"

"Denise!" She looked at me with one of her knowing smirks—the same ones I got from Neil.

I raised my hands helplessly. I knew better than to argue with Judy Heumann, one of the leading disability activists in the world. Neil had known her since he was five years old. They went to elementary school together, and at lunchtime Judy, whose arm movements as well as her legs were hampered by the effects of post-polio, would feed Neil and three other kids with CP. Neil proclaimed Judy as the best feeder he ever had. They called each other sister and brother, which, in other words, meant Judy was my "sister-in-law."

After I had a chance to think about it, I decided she was right.

What better way would there be to welcome David into the community and share my joy? Besides, we needed so much stuff that I didn't even know where to begin. I gave Judy a list of people and things that I thought we needed. I left the rest up to her.

Over one hundred people filled the barely furnished, brown-carpeted conference room at the Center for Independent Living on a Friday evening. Even people who hadn't been on the list called to invite themselves. Just like the Three Wise Men (times thirty-three or so), they came bearing gifts: clothing, stuffed animals, baby blankets, a bassinet, a stroller, a port-a-crib.

I appreciated everyone's warm generosity, but I was still anxious. I worried about baby care. We couldn't afford full-time help, and even if we managed to eke out a few extra dollars, who could we find to work on weekends? And for what hours? I hadn't had a chance to talk to Neil about it in any detail—just another one of our unfinished conversations—but at the shower, in the midst of the wondrous celebration, I got up enough nerve to pass around a sign-up sheet asking for volunteers who might be available to lend a hand. Yet, even as the sheet went around, I argued with myself: had I committed a horrible breach of friendship etiquette?

The list circulated back to me with at least eight names. A few were close friends, whom I knew I'd call in a pinch, and the rest were acquaintances I'd known for years. I was struck by people's generosity and somewhat in awe that David's little being—whose early weeks had been so precariously eventful—had magically sparked all this attention. I only hoped that his presence would also help me reach out and allow me to feel deserving of their assistance.

Even Chavallah, our housekeeper, seemed to be getting into the spirit. One afternoon when she came to start dinner, she engaged me in conversation as she scurried and flurried around the kitchen rattling pots and pans.

"Is he circumcised?"

For anyone but Chavallah (and perhaps my mother-in-law) the question would have been absurd.

"Yes," I answered, biting back a smirk.

"Very good," she approved. "You know, Devorah, I was thinking that if you want, I could do some massage therapy with him and give him warm baths. It will relax his muscles."

I perked up at her offer. "That sounds good." To me, her idea made more sense than the prescribed physical therapy of stretching him from limb to limb to loosen his tight muscles. I knew hot tubs really relaxed me; I felt like Raggedy Ann after I got out of one . . .

I watched her turn from the sink to the adjacent stove as she put the freshly cut vegetables up to boil. Her massive, black shoulder-length curls bobbed back and forth as she reached for spices on the rack above the sink's counter. "Um," I began tentatively, "I was wondering, Chavallah, have you ever worked with babies?"

When we had first interviewed her, Neil and I assumed that whatever child we adopted would be older, so we didn't ask if she had any experience with babies.

"Oh, sure," she answered. "Well, I mean, I used to work with toddlers in the nursery on the kibbutz."

I found myself softening. Maybe it wouldn't be so terrible to have her stay on. Maybe if we spoke to her and made things clearer about what we expected from her, what I expected from her . . . it would avoid having to fire her. More notably, it would relieve us of having to search for a new au pair.

The three of us sat down after dinner one evening and had a discussion. Neil did most of the talking, Chavallah listened with her far-off gaze, and I anxiously clenched my napkin under the table.

"I know when we hired you, we told you that we were interested in adopting a toddler, and we thought it would take a while," Neil began. "Now it's pretty definite that we'll have a baby in about three weeks. How do you feel about that?"

"God certainly does work in mysterious ways." Her thin lips parted to let out a little laugh, and Neil and I hummed and nodded our agreement. "I feel that it's a blessing."

I pushed my nerve from my stomach to my throat and spoke. "I do have some concerns. . . . Right now, I don't know how much help I'll need during the day. It's obvious I'll need you more than I do now. I'm also aware that when we first spoke, you thought the hours we needed were perfect because you wanted to devote most of your time to music. So, how do you feel about working longer hours?"

Chavallah sat picking minute crumbs off the table. She cleared her throat. "I feel fine working more hours. I think we need to talk about money."

"Okay," Neil responded with his usual pragmatism.

I sat in silence, listening to Chavallah question Neil regarding the value of the rental she was living in behind our house. Right now she lived there rent free in exchange for doing our very part-time housekeeping. "It would rent for about three hundred fifty dollars," he said. His response satisfied her, giving her the assurance that she was being compensated equitably.

I let Neil negotiate. He offered her one hundred dollars more a week. Room, board, utilities, and four hundred dollars a month for six to seven hours of work a day, five days a week. I thought it was a lot, more than we could afford, but Neil knew our finances better than I did. Chavallah seemed pleased.

I had a gnawing feeling that I couldn't verbalize. Of course, Chavallah had every right to be paid for her work, I reasoned, and if she didn't get what she thought was fair, she would feel resentful. At the same time, it troubled me. Did it bother me that it all boiled down to a monetary negotiation for her, or was it something else?

"When are you going to pick out a color for the baby's room?" she asked, changing the subject.

"Probably this weekend," I answered. "Do you want to come with us?"

Why on earth did I invite her to go with us?

"I'd like to," she said. "Since I'll be spending a good deal of time in there, I should help make the decision."

The decision is Neil's and mine!

Yet maybe she had a point. I didn't want to be juvenile about it. I should be glad that she took an interest.

Luckily, she agreed on the colors I chose: mauve with a dusty rose trim.

We enlisted a few friends to clear out the room soon to be David's nursery. The room, a cozy office off the dining room, even with its mismatched furniture, had been my favorite place in the house. Dark blue industrial carpet covered the well-worn wood floor, and creamy home-sewn chintz curtains hung from the picture window overlooking our secluded backyard. In the square room, Neil's solid wooden desk took up the whole length of the window and the walnut laminated computer table occupied the only uninterrupted wall. My unfinished pine desk fit snugly between one bathroom door and a built-in closet, while an old chest of drawers (the one piece to remain in the room) sat beside the wall heater. It was probably the warmest room in the house: basking in the afternoon sun, insulated from the winter draft by rooms on each side, and heated the most sufficiently by our one heater (which went through to the open living room). Except for the bathroom and our bedroom, it was the only other room in the house with a door.

I had spent a good part of my days in that office: thinking, writing, making phone calls. Now the desks, the computer, and I had no other choice than to relocate to the three-sided, 8' X 10' alcove of the front entryway, which opened onto the living room and dining room. Those three rooms spanned the entire length of the house.

I didn't like change when it seemed beyond my control; it felt disrespectful and inconsiderate. Just like the computer, my place was reassigned without acknowledgment. Except I didn't quite know what I should be acknowledged for. I was only giving up a room. I still would have privacy most of the day, when David napped and Chavallah wasn't around, to work on my writing in the alcove. Yet for me, the whole situation had its roots in a deeper issue.

Unlike Neil, who had established himself in the world, I still didn't feel that I had carved out my niche. Certainly, I had had successes in my life, but I was still haunted by the words of that doctor, the one who prophesied that I'd be a vegetable for my adult life. I had greater expectations, and perhaps now at thirty-six, with motherhood impending so suddenly, I feared that the dreams I had for myself would never be realized, not just because of motherhood, but because of inadequacies within myself.

I could no longer go into the office and focus on my work, centering on my desire to be a writer. I had rediscovered that dream from my childhood in recent years. My mother had had that dream for me, but it was only when I could own it for myself that I began to take it seriously. As any egocentric kid, I found encouragement in my mother's praise, not to mention the accolades from the teachers in my special school. But was I good enough for the outside, nondisabled world? Did I know enough? I didn't think I did and I was so afraid, especially after my mother died, that my ignorance would be discovered. I had been petrified of criticism, not realizing in my younger years that writing is as much a craft to learn as an expression of thoughts and ideas. Like a baby chick hatching, I felt my shell of insecurity slowly beginning to crack. I found a teacher, Sandy Boucher, and joined her continuing writing workshop. I met other women there who, like me, attempted the humbling search to reveal their own "voices" with tempered impatience (though Sandy questioned whether mine was tempered at all). I fell in love with writing as my "voice" became louder and clearer; I painstakingly discovered that with each draft, my work became more audible and articulate. After three years, I started getting a few things published, but now there would be a big change in my life. I feared that my writing would lose its importance and validity; I wouldn't be able to devote enough time and energy to it. I would have to give it up, just as I gave up my office.

As I sat at the computer in its new spot, it was harder to shut out my self-doubt, and not just about my work. When I looked around the doorless room, I saw a house that was not the home I wanted. Although we had lived in this house for almost four years, it still felt as unsettled as a college dorm room.

We had bought the small, two-bedroom house from a widower and his teenage son. Neil saw its potential immediately, even with the shabby, overcrowded furniture, sickly blue walls with butterscotch trim, and orange and brown Carpet-tile stuck to the bathroom floor. The layout, though, was perfect—no narrow hallways or sharp corners to maneuver around.

The fifty-year-old house had charm, with its stone fireplace in the dining room, box-beam ceilings, and diamond-pattern-trimmed windows. In the years we had lived here, the house brightened with two coats of warm but mundane cream-colored paint, a remodeling of the entire funky kitchen, and the refinishing of the natural blond wood floors that sprawled through the barely defined front rooms.

Yet when I looked around the house at times, I became discouraged; I was thirty-six years old and still living with a hodgepodge of furniture from Neil's first marriage and an assortment of our own: a country rocker, a gray tweed sofa-bed, an antique lamp with a broken-paned Tiffany shade, an off-white leather lounger, a cheap brass floor lamp, and a deep-seated pin-striped chair ("on loan" from a friend). The oversized, somber table in the dining room seemed more suited for a monastery dining hall than our humble little abode. Heavy, nondescript beige curtains from JC Penney's covered the house's best and worst feature: the many windows, which let in the bright morning sunshine in the front room but took up most of the wall space. I kept the drapes in the living room opened most of the day, but the ones in the alcove remained closed, to block my view of the bland, stucco apartment house with its seedy looking residents on the opposite, nearby corner. The drapes did little to keep out any of the cold winter air.

Then there was that ugly off-off-white carpet on the doors and thresholds (from bottom to top of wheel-rim height) to protect them

from the too many run-ins with our wheelchairs. As Neil and I sometimes whizzed through the house too distracted by a ringing phone
or late-night fatigue, we'd misjudge our clearance and leave long-
lasting memories of our minor collisions chipped in the paint and
wood. I couldn't decide which was less unsightly: the gouges or the
dirty, shredded carpet.

I wanted a nice, warm, friendly house with ambience, one I could
be proud of when real company came (like my in-laws). But I didn't
even know where to start! I never felt sure that I knew what I was
doing—not as a homemaker and not as a house manager.

"You're not a *baleboosteh*," Neil responded with a tone of revelation during one of my house-related laments.

"What's that?" I had heard that Yiddish word used in references
to my great aunts. I had an inkling of what it meant, but I wanted to
be sure.

"You know," my dear husband replied. "Someone who runs the
house, takes care of the family. Sees that everything gets done the
right way."

"Sounds like a `ball buster' to me," I said.

"Yes! Exactly!" He thumped his hand emphatically on the dining
table. "My mother was a *baleboosteh*. So was yours."

I clenched my teeth hearing him talk about my mother and his in
the same breath, but admittedly he was right: they were both *bale-
boostehs*, though Neil's mother certainly out-chutzpahed mine.
Clearly, Neil admired both of them for their ability to do what they
did, and he wanted me to be more like them. But his perspective also
smacked of male chauvinism; I knew there was a flip side to his
desire to have me take charge: I wouldn't bother him with *those*
annoying, insignificant details.

I wished I could have found some of his mother's chutzpah within myself, especially when it came to Chavallah. Little by little, she
did the things I asked: she washed the new baby clothes and put pull
tabs on the zippers of David's new sleepers (small rings of yarn tied
through the metal zipper holes to make them easier to grasp). Every
time she completed a sleeper I felt a small weight lifted off my shoulders.

"I did a few more last night, Devorah," she announced, display-
ing the pile of five she had brought with her when she came to work
one afternoon. She had twenty more to go.

"Thanks," I smiled.

She put them away in David's newly painted room. I waited for her in the kitchen.

"Chavallah, would you mind changing the light bulb that blew out last week in the kitchen?" I pointed up to the ceiling.

She pushed her blue-rimmed glasses back up on the bridge of her nose. "But Devorah, there's plenty of light in here," she said, referring to the two other light fixtures. "It's foolish to waste energy."

Like a shamed puppy, I retreated with my tail between my legs.

I tried talking to Neil about the incident after she left that night, but it sounded so trivial when the words came out of my mouth.

"She wouldn't change the light bulb in the kitchen."

"Why?" he asked, slouched down in his seat. He hardly seemed interested at all.

"She said there was enough light in there already," I answered. Then I began to justify myself to him. "It's the light right over the counter where I read the paper in the morning. The print's hard enough to read as it is. And besides, all those bulbs were put in at the same time. They're due to all burn out soon. If it's on a weekend, we'll really be in the dark."

Neil shrugged. "Just tell her you want it done."

He just didn't get it. "But she intimidates me."

"Why?" He asked simply.

Why? I didn't know why. Did I have to come up with a reason in order to get his assistance? "She just *does*, that's all. . . .

You can get people to do almost anything. Can't you give me a clue?"

"Yeah," he nodded, as a smile caused wrinkles over his freckled nose. "Don't make it heavy."

I didn't know exactly how to do that, but I knew he was right. I was making more out of it than I wanted, perhaps trying to push away a more gnawing question: if she wouldn't change a light bulb at my request, could I trust her to follow my wishes in taking care of my baby? My intuition knew the answer, but I resisted listening. Neil didn't see a problem, so why should I create one. I had enough on my mind, and besides, if I fired Chavallah, I might get someone worse or no one at all. I knew I was slipping back into "poverty mentality," as Jose, my old therapist, used to call it. I ignored my own instincts, persuading myself that I *should* be able to make the situation work.

The next day when Chavallah came in, I insisted, as lightly yet firmly as I could. "I really want you to put in a new bulb."

She nodded before admitting, "I'm afraid of heights."

I couldn't understand why she didn't say that in the first place. Why was it so terrible to admit a weakness? And I had other options: I could have asked a friend or neighbor. In fact, I offered to do that, but by the end of the day she had managed to screw in a new bulb.

I didn't have much time to dwell on my distrust of Chavallah. When she was out of sight, Chavallah only crept into my mind when I saw the still unadapted sleepers piled up on the blond wood of David's new custom-made oak crib—a crib that was in itself a work of art.

Designed by Neil and crafted by the husband of one of Neil's coworkers, the crib had a sliding gate that opened vertically and an adjustable mattress platform. Neil and I would be able to roll right up to the crib, since it was high enough for our knees to fit under, slide open the gate, and be as close to it as possible so David would never, for a split second, be in danger of falling out. The gate's tracks attached along an open-shelved storage space as high, wide, and deep as the crib side. The mattress could be lowered when David got older so he would be able to get in and out of bed by himself. We could use the crib until David outgrew it.

The crib was presented as a gift along with many others, at yet a second shower given at Neil's office. Aetna, Neil's boss, enjoyed every moment of trying to keep Neil in the dark while scheming and plotting and sending memos to his colleagues as Neil whizzed in and out of their offices.

"I think something's going on at work," Neil said one evening.

"What?" I asked, as innocently as I could.

"I don't know," he replied. "But I saw something with a drawing of the crib on someone's desk."

Aetna had mentioned that she had seen it, too, when I spoke to her on the phone the day before. She had a fit. "I told everyone it's to be a surprise, so what does Richard do? He leaves the invitation memo right on his desk!"

I didn't tell her Neil suspected anything. She had put so much of her time and energy into keeping it a secret — even making sure he was always with someone else when she called me, and never leaving a message on the answering machine when I wasn't there, afraid that he might get home before I did.

The event took place at noon in one of the conference rooms at the bank. I "snuck" in (as quietly as I could in a motorized wheelchair) a few minutes before. Neil was busy with a problem that Aetna was supposedly going to manufacture but, as fate would have it, really did exist. More than fifty of us waited for him to appear. He opened the door to a big "Surprise!" and sat in the doorway for at least a minute in silence, completely overwhelmed.

When Neil's colleagues had drifted back to work, Aetna ushered Neil and me into the privacy of her office. She handed us an envelope. "This is a remainder of the money I collected that we didn't have time to spend," she said. "There's enough in there to buy a microwave if you don't already have one."

For the last four weeks, I had pestered Neil, every few days. "Neil, when are we going to get the microwave? Kate said we'll need it to warm up bottles. It's good for reheating food, too." I would get a shrug or a roll of his eyes, telling me he didn't consider a microwave a necessity. Since there were thousands of things on my mind, I never pressed him on the issue. I eyed Neil now, who was grinning sheepishly at his boss.

"Oh, Neil," Aetna's voice oozed with sarcasm. "This is the twentieth century! Are you really going to risk second-degree burns from boiling water every time you heat up a baby bottle?"

That was all it took convince him? Just a word from his boss! I swallowed a twinge of resentment; it shouldn't matter anyway, as long he changed his mind.

Three days later we went to Sears.

The benevolence the people had showed us was more incredible than we could have imagined. Yet for some reason I couldn't explain, it didn't surprise me. All babies are special, but it's rare when people beyond family and close friends are touched by one baby. David had touched so many people. It was too unfathomable to understand, and yet I knew he would. I felt it, those first moments when I held him, and my walls of doubt and reason melted away. Yes, he was just a baby, but David seemed to have a radiating effect on people he hadn't even met, quite like a small stone dropped in the center of a large pond making rippling circles that reached to all shores.

Chapter Six

The Belabored Run

It was my next to last leisurely morning. I had just made myself a cup of instant coffee (with my same old Sunbeam Hot Shot) and was about to slide it onto the attached wooden platform when the phone rang. I left the cup and answered the phone on the counter a few feet away. It was Jane, Rita Sue's assistant from the adoption agency in St. Louis.

"Denise, good news," she said. "We received all the papers from Sacramento. The judge will look at them today and sign the release. The baby can come home tomorrow."

My breath constricted in my throat and my eyes welled with tears. It was hard to talk, but I didn't even have to.

"I know you're happy," Jane responded for me.

"Yes. Yesss!"

As soon as I hung up, I tried Neil. I got a damned busy signal. I called his beeper. No sooner than a minute later, my phone rang.

"Tomorrow, tomorrow," he squealed.

"How—?" I asked in astonishment.

"Rita Sue just called," he explained, followed by one his cocky guffaws.

"Don't be so smug," I jokingly scolded.

Actually, Neil had every right to gloat. When I had returned from St. Louis on February 21, he did determine that David would be home by March 20, which was tomorrow. Of course, I had been skeptical. I rarely had the experience of anything going according to plan. Besides, I didn't think we would be ready for David's homecoming by March 20.

I called Kate after I spoke to Neil—so what if my coffee got a little colder.

"I'm all packed and ready to go," she said. "I just have one question. . . . Do you mind a baby with chicken pox?"

I groaned. When I spoke to her earlier in the week, Kate told me that her daughter, Andrea, had caught them from a classmate. David was bound to get them.

"I already had them," I answered, remembering the day I missed Children's Hospital's annual Easter party when I was ten because my mother's keen eyes had noticed one small red bump on my belly, and in the short time it took for her gaze to travel up to my face, I was covered and very itchy. "And Neil had 'em, too. So, bring him. . . . Is he okay?"

"Oh, sure. He's a little more fussy than usual, but he's still the best baby I ever had," she assured. David was a very asymptomatic baby; even when he had an ear infection a few weeks before, it wasn't detected until Kate had to take another infant to the doctor and took David with her. She insisted he look at David's ear, though he wasn't crying and had no fever; he just `wasn't sleeping and eating as usual.'

". . . The one problem I'll have is keeping Rita Sue from noticing his spots; she's coming to say good-bye. But with her, it shouldn't be too hard; I'll keep the curtains closed and the lights off when she's here... I hope the plane won't be too crowded so I can seclude him. They won't let him fly if they find out. But don't worry, we'll be there."

My coffee wasn't even lukewarm when I got to it, but I couldn't pour it out until I drank it half way, otherwise I'd spill it before I reached the sink. I began gulping. The phone rang again.

"It's Jane, honey. I'm afraid I have some bad news," she began. "We're missing two documents from the papers we received from AASK (the local chapter of Aid to Adoption of Special Kids designated as the supervising agency). I've already spoken with them and they are going to send them, but the documents need to be sent through the Office of Family Services in Sacramento. It will take a couple of days for them to get here. I'm sorry, honey."

My tears didn't well this time, they streamed. "Can't the judge give temporary approval?"

"I'm afraid she can't," Jane answered with sympathy. "But it will only be a few more days, Denise, and then he'll be home for good. I promise!"

I learned a long time ago not to believe in promises no matter how desperately I wanted to. There were just too many excuses for them to fall through—"Too rainy to walk to the movies," my mother would say, "we'll go another day" (a day that never came before the film changed), or "I'll buy you a puppy when you can walk," Aunt Tootsie vowed (Christian Science practitioner), and now "just a few more days then he'll be home for good." Frustration choked my throat.

"Denise, just be patient a little while longer," Jane urged. "Do you want me to call Neil?"

"No," I sniffed. "I'll do it."

Neil didn't take it very well. The oomph went out of his voice as if he'd been slammed against a wall by a Mack truck. I couldn't bear picturing him slumped down in his wheelchair with his bearded chin resting on his sunken chest. There was no way I could console him. It was a very brief conversation.

It was probably for the best, I decided while swallowing my cold coffee and scanning the comic page of the newspaper. He shouldn't travel with the chicken pox. He'll be practically over them by Monday or Tuesday. We haven't even met our pediatrician, yet (Neil was told to call as soon as the baby arrived), and it would be awful if we had to call her over the weekend. Then, too, there were so many little odds and ends to take care of, and Neil and I hadn't even thought about a weekend attendant (we assumed Chavallah wouldn't want to work on weekends). It would also be nice to have one last weekend alone with Neil.

By the time I read Dear Abby and the book review, my logic had succeeded in suffocating my disappointment, until the phone rang, once again.

"Wanna take a ride to Sacramento?" My husband sounded a lot more cheerful than he did when I last spoke to him a half hour ago.

During the past thirty minutes, he'd been on the phone to St. Louis, Oakland, and Sacramento finding out which missing documents had to go from where to whom. "They forgot our fingerprints and the doctor report," he told me. "The woman in Sacramento said that Federal Express picks up their mail at three. We could make it!"

For a second or two, I had the impulse to counter with my logic. I quickly dropped the thought—it would just waste time. I glanced at the square-faced kitchen clock hanging above the window. Almost ten. Neil could make it home on BART in forty minutes. We could stop at AASK for the papers, and be in Sacramento by two.

"I have to go get dressed. Bye."

Leave it to bureaucracy! We had had our fingerprints done—and redone several times (I made the most smudges)—months ago. They had cleared through Sacramento and the report was sent straight to AASK.

The medical report had a more complicated story. The medical form was among the many papers we received from AASK and we, in turn, sent it on to our doctor assuming that the information wanted and the reason for it was self-evident. We didn't think a phone call was necessary since, for one thing, Neil and I were not keen on calling a busy receptionist of a large multi-doctored practice to explain a non-medical matter. We had only begun to use this doctor after we got married (on the recommendation of a disabled friend of Neil's), but he seemed pretty comfortable when I mentioned I was interested in getting pregnant. "Come in when you're ready," he said, an indication to me that he was open to the idea of us having children.

The completed medical form came back to us about a week later. A lump rose in my throat as I read his answer to the last question: Is there any reason why this couple should not be considered for adoptive parenthood? His scribble read, "Couple's cerebral palsy presents a potential hazard in raising a child." Neil took it calmly. I saw red.

"Aren't you angry?" I asked him after he read the returned form.

He shrugged. "Why? It just tells me he's not as aware as I thought he was."

"But don't you have feelings about what he wrote?" I persisted.

"Nah, that's the way he sees it."

I gritted my teeth and shook my head. Discussions like this always frustrated me. We had them periodically, starting with the one we had so many years ago on our first date.

"My father always told me I was ugly," Neil had shared with me, sometime before our conversation had turned toward adoption.

I was horrified. How could anybody say that to their own son? Besides, it wasn't even true! "Weren't you hurt or angry?"

"Why?" Neil asked blankly.

"That's a rotten thing to tell someone," I indignantly replied, "especially to your own son."

Neil matter-of-factly explained, "He was trying to prepare me for the way the world would see me. Don't forget, he was a Survivor. He saw what Hitler did to people like us. We were the first ones to be killed."

I saw the adoration on Neil's face when he talked about his late father: a grocery store owner who brought home candy every night for the neighborhood kids. Unlike Neil's mother, who carried her bitter memories of the war with her every day of her life, his father determined to let it remain in the past.

"Oh, he didn't say it to be mean. But to my father, my cerebral palsy was ugly, and he had to live with that." Neil's eyes shone brightly. "My mother would always tell me again and again that I was so handsome. I never believed her. . . . Yet I remember one time my father came out by himself to visit me at college, 'cuz I never went home, and he and I went out to eat. For the first and probably the only time in his life he said, `Neily, I'm proud of you.' That was all, but for him it was a lot. . . . He almost cried."

I was touched by Neil's poignancy, but I couldn't help thinking that while Neil appreciated his father's own honesty and motivation, he failed to see the harm involved in his father's words to him. It's not as if Neil had no awareness of how people saw him before his father said he was ugly, for as disabled individuals we inherently sense how we're seen from the time we are children, but the closer you are to the source of a remark, the more impact it has on you in very subtle ways. We internalize those inadvertent comments into self-hatred and self-doubt that remain with us even when we succeed. I'm sure Neil would have rolled his eyes if I had suggested a connection between his father's opinion of him and his own adult body image as well as the intimacy issues we had in our marriage. But I knew the link was there.

When I read the doctor's response on the form, I felt the same old impotence of discouragement. The words he had written echoed my own self-doubts about parenthood but, because I was disabled, I couldn't just worry about my concerns, I had to worry about the implications of his. Somewhere, down deep in those feelings, was my outrage, too; the anger of being dismissed by the flick of his pen.

After months of putting off what to do about this (since it happened before David was even born), Neil phoned the doctor's office for an appointment to talk it over with him. I chose not to go; it called for too much diplomacy.

The doctor's reservations, according to Neil, concerned not so much the physical safety of the child, but his or her psychological and emotional well-being. Would the child talk like us? No, Neil explained, because of exposure to TV, radio, the people who'd help us: "Kids who grow up with parents who have foreign accents don't inherit the accents, and besides do you think it's so easy for someone without cerebral palsy to talk this way!" What about being teased by other kids? Neil responded asking if the doctor knew of any kid who had grown up without conflict.

I didn't quite buy the doctor's reservations; they didn't sound like "potential hazards" to me. I suspected that the real issue stemmed from a recent news event concerning a couple who battered and killed their adopted child. Authorities, upon investigation, discovered that the "woman" was a physiological man. The physician in that case was being held responsible for not disclosing the wife's actual gender before the couple had been approved as parents.

The doctor, even after talking with Neil, refused to reconsider his answer (perhaps fearing that he would be held liable if any harm came to a baby in our care). He also sent us a bill of $50 for his time. Neil, in turn, billed the doctor for a $50 consultation on disability awareness. A week later we received a note back; payment was suspended, and we needed to find another doctor.

I had phoned a doctor I had gone to once before. After a thorough exam and going through the form with us, he came to that infamous last question: Is there any reason why this couple should not be considered for adopted parenthood?

"Can you both use a phone?" he asked. Neil and I nodded at him quizzically. "You know, just in case there was ever an emergency," he explained as he wrote `no' for his answer on the form. "And by the way, I also do fertility work if you ever want to have one, too."

AASK had received his report well over a month ago. . . . Well, at least I'd get to spend one of my last childless days alone with Neil.

I hurried to get dressed while Neil was en route, interrupted only once by a phone call from Neil's boss Aetna to let me know that she spoke to the woman in Sacramento and told her we were on the way.

"I had her put the Federal Express charge on my Visa account to save you time," Aetna explained, and then added with a chuckle, "She couldn't understand what the big rush was since, after all, `it was only a matter of a few more days.' I responded with `I take it you've never met Neil.'"

Twenty minutes later, Neil whizzed through the door with a greeting of, "Are you ready yet?" Without wasting a word, I hooked on my cumbersome footrests, grabbed my jacket, and headed to the van. Neil followed, not even one wheelchair length behind, giving me barely enough time to slide into the passenger seat. I never saw his stiff legs shuffle him so quickly from his wheelchair to his driver's spot. We buckled our seatbelts, he revved the engine, and we were off on our first stop to AASK. Their program director, a rather talkative, good-hearted soul, met us downstairs (AASK's office was not wheelchair accessible). She handed me the manila envelope through my opened window. I grabbed it as Neil gassed the engine. Next stop, Sacramento.

We made the usual hour-and-a-half trip in an hour and fifteen minutes. It took the extra fifteen to find the right building in a maze of tall office complexes with look-alike, speckled marble-floored, glass-enclosed lobbies. Another ten to find the room and floor on the massive lobby directory. All the while, I needed to keep a steady eye on Neil as I trailed behind him, for even though our chairs were virtually the same speed, he typically outwhizzed me—without a look back to see if I was there. (I never had to worry about turning into a pillar of salt.)

We reached the right office at 2:04.

"This is a real treat for me," a dark-haired, thirtyish woman greeted with a smile before leading us into her cramped office with an oversized gray metal desk. "I never get to meet the families."

"Oh, yeah?" My husband responded with interest, so adept at getting other people to carry the conversation.

"Yes, I get to know a lot about the people, but this is rare . . . ," she explained.

In more ways than one: I held in a chuckle.

Neil handed her the manila envelope and, as she looked at the contents, I suddenly wondered with a bit of apprehension how much approval power she had. I swallowed with relief as she reached for the Federal Express mailer and slipped in the documents.

"Can we take that down to the Federal Express office for you?" I asked, eyeing the clock on the wall at 2:26 and fifty-two seconds.

"I'll call them and they'll send a messenger." She caught Neil and I giving each other dubious looks and assured us: "They're just a block away and they always come by for the three o'clock mail."

Neil raised his eyebrows at me in response to my shoulder shrug while the woman made the call. We had to let it go now. It was out of our hands.

Chapter Seven

The Welcoming Home

Janet appeared at my door Friday afternoon, about a half an hour later than I expected her.

"I forgot to bring my camera with me to work this morning," my former roommate said, "so I had to go home and get it."

I grinned. I had reminded Janet to bring her camera every time we spoke that week (having regretted that my first moments with David were not captured on film); it was one of the reasons she was coming along. The other two reasons for wanting her with us were to give us moral support and to drive, just in case Neil's excitement at meeting his son snowballed out of containment and prevented him from focusing on the road during the ride home.

"So, how are you?" she asked, bending her wiry frame for our usual hello kiss.

"Nervous."

"Neil's at work?"

"All day," I sighed. "But I'm glad; he would have driven me nuts if he stayed home. Besides, this is his last day for the next two weeks."

"I can't believe he's taking two weeks off," Janet commented—for the both of us. One week of vacation at a time had always been more than he could bear (he was entitled to four). "So, are you ready to go?"

"Almost. Just waiting for Chavallah to get here." I pressed my lips tightly together.

"How's that going?" Janet asked in a lowered voice.

Before I could answer, we heard her sandaled feet shuffling up the ramp. My stomach muscles tensed in reflex. But as she rounded the corner of the porch, I felt a moment of relief; she carried a pile of infant clothes in her arms.

"I just finished putting the tabs on all the zippers," she announced.

"Oh, thank you," I said, trying to keep any sarcastic thought from creeping into my head and out of my mouth. "Janet and I are ready to leave for the airport. The plane's due in at six, so we should be back by seven-thirty. Are you okay with the shelves and bottles and stuff?"

Chavallah shook her head of thick, black curls. "I'll clean first, and then I'll paper the shelves. I can sterilize the bottles while I cook dinner."

I wondered how she would do it all in three and a half hours, but I needed to have more faith—she did get the zippers finished. Besides, I didn't have time to worry about it now; Janet and I had to pick up Neil by five. We had to get going to beat Friday rush hour traffic.

As Chavallah went in to begin her work, I dug my van keys out of my side pouch and handed them to Janet. After several perspiration-dripping attempts at learning how to drive, I had decided that I had inherited my father's nervousness when it came to getting behind the wheel, and so I resigned myself to being a permanent passenger.

Janet took the driver's seat as I positioned myself behind the passenger seat and locked the brakes of my wheelchair. I heard the ignition start while my eyes focused on the seat in front of me—the only other seat in the van. It had been my seat: the seat I had sat in for long rides, the seat I had sat in to adjust the right rearview mirror, tune the radio, control the heat and air conditioning while Neil was behind the wheel. My seat wasn't emptily waiting for me now. An infant carseat, facing toward me, took my place. I swallowed some emotion: sorrow? resentment? childish hurt?—realizing the seat wouldn't be mine again for a long, long time.

We picked Neil up in front of his downtown office building and headed for SFO. Rush hour had just begun, but we made it to the airport with time to spare—too much time. To add more anxiety, the plane had to make an unscheduled stop in Reno to refuel, meaning a half-hour delay.

"He's too young to gamble," Neil wisecracked.

I tried to find it amusing, but I was never much at ease where planes were concerned, especially at the thought of one suddenly running out of fuel, with my baby on it.

"Let's go for coffee," I suggested.

We sat at a small, dirt-smudged, Formica table at the snack bar. Neil and Janet had begun a conversation that I wasn't paying attention to when a woman's voice interrupted.

"Excuse me," she said. We all turned our heads to look at her. "Are you Denise and Neil?"

I caught Janet's mocking here-we-go-again glance. Neil and I had developed a kind of celebrity status from our presentations over the years on disability-related topics at classes or conferences.

"Yes," I smiled, ready to brag about the reason we were there, except I never got the chance.

"I'm Maggie, Kate's sister." As soon as she said it I could see the resemblance—same green eyes, thin face, but more reserve. "It looks like we're here to meet the same plane."

She joined us with her own cup of coffee as we waited for the plane's arrival time to approach. I checked my watch every few minutes. After what seemed to be an endless half an hour, the four of us headed toward the gate.

It was dark outside, and the large glass windows had turned into mirrors reflecting harsh circles of ceiling lights, thin brownish gray carpeting, and images of greeters awaiting the landing of TWA flight 28. Few of them could have been more anxious than the four of us waiting behind the last row of chrome-attached chairs to avoid the stampede of arriving passengers.

I placed my cold, clammy hand on the arm of Neil's tweed jacket, needing some human contact to keep me from jumping out of my skin. I glanced at him every now and then. He sat hunched forward with his eyes fixed on the opened jetport, intensely silent, beyond my reach. I felt alone.

Passengers poured out in an endless stream. We waited. Then there were the tricklers. We waited. Some of the clean-up crew headed down. We waited.

Finally I caught my first glimpse of Kate cradling a white bundle in her arms, flanked on one side by her youngest daughter, Andrea, and on the other by a flight attendant weighed down with carry-on baggage. They walked steadily, but slowly, up the jetport walkway. Kate moved regally with her head high and shoulders back, looking so formal in her dark green suit. As she came closer, I could see David's little head in a blue bonnet poke out from the white blanket.

I swallowed, grinding my teeth together, and jerked my hand

from Neil's arm to clench my fingers around the chrome of my wheelchair. I braced myself, my eyes never straying from Kate's advancing figure as she crossed the metal strip of the threshold and strode across the carpet in her black pumps without pause. My vision narrowed with each step that brought her closer to me, my eyes latching onto my son, David.

"Who wants him?" she asked, stopping in front of Neil and me.

Silently, we gazed at David. He didn't look exactly as I remembered. The baby bonnet he wore fit too snugly on his head, and tied with white ribbon under his chin, made him look pudgy. Faded pink chicken pox dotted his forehead and round cheeks; his face paled under the harsh cones of ceiling light. I knew it had been such a long trip for him, yet my heart sank a little—I wanted something to recognize, to reconnect me with David.

Remembering Kate's question, I gestured to an awestruck Neil; it was certainly his turn to hold his son, even though he didn't look quite ready.

I watched David's face as Kate bent over to place him in Neil's arms. David's inquisitive blue eyes examined every face around him—Janet's, mine, Maggie's. With a tiny movement of his head, David looked up at Kate for reassurance. Blocking my view for a moment, Kate straightened up again to reveal David in the crook of Neil's arm. David finally focused on his father's face; their eyes locked onto each other in a long, unbroken gaze. A whimper escaped my lips.

Part of the blanket fell away through Neil's large fingers, revealing David's short blue outfit, rounded bare leg, and a white ankleted foot fitted with a blue slipper marked in blue with a capital B. I took off my glasses and wiped my eyes with a crumpled tissue.

I moved closer to them as Janet clicked her camera. I covered David's tiny hand with my own. He looked up at me. My lips brushed his smooth, round cheek. I smiled into the camera lens.

During those few moments when Neil, David, and I were enraptured, Kate had a chance to greet her sister and introduce Maggie to Andrea. I overheard Kate making arrangements for Andrea to stay with her newly acquainted aunt, who lived about twenty-five miles from us; Kate was spending that night (and probably a few more) with us. I protested: "There's room for both of you at my house."

"No, no, no," Kate emphatically shook her head. "Andrea will be just fine at Maggie's. What you don't need right now is a precocious eight-year-old around the house."

I didn't feel right about it, but I knew Kate couldn't be talked out of her decision. It was probably for the best, I thought anyway, not knowing how relieved I'd be to have Kate all by herself just a few hours later.

Neil drove the van home. Janet sat on the floor between the two front seats, and Kate sat beside me in Neil's wheelchair. While we drove along the lamplit highway, my eyes never left David's face. As he faced me from his carseat, shadows of passing vehicles covered and revealed his face. His alert eyes never closed, too busy taking in the sights of streetlights and their reflections in the night.

"He hardly slept on the plane," Kate chatted easily. "He just wanted to look around and see what was going on. People kept coming over to see him, and I kept shooing them away so they wouldn't see his chicken pox. . . . And then when we landed here, the flight attendant insisted on helping us off. . . . I was afraid they might make me pay a fine if they found out, but anyway, I warned her that she was going to walk into a very emotional scene," Kate gave a little chuckle, "and she said she'd been a flight attendant for twelve years and had seen everything. I didn't argue with her. I just let her carry the bags. After I put David in your arms, Neil, I caught a glimpse of her hanging onto a coworker, sobbing."

Neil pulled into our usual parking space in front of the house and I was the first to get out of the van. I rolled up the wooden ramp and opened the front door to a wonderful smell of Friday night—of roasted chicken and potatoes: the smell of *Shabbos* that I grew up with. The lights were on throughout the house. I moved into the dining room just as Chavallah met me at the kitchen doorway. Beyond her thick frame, I caught a glimpse of pots and pans, on the stove, in the sink, on the counter. Everywhere!

She greeted me with her moon-faced smile and a flood of disconcerting information concluding with, "I didn't know how long to boil the bottles, but they've been in hot water for about an hour. . . . And I didn't know how to put the contact paper on his shelves . . ."

Before I could think of what to say, Kate, Janet, and Neil, with David on his lap, paraded into the house. Kate mentioned that David needed a diaper. Neil rolled directly toward David's room, with Kate and Janet right behind. Chavallah and I followed. Neil got David onto his crib easily enough and took off his jacket and tie before he started to undress David. He had no trouble unsnapping David's one-piece outfit, but having four people watching made him nervous. He looked at me grimly and mumbled in an irritated voice, "Denise, I don't need an audience."

I took my cue. "Come on, let's all go into the living room."

Kate and Janet were first to exit, and before I turned to go, I caught Chavallah peeking over Neil's head. I knew she was checking out David's circumcision. *That, apparently, was all she gave a damn about!*

"Denise," she said, following me out into the dining room (I put a stop to `Devorah' a few weeks ago), "Dinner's in the oven. . . . Do you mind if I leave now? There are some Israeli dancers I was planning to go see."

"Go ahead," I said, fighting my urge to tell her, among other things, not to come back. At that moment, I despised her, not because of her incompetence, but because she was spoiling the joy of David's homecoming for me. I watched her practically fly out the door as the wind slammed it behind her.

Kate and Janet looked at me for an explanation, but Neil had just called for help. He couldn't get David's arms out of the outfit he had worn home. Kate went in to assist while I joined Janet in the living room. A minute or two later, Neil rounded the corner of the living room archway with David sitting upright in his lap and Neil's long arm draped casually over him. David's back fit so naturally in the curve of Neil's sunken torso, as if the two had been made for each other.

It didn't take long for Neil to notice Chavallah was missing. He looked at me with raised eyebrows. "Where is she?"

"She left," I said, relating her conversation with me.

I led the way into the kitchen to show them her mess and eyed Neil carefully. He pressed his lips together for a long minute, his arm twitched with a familiar sign of anger and anxiety, and then finally he uttered the words I had wanted him to say over a month ago: "She's outta here."

Without any awkwardness or hesitation, Kate went right into the disaster area and surveyed it. "Oh, it's not that bad," she lied. "I'll take care of it after dinner."

I wanted to object. She had traveled all day; she had to be tired. It just wasn't right that she had to come into our house for the first time and had to clean up someone else's mess. But I had no other choice than to let her and, in reality, I felt blessedly relieved that she offered.

First it was time, Kate announced, to make David's bottle. Janet and Neil went in the other room while I stayed to direct Kate to where things were and to learn what to do, so that I could instruct somebody else when the time came (I quickly learned from this latest Chavallah incident that I couldn't trust people to know what to do).

I watched Kate move around the kitchen, admiring her competence and ease: fishing out a small bottle, white collar, and orange nipple from one of the big pots Chavallah had left on the stove, mixing up the formula, adding two teaspoons of baby oatmeal (which filled David up enough to sleep through the night), and finally assembling an almost ready-to-drink bottle. She twirled it on its side, to make sure it didn't leak, before popping it in the microwave for thirty-five seconds.

She talked through the whole procedure. I hung on every word, trying to store up all the little, but important, details along the way: "It's not necessary to sterilize bottles when you have a dishwasher," she had pointed out when she began. "Just do an extra rinse cycle to make sure to get off all the soap residue." She ran the can of Similac formula under hot water and dried it "to clean away any grimy scuz," before puncturing the top with the can opener. She used an orange nipple for the oatmeal bottle, because "it has a bigger hole to let the thickened formula flow through."

The microwave beeped. I watched Kate remove the bottle, shake it up, and pinch the nipple to make certain it hadn't clogged up. She tested the temperature, sprinkling some drops of the milky substance on her forearm (and then on mine). When she finished, she handed me the bottle. I took it into Neil.

I was so thankful for this woman, so grateful she was there; it was like having a small miracle. Kate had entered our house, immediately plunged into a tense, precarious situation, and did what needed to be done. She took charge without taking over. At the same time, I knew it couldn't have been easy for her. I appreciated her silence, for not voicing the serious doubts that must have been plaguing her, at the moment, about bringing David here.

Cradling David with one arm, Neil's right hand steadily held the four-ounce bottle up to David's eager lips. Neil's eyes never strayed from David's face as he watched his son guzzle more than half his bottle. Kate, Janet, and I looked on.

"It's time to burp him," Kate said.

"Oh, yeah?" Neil glanced at her; it was all new to him.

With some misgiving, Neil pulled the nipple from David's mouth, evoking some tiny grunts of protest. I took the bottle as Neil sat David up on his lap and began to gently thump David's sturdy back with a closed hand. In synch, tiny sounds reverbated from David's vocal chords.

"Aargh!" David burped once, and then again.

"You're a natural," I commented to Neil, as David, cradled once more in his father's arm, drank the rest of his bottle.

Neil settled David in his infant seat in the deepness of the striped lounge chair using the "grab and glide" technique. It was the same method that I had come up with to get David from one surface to another: grabbing a healthy fistful of the terry-cloth material of David's sleeper to glide him face up through the air. David's eyes flickered with recognition, and he burst into his familiar two-syllable laughter in midflight.

He's really going to like it here!

From his tilted infant seat, David's eyes scanned the living room and dining room, but his lids slowly began to droop. Janet snapped a few more pictures of him and then she had to leave.

With David finally settling in, Kate served Chavallah's roasted chicken dinner in the dining room and we sat down. Neil and Kate began eating immediately, but I wasn't hungry. I just picked at the dark meat with my fork.

"Well, I'll say one thing for Broom Hilda," Kate quipped. "She's not that bad of a cook."

"Yeah, but you haven't tasted her meatloaf!" I smirked before letting my fork drop to my plate, then rubbing my opened palm melodramatically across my forehead. "*Oy gevalt*, what are we going to do?"

"Now, don't worry," Kate assured. "Everything will work out."

I sighed forlornly. "When do you need to go back to St. Louis?" I asked.

"My plane reservation is for Wednesday," she answered. "But don't you worry, I'll stay as long as you need me."

"About twenty years?" I suggested with a snort.

"Listen," she said, "you wouldn't want me meddling for that long."

I wasn't so sure about that!

Neil just gobbled down his dinner and then, as usual, gave our guest most of his attention, asking things about Kate's family that I already knew. I drifted in and out of their conversation, trying to restrain my resentment at his apparent nonchalance over our situation. I wanted him to *say something* to relieve me of the burden I thought I was carrying by myself. Where was the Great Problem Solver who whizzed through those high tech computer glitches at the bank? Feeding his face and playing Pearl Mesta, and paying no attention to me.

My gaze wandered off to the living room. Not more than ten feet away, I saw my son in his infant seat under the soft yellow glow of the lamp. His eyes had finally closed and his chest rose and fell with each gentle breath. His tiny open hands rested on a white flannel blanket. Suddenly, I could feel his comfort, as if that blanket had been snugly tucked around my own quivering heart. David slept peacefully. After those first weeks of uncertainty, after his three-month sojourn at Kate's, after an adventuresome day on a plane, and even after his welcome into a rather chaotic scene, somehow he must have known he was finally home. . . . I had a lot to learn from him.

Chapter Eight
Two Cripples and a Baby

Our Saturday morning volunteers, Teri and Nora (friends from my writing group), had arrived by nine and were ready to put in two very full hours of bathing, exercising, and dressing David under Kate's meticulous instruction. She would also have them make another batch of formula and fill the bottles to store in the refrigerator; the mixture would stay good for forty-eight hours, Kate said, although with David's healthy appetite, I doubted that a batch would last that long.

Kate toasted English muffins and brewed coffee, but I wasn't hungry. I tossed and turned all night, too excited about having David home to fall into a deep sleep. Still, I sat with everyone at the table, slowly chewing little bites of buttered muffin and sipping my coffee to help wash them down; my body needed something more than adrenaline to keep me going.

Kate mentioned that we needed a few things from the drugstore. Eager to demonstrate his usefulness and escape from a house full of women, Neil readily offered to go. Besides, he would have done anything for Kate; she was his kindred soul, he discovered, after watching Kate put as much sugar in her coffee as he put in his.

Kate gave Neil a list of items he had never bought before in his life: A & D Ointment, baby wipes, disposable bottle liners for the two sets of bottles that Colleen had sent along as a very practical gift. (The bottle didn't need to be held up in midair while David sucked.) I was skeptical about sending Neil off alone, but I had no intention of leaving David, even though I had no idea of what use I could be staying home.

Since David had arrived, I receded into a passive motherhood. I hadn't even held him in my arms the night before; Neil had diapered him, fed him, and burped him. Neil was the one who put David down in his bassinet in our room (to be closer to us if he awoke during the night). I did give David his early morning bottle as he lay on Neil's pillow while I cooed to him softly. It was Neil, though, who had gotten up to get him, since the bassinet stood between his wheelchair and the wall (the only place it fit in our cramped, crowded room). And I let Neil whiz through the house (not that I could have stopped him) into our room when we heard David, alternately kvetching and gurgling, as we sat eating this morning.

In one way, I gladly relinquished my physical role. I knew that in two short weeks, when Kate would be gone, when friends' visits would be less frequent, and when Neil would be back at work, I'd have David to myself most of the day. I figured that I should take advantage of having other people around to help while I could. Yet deep within me, my acquiescence wasn't that simple to explain.

My family had never considered assertiveness an admirable trait. They might have encouraged me to use my intelligence, but never my assertiveness; I suspect they had mistakenly equated assertiveness with traits like selfishness and rudeness. Besides, it had always been easy for me to take a back seat, to relinquish my power. It made it easier for everyone. I played along in my role of the "handicapped daughter," not wanting to cause friction, not wanting to be rebuked or criticized. It was clear, though, that while my disability may have amplified my submissiveness when I was younger, it motivated me to struggle to overcome passivity when I got older. I had come a long way, but obviously, I had miles to go, and with David here, I couldn't stop now. It was just that, at present, I had lost my sense of direction.

I watched David bathed in the bathroom sink. Teri gently lathered his smooth, white skin with a washcloth and baby soap. She sang little rhymes. He laughed and played with one of the strawberry blonde curls of her hair. A baby in bathwater, I observed, was as slippery as a clinged peach, and I determined with little regret that I was glad *someone else* got to do this particular task. While poor Teri tried not to let David slip through her fingers, I marveled at the round shape of his fuzzy, golden head, the curve of his little ear, and the solidity of his compact little body. When Teri finished, Nora wrapped David in a pointed, hooded towel (giving him that "seven dwarfish" look) and put him in my lap. I hugged him tightly and kissed his covered head, savoring the fresh sweetness of the

Johnson's Baby Bath with David's familiar almond scent.

I brought David into his room and let Nora diaper him and put on his tee-shirt. This time David's tiny hands reveled in Nora's long, dark tresses.

Neil returned just as Kate was about to show Teri and Nora David's exercises. I took the plastic bag from him and ushered him toward David's room. He scowled with reluctance. I pursed my lips. He was David's father; he wasn't getting out of this.

Kate spread a soft blanket on Neil's old camp trunk that sat on the opposite wall of David's crib. She took out the Xeroxed pages of exercises and reviewed them with Teri and Nora while she demonstrated with David. Kate said that the doctor and therapist in St. Louis had seen a 'noticeable' change in David; his arms and legs had more flex to them, and his torticollis was now so slight, though he still preferred turning his head to the right.

Neil's arm twitched. I reached my hand out to comfort him. His eyes flickered at me before he hung his head down. He could barely watch *(and this man wanted a disabled child!)*; I hoped Kate didn't notice. Kate and her whole family had worked so religiously on this exercise program, three times a day. I didn't want to hurt her feelings; I wanted her to know that we appreciated her efforts. Most likely our doctor would discontinue the exercises (in favor of a more contemporary, less stressful treatment program), but I felt Kate needed to know that she had done her best for my son.

Worn out and hungry from his workout, David drank another bottle. I put David down on his stomach and rubbed his back; my one hand covered most of it. Seconds later, he was asleep. I slowly closed the crib's gate; it was his first nap in his new bed.

Teri and Nora went home (probably to recover) shortly after, leaving Neil and me sitting at the table in the shaded dining room. The house was quiet once again, with only the sound of a rustling plastic bag and hollow footsteps on the kitchen linoleum just a few feet from where we sat as Kate unpacked Neil's purchases and put them away.

"Oh, Neil," she called in to us, "are you sure you bought a big enough size of this?" She held up a jar of A & D Ointment. It had to be well over a pound. "This should last through the diaper years!"

Neil grinned. "Well, you never told me what size to get."

Kate finished up in the kitchen and joined us. She offered to make lunch, but neither Neil nor I were hungry. Instead, I persuaded her to call her brother who lived in Berkeley.

"He could pick you up; it's not that far. You can spend time with him," I said. "We'll be fine. More friends are coming over this afternoon."

She eyed me warily. "You know, I didn't come here to be with my family. I'm not worried if I see them or not!"

"I know, I know, but this would be the perfect time," I reassured. "David's out for at least two hours, you've made extra bottles, and Neil and I will be able to handle David when he wakes up. Right, Neil?"

Neil nodded.

She finally agreed and called her brother. Ten minutes later, Keith honked outside our door and Kate left, though not without making sure we had his phone number.

I sat with my head resting on the table, my body slumped with fatigue. I felt suddenly drained of the adrenaline (and caffeine) that had been rushing through my body all night and morning long, though it remained racing through my brain carrying no specific thoughts, just wordless spurts of frenzy: a baby slept in this house. My baby!

I lifted my head to look at Neil, slouched at the head of the table. His bearded chin rested on his red velour shirt. One arm relaxed along his body. The other bent so that two of his fingers, his thumb and middle, gently pinched the bridge of his nose.

"You're crying," I said, fighting back alarm.

He nodded.

I tried to maintain an even voice. "Why?"

"This is so heavy!"

I wished he could be a little more verbose. "Why?"

I saw the movement in the arm at his side. "I'm scared," he admitted. "I always dreamed I'd be a father, . . . but now it's real—"

"It sure is!" I jerked my head in the direction of David's room. "Can't back out now. You gotta put your money where your mouth is."

I saw a flicker of a smile on Neil's face and felt a wave of relief. I always thought of Neil as the strong, logical one; it had unnerved me to see his vulnerability just now. It had been me who had had the fear and doubt: worrying, wondering, and grappling with the decision to adopt David. I guess now it was Neil's turn to face his doubts and, knowing him, I knew he would conclude the same thing I did: even with the struggles we faced—the imminent firing of Chavallah on

Monday (assuming she wouldn't show up until then) and no replacement for her in sight, the uncertainty regarding David's real or unre-
al disability, and whatever raising a child would entail for us—David
belonged no other place than in our home. It was nice, though, to
have a sign that my husband was as susceptible as I was to human
frailties, at least once in awhile.

A living room full of people greeted David when he awoke from
his nap. His eyes widened as he looked around at the faces of friends
who had come to welcome him. He remained on Neil's lap at the
beginning but, as the afternoon wore on, he happily bounced from
one lap to another, finally ending in mine for his four o'clock bottle.

By the time Kate returned, everyone had gone. David was napping again, and Neil and I collapsed on the couch. We were
exhausted.

"I found someone!" Kate announced triumphantly.

Neil and I stared at her.

"My brother's girlfriend is a licensed practical nurse who took a
leave of absence to go back to school. She has time and would be willing to help out until you find a replacement for Broom Hilda." Kate
took a breath before she added, "I think she must be sent from heav-
en."

I had to silently disagree; with tears blurring my vision, I could
almost see a halo above Kate's brown head.

Within twenty minutes of Kate's call to her brother's, Lydia
appeared at our door—tall, blonde and spunky. Neil and I glanced at
each other. *This was more like it!*

Kate went through David's whole routine with Lydia, from formula bottles to his exercises (which she aptly coined as "putting him
through his paces"). We agreed that she'd start out coming two hours
in the morning and late afternoon, and an hour in the evening to get
David ready for bed.

After she left, I was ready for dinner.

I had a better night's sleep, too, and after breakfast the next
morning, the four of us, Kate, Neil, David, and myself went out into
the warm sunshine of early spring. David sat on his father's lap as we
followed a familiar route along the narrow side streets to the larger
shopping area of College Avenue only three blocks away. Our mis-
sion: to find a baby carrier.

A few neighbors were out working in their gardens or jogging.
We knew most of them by sight and they usually greeted us with a

friendly hello as we passed, but today they came over to us. They welcomed David into the neighborhood with their smiles and praises. I thought of how lucky Neil and I were to be living out here instead of someplace like New York, where we had grown up—where it was so hard to get out and about that, when we did, people stared at us and stayed away. I cringed to think how they would have reacted if they had ever seen us with a baby.

We soon reached the children's store and looked through a jungle of baby snugglies and backpacks. None were right; either they had too many straps to fasten and compartments to snap, or they weren't usable for someone who maintained a sitting position in transit. Then I spotted a large piece of purple material with a price tag on it hanging from a hook.

"What's that?" I asked the salesperson who was helping us.

"It's a carrier called a Kacoon," she answered, taking it down for me to look at. "It's used in India and Africa. See, it's a sling."

She demonstrated it on me. It slipped on like a sash; no snaps, no straps, no ties. Kate picked David up from Neil's lap and slid him into the Kacoon. He almost disappeared into the folds of heavy purple cotton, but my arm cushioned David's head (with added support from my chair's armrest). For the first time I felt at ease in cradling him, just like other mothers held their infants. I'd be able to take him for walks and he could nap in my arms; I could feed him a bottle if he got hungry. I could look down at his face to smile and reassure him. I had no idea, yet, how I would get him into it by myself, but I was determined to make it work.

"Maybe if we inserted a pillow, the material wouldn't swallow him up," I suggested.

Kate nodded. Neil wore his skeptical look, which usually made me reconsider. I refused to be discouraged this time. I stared at him defiantly. He gave me one more wary glance before he took out his checkbook.

In the afternoon, after several nearly successful attempts (it *would* work with practice), Kate helped us get David in the Kacoon. Then Neil, David, and I ventured out for another first—an outing by ourselves. Neil coveted David again, cradling him snugly against his chest in the Kacoon with a pillow inside. With his head hidden by a flap of still abundant material, David fell asleep immediately. The three of us, or as Neil wryly mused, "two cripples and a baby," headed for our favorite cafe.

Moving a chair off to the nearby wall, Neil settled himself side-ways at a square wooden table. It was just a few feet away from the glass display counter where I got in line.

"The usual?" the young server inquired as his head peeped over the counter. "Two mochas—heavy on the syrup."

I nodded. It was so good to be known, and not have to shout above Patsy Kline's wail over the loudspeaker.

"Hey," the guy called when he spotted Neil. "What's in there, . . . a baby?"

"Yes!" Neil and I burst out together.

Counter service stopped while two more servers peeped over the display case. Neil turned back the flap so they could see David's face. Like a scene from the Three Stooges, their dark eyes popped out and their mouths hung open before they found their voices to admire David. David opened his eyes, looked straight at them, and laughed.

We sipped our chocolaty mochas through straws as David lay in his father's lap mesmerized by the moving wooden blades of a ceil-ing fan.

"What a beautiful baby!" the woman at the next table remarked.

I beamed proudly and agreed, "Yes, isn't he?"

"Denise!" Neil's voice reprimanded drolly.

I looked at him for a second before realizing I was supposed to be modest. "Oh."

"How old is he?" the woman asked, seeming to have missed our private little exchange.

"Three months," Neil answered.

"You know, he looks like you," she said to him. "Especially when he smiles."

For a moment, I looked at father and son, reflexively checking for a resemblance. An afterthought reminded me that David had come with a different set of genes. (*And I had been afraid that I would never have a complete bond with a child that didn't come from my body.*) I was a little hurt, though, that she didn't say David looked like me.

The showdown with Chavallah took place on Monday afternoon when she reported for work. Neil and I were sitting around in our bedroom with David and a few friends. My stomach churned as the front door creaked open and closed, as she then found her way to our voices.

"Hi," she greeted from the doorway, her thick middle-aged body blocking out the daylight from the living room. "How is everything?"

It amazed me that she stood there with such obliviousness. She hadn't made one inquiry or offered any kind of assistance all weekend. *What kind of person was she?* I couldn't even look at her, let alone answer her.

"Why don't we go into the kitchen?" Neil suggested immediately.

She turned and led the way. Neil followed. Before I joined them, I eyed my friends for nods of support and assurances that David would be looked after.

Chavallah squatted down next to one of the kitchen counters, letting the blue midlength smock she always wore brush the floor. She looked up into Neil's face as he began to speak. "Denise and I both feel that this job may not be right for you."

She adjusted her thick blue-rimmed glasses and replied, "I'm perfectly happy here."

"But I'm not," I said, straightening my spine and grasping the chrome sidearms of my wheelchair.

Unwittingly, my words unleashed a wild woman. Her dark curls flew out in all directions and her long earrings tinkled against the shells of her necklace as Chavallah crouched and lunged around the kitchen—like a jungle cat circling its prey—spewing words as sharp as daggers. "She's spoiled and selfish," she complained about me to Neil. "She always wants things her way. She's too stubborn to listen to anyone who has a different view."

It wasn't true! It wasn't true, I wanted to cry. I wanted to remind her of all the times I tried to accommodate her at my own expense: she had complained about bending to gather the old newspapers from a large wicker basket, so I agreed to stack on the spare table in the living room (the pile resembled a mountain of earthquake rubble by the end of the week); at her insistence, I bought extravagant cooking ingredients and kitchen gadgets; Neil and I paid for an expensive oak closet for the studio apartment, which she picked out. I wanted to remind her, but my anger and hurt choked my throat, just as it did when I was younger.

"You're a liar. You're a liar," were the only words my rage would let me utter as I spun around to face her.

"I've done my best, but she's very demanding . . . ," Chavallah raved on to Neil as if he were her ally and I were just a hysterical woman.

"That's a lie," I screamed. "You're a liar!"

When my husband, sitting in his slumped-down-so-that-his-butt-is-hanging-off-the-seat position, finally had enough, he raised his hand. "The fact is, Chavallah, this is her home."

That was it? That was all he was going to say on my behalf?

Chavallah attempted, again, to persuade Neil that I was unreasonable.

"This is Denise's home," Neil repeated.

I lowered my eyes and cupped my chin in my palm, feeling my shallow breath tickle the back of my hand. Chavallah crouched down in front of Neil; he had succeeded in her acquiescence. She started to negotiate with him her terms of moving out of the little apartment. When he agreed to giving her a month, rent free, to find another place, I left the kitchen. I couldn't stomach any more.

Neil had been so detached and logical. He reduced a volatile situation down to one sentence: "This is Denise's house." There was nothing Chavallah could say to change it. With that one sentence Neil resolved the issue, but again, for me, there was much more involved.

Instead of feeling relieved, I felt cheated. Like so many times before, my unwieldy emotions had rendered me impotent; they prevented me from saying what I had to say, what I *needed* to say, in order for me to let it go. My slow, deliberate speech had also failed me; I couldn't find the words fast enough to relay them from my brain to my tongue because of those strong emotions in between. Days, even *years*, later, I knew I would think of this scene with Chavallah and feel the same noxious heaviness in my chest that I felt now, wishing I had been able to confront her for her disregard and irresponsibility.

I also felt used, not only as a target for Chavallah's vehemence, but as a scapegoat for Neil. What had happened to *his* anger? It had been there Friday night when Chavallah had walked out and left us with the mess she made. Yet he hid behind his logic—distancing himself from the ugly emotions in the room—and said nothing to her to put his "good guy" image (that he so proudly adopted from his own father) at stake. His statement, "This is Denise's house," may have resolved the situation, but it still left me bearing the brunt of Chavallah's wrath. Neil made no attempt to divert her hurtful rage away from me.

For now though, it bothered me that I had been reduced to such infantile behavior. I was fifteen again, just three months after my mother died; my sister and my father were going to New Year's Eve celebrations. I resented them making plans, giving no thought to me. I would be alone to welcome the New Year. I pleaded with them not to go, not to leave me. "Nobody cares about me!" I sobbed. "Nobody cares about me!" Instead of consoling me, they attacked me with words. "Neisie, you're being unreasonable," my father yelled. "You only think about yourself!" My sister screamed that I was "a jealous little brat!" Had their actions been any less selfish or self-serving, I wondered? But I couldn't defend myself. Their words devastated me, like Chavallah's did moments ago.

All I could do was cry, afraid that their perception of me was shamefully accurate. Who knew me better than my own family? And they conveyed to me an all too obvious message: I was a burden for them, maybe not all the time, but a burden, nonetheless. They had just made it clear that they thought I had taken up enough of their attention with the necessities involved in living with someone with a disability; they needed a break from me. But what about me? I lived with that disability too, but I couldn't run away from it. I *had* to deal with it.

My disability forced emotions to rise to the surface for my family—anger, frustration, guilt. Yet instead of dealing with those feelings to strengthen our bond, my father and sister ran away from them. My disability served as the scapegoat, making their behavior excusable just as it made my behavior insufferable. It also served as a deflector for our grief over my mother's loss. Shelley and my father were going out to escape it; I couldn't. Years later, I realize my sorrow that night wasn't just about being left alone. My grief was about the kind of family I had—a family who knew too few skills to cope with each other's needs and feelings, who knew too well how to displace and bury their pain, and who sought happiness and solace from outsiders rather than from one another. That night, though, under a barrage of wounding accusations, I had no other choice than to accept the yoke of blame.

Chavallah's harsh words had brought my dark, shadowy feelings of shame, hurt, and unworthiness into focus. Feelings that remained inside me even after the years I've spent trying to purge myself of them. It was even more infuriating that I had reacted as I've always reacted: hysterically. Those old tunes from childhood still haunted me, and though I could now acknowledge their existence, I had yet to figure out how to avoid their seduction, how to stop dancing the same old dance. I certainly didn't want to pass the same songs and steps on to David that my family had passed on to me. I wanted our bonds to be stronger. I didn't want my son to be crippled by the same self-doubts that still betrayed me. I vowed to start him off with a completely different set of tunes.

"Is David okay?" I asked my friend, Lillian, who was holding him when I got back to my room. I was concerned the shouting might have upset him.

"He's fine," she assured me. "He definitely knew something was going on because his eyes widened every time your voices grew louder."

I took David from her and settled him in my lap. My lips brushed his fuzzy head while my heart ached for whatever discomfort the little tirade could have caused him. The constricted muscles in my chest relaxed as I let myself breathe. At least Chavallah wouldn't linger on as she had for the past two months. At least I wouldn't have to tolerate the thought of her taking care of David. Thanks to David, she was gone!

Aside from that unpleasant episode, everything else began running smoothly. We settled into a routine much quicker than I anticipated. David was a very accommodating baby, thanks to Kate, who had started him on such an easy routine during the first weeks of his life. She wouldn't take any credit, though. "All babies are like this," she claimed. "They only cry when they're hungry, tired, in pain, or need a diaper." She also tipped me off about feeding him warm water. She swore by it. "Relieves gas. Moves it right along!"

Kate spent Monday night at her sister's, and everything at our house went perfectly. Lydia's third and last visit of the day came a few minutes past eight o'clock. She washed David and dressed him in a clean diaper and sleeper after his exercises. Then she prepared his bottles for the night and early morning, including his oatmeal bottle for his next feeding. Making sure everything was put away, Lydia left Neil, David, and me to spend our first night alone.

I sat with a pillow on my lap on the couch under the dimness of the floor lamp and waited for Neil to land David on top. Neil glided him with confidence now, and David was so used to it he didn't bat an eye. Despite my fear that Neil and I handled him too roughly, it didn't seem to bother David. The more he got tossed and jiggled around, the louder he laughed and gurgled. Positioning his head on the pillow, I held the bottle to David's lips while the little pink cushion Aetna made with a wide elastic band steadied both my hand and

the bottle. I was so proud watching him drink. I grinned triumphantly when I burped him. But when he fell asleep in my lap, I felt
awestruck at his comfort, his acceptance. All our lives, Neil and I
struggled for acceptance, perhaps never really knowing what it
was—until now.

So we thought that we had this idea of parenting down pat, but
the next night we hit a snag. Around seven-thirty, David started crying. We tried a bottle, but he apparently wasn't hungry. Neil changed
his diaper, but David was neither wet nor poopy. Neil rolled back and
forth through the house, but David's tears kept streaming down his
red face.

"Call Kate, call Kate," I heard a panicked Neil yell from another
room.

All my instincts told me to wait (Lydia would be here soon), or
that I should call Jo Anne who lived across the street instead of Kate
who was at her sister Maggie's, twenty-five miles away. Somewhere
in the midst, warmed water even crossed my mind. But it would be
impossible to reason with an overwrought Neil. I called Kate from
the phone in the bedroom.

"Okay," I said, meeting Neil with poor screaming David in the
living room. "Kate is on her way."

"Kate! Why'd you call Kate?" he yelled as his veins bulged from
his forehead.

"You told me to," I shouted back.

"No, I didn't! I told you to call Jo Anne," he said vehemently.
"Now, go!"

Steamed, I returned to our bedroom and called Jo Anne.

I went back to the living room to wait for whomever showed up
first, and demanded, "I want to hold my baby." Neil had hogged him
for the past four days. He carried David whenever we went out. He
held him in the house. The only time David sat with me, it seemed,
was for his evening feeding.

Neil hesitated before I glared him down. Then he grabbed
David's sleeper and lifted. My arms went out to receive my son.

"Aaargh!"

I never knew such a loud burp could come from such a tiny body.
Suddenly, as he landed in my lap, David's screams were stunned by a
momentary silence, followed by delighted gurgles, . . . as Jo Anne,
Lydia, Kate, and her niece (along as chauffeur) rushed through the
door to the rescue.

"It was gas," I explained meekly while Neil bowed his head wearing his Stan Laurel grin. "He's okay now."

Neil and I certainly learned a lesson. We always kept a bottle of water ready and, no matter how David screamed, we didn't panic— at least, not to the same extent we did that night.

I felt that we had passed the test when Kate announced that she was indeed going home the next day. We arranged for her sister to drop her off in the morning so that Kate could spend an hour with us before Maggie drove her and Andrea to the airport.

We sat in the living room—Kate on the couch, Neil and I parked not more than a foot away, and David upright in Neil's lap, his head and back resting on Neil's velour shirt with Neil's arm around him. Kate was saying that David's pediatrician, Ann Parker, whom we had first seen the previous day, had called her earlier in the morning.

"She seems wonderful," Kate remarked. "Knows a lot about CP and child development."

"Yeah, I was very impressed," Neil said. Of course, he was; Dr. Parker nixed David's present physical therapy program. "You know, she wasn't taking any more new patients, but when I called her assistant, I said that I thought Dr. Parker might be interested in seeing us. I told her David had a good chance of having CP, and I had CP. Then she asked, `What about your wife?' I answered, `oh, she has CP, too.' Within five minutes she called me back to say Dr. Parker will be happy to see us."

I liked Dr. Parker but I wasn't that impressed. Doctors were doctors, with all their judgments. And we were a novelty. My verdict was still out. Besides, I thought it was a little ridiculous to be told to call the office every day to "check in." (I doubted other new parents were instructed to.) Yet she had been more positive about David's disability than the doctor in St. Louis. She didn't seem judgmental about his prognosis, making no guesses or assumptions about whether he'd walk or not (unlike the therapist I met a month ago). "Let's just see what happens," she had said, as if we were on an adventurous journey.

As we talked, Kate's eyes strayed magnetically to David.

"You want to hold him, Kate?" I interrupted.

"Oh, yes," her strong voice cracked. "These past few days I did-n't want to interfere, but oh, how my arms ache from not holding him!"

I understood. I felt that same ache, an ache of emptiness, when

David slept too long, or when Neil hogged him. My arms would long to cuddle and snuggle David, to feel his solid, round body against mine.

Kate stood up and bent over Neil. Gently, she lifted David and, cradling him, she sat down again. Sucking his pacifier, David turned his head as he stretched his neck to see his parents. He let Kate hold him, but his deep blue eyes remained fixed on Neil and me.

I wiped tears as they trickled down my cheeks and heard rasps of choked emotions involuntarily escape Neil's throat.

"My job is done," Kate sniffled as we all tried to smile. "David's home!"

We hugged and kissed when it was time for goodbyes. I walked her to the door and watched her go down the front steps and get into Maggie's car. We waved to each other before the car took off. This chapter had closed and, once again, I felt alone.

Chapter Nine
Old Familiar Roads

D uring the next two weeks, while Neil was off from work, David had probably been seen by as many pediatric rehabilitation specialists as his two parents had seen in their lifetimes. Since we had so many contacts, Neil and I decided to call on a few for their opinions. They were all eager to see our baby anyway, and we were just as eager to show him off. The sessions were quite different, too, from the ones Neil and I had been subjected to when we were kids. Instead of gray-headed doctors in white coats surrounded by somber medical students, there was laughter and chatter and fussing over a beautiful, alert three-month-old who captured almost everybody's heart with his charming smile and magnetic blue eyes.

David's first informal evaluation took place on the double bed in our crowded cream-walled bedroom. He had just awakened from his nap making little hungry squawks. As soon as Neil propped his bottle against the pillow, David's mouth snatched the nipple. Immediately gratified, David focused his eyes on the new faces in the room and some very fascinating looking video equipment.

Hal and Megan Kirschbaum, former colleagues of ours, ran an organization called Through the Looking Glass, which offered a variety of services to families with disabled children. A state grant had also provided them with funding to videotape disabled mothers (and fathers) caring for their babies from infancy through their first year. Neil and I agreed to participate in their project (and get copies of all the tapes), so we invited them over. They offered to bring their physical therapy consultant, Kathy, a young woman with curly hair and sparkling green eyes.

"He's so alert," Kathy marveled as she watched David, who was now on his father's lap being burped. David's eyes were fixed on

Megan while she scurried about pulling down the window shades to block off the glare of the strong afternoon sun, that is, until he caught sight of the blinking red light of Hal's focused camera.

After David produced a pair of loud, healthy burps, Kathy, with an inviting smile, reached out for him. He went to her with a gurgle and outstretched arms. She tousled him playfully first, and then laid him down on the bed.

She reached into her carpetbag at the foot of the bed and pulled out an array of baby toys—a yellow rubber duck, a red ring with a small blue ball in its center, and other multicolored thingamabobs.

"I'm doing the standard test used to record infant development," she spoke as she watched David reach for a squeaky yellow duck.

"Dr. Parker did it, too," I said. "She told us that David's cognitive development is where it should be. He had a little more trouble following the dangling red ring a few days ago, but she even said it could have been due to the changes he's gone through. You know, adjusting to a new home. . . ."

"He really concentrates," Kathy remarked. "I was noticing when Neil sat David on his lap to burp him. David was very interested in what was going on. He's very social, smiles and makes eye contact."

My mind flashed back to my first spellbinding eye contact with David on the plane. I swallowed a chuckle while I scooted closer to get a better view.

"Now, let's see about those arms and legs everybody's been talking about," Kathy murmured as she slipped off his red cotton sleeper.

Such soft, plump skin, I thought, as his flexed hands extended from the creased wrists of his bare forearms to play with the dark golden curls of Kathy's bent head; skin like my grandma's—with the sweetness of her soul.

Kathy knelt on the floor beside the bed and gently began bending David's limbs.

Kathy was handling David with such obvious delight. Dr. Parker had, too. There was warmth in their smiles, joy and acceptance in their faces. A look I could never imagine in the eyes of the doctor who had written the initial medical report; just the tone of it sounded so detached, so morbid, so hopeless—and sadly and clearly, too objectively subjective.

Kathy had changed to a sitting position on the bed and took David on her lap to move his little body around some more. Several times over, Kathy's hands gently bent and flexed David's elbows, wrists, arms, legs, knees, and ankles. First arms, then legs. First right side, then left.

"I'm feeling a little more rigidity in his arms than his legs," she said, glancing up at Neil and me. "Still, it seems so slight."

"When Dr. Parker examined him, she felt the increased muscle tone in his legs, not his arms."

Kathy nodded. "It's hard to tell with babies because they can change so much from day to day. I bet David might be one of those kids who baffles the medical profession. I've seen it before, where kids don't bother reading their own case histories and grow up without a sign or symptom, despite all the evidence." So that day it was his arms. Two days later when we took David to see my friend, Alice, the director of the OT Department at Stanford's Children's Hospital, the tightness was on his right side and, Alice assured me, "he's very bright." *Of course, I knew that*—but I was his mother. I looked at her skeptically. "How in the world could you tell that a three-month-old is very bright?"

"Because he has a sense of humor," she answered, as she teased him with yet another dangling red ring. "Look at the way he's laughing. A sense of humor in babies is a sign of intelligence."

I liked having a fact to back up my intuition.

At the end of Neil's two weeks off, when it seemed like we'd been exposed to a dozen dangling red rings and squeaky yellow ducks, the word on David was as inconclusive as the first doctor's report. As for Neil and me, we decided to stick to our own individual theories about David's alleged disability. "Well, you know, he had to get to us some way," I'd offer with a shrug of my shoulders and roll my eyes up to whatever powers might be out there.

Neil's explanation of course, was more pragmatic than mine. He concluded, referring to all the expertise: "If you look for something hard enough, you'll find it!"

Everyone seemed in agreement about one thing, though—David should still be considered an "at risk" infant; it would make him eligible for state-supported services from the Regional Center.

Neil contacted the Regional Center, set up an appointment, and filled out all the forms. He did most of the talking at the intake interview. I willingly took a back seat, feeling a twinge of envy at his ease in handling everything so confidently and admiring his ability to establish a rapport with people who were part of "the system."

I watched Neil; I studied his manner during every encounter, hoping to learn what to say, what to do—how not to feel old pangs of fear and intimidation. In childhood, I was taught to be accepting of what was offered, especially when it was for free; "Beggars can't be choosers," I was always told. I never learned how to stick up for myself. In adulthood, although I had steadily acquired more skill at assertiveness, I was still finding that habit of silent submission so painfully hard to break. Perhaps, for both our sakes, David could help me with this lesson.

The Regional Center's acceptance of David as a client meant that the agency would purchase twice-weekly physical therapy sessions for David and four hours a week "respite care" (to give the parents of a `special needs' infant a break). The services would be provided through private vendors, considered to be `qualified' (but not supervised) under state regulations. In other words, Regional Center would pay the expenses, but Neil and I wouldn't have much choice in selecting David's physical therapist or weekend home care worker. . . . And it also meant that when Neil went back to work in his neat corporate world, I'd get stuck with having to work out a mess of details.

In two weeks' time, we received word that David had been approved as a Regional Center client, for better or for worse.

"But how am I going to get him to Whitten School for physical therapy twice a week?" I lamented in an exhausted voice, just thinking about packing up extra clothes, diapers, bottles, then getting David into his Kacoon and settled on my lap for a forty-minute BART (Bay Area Rapid Transit) train ride that would leave us off a half a mile from Whitten, in a neighborhood I might feel safe in with two police escorts and a bulletproof vest.

I called Debra, David's Regional Center assigned case worker. I found courage to ask if a therapist could be sent to the house.

"We can't do that," she told me apologetically. "It's not our policy. . . . Let me see if we can purchase van services," she said. "I'll check with my supervisor and call you back."

My heart sank. In recent years, if I couldn't use public transportation to get somewhere, I'd ask a friend to drive me or I'd hire my own driver. I avoided using private van services at all costs. I had never liked them—the drivers would always show up late with no apologies, call me "baby" or "sweetheart," and handle me with little respect as they strapped the seatbelts tightly around me, showing no consideration or discretion for touching even my private body parts.

Most of the time the drivers wore sunglasses to cover up their blood-shot eyes and sucked mints in an attempt to mask the odor of pot or alcohol on their breath. Whenever they stopped at red lights, their heads would turn to ogle well-developed women. Of course, there was a camaraderie among them, so it did little good to call up and complain; the managers and dispatchers would assure me that their drivers were all reputable and typical "good guys." There was almost no alternative but to tolerate their overpriced, inadequate services.

It was not something I felt that I could readily explain to Debra. The Regional Center purchased van services for other disabled clients and knew the system wasn't perfect, but what could someone expect from underbid contracts? Certainly not quality!

I was hoping Debra wouldn't get her supervisor's approval.

The phone rang minutes later.

"Good news, Denise," Debra said. "We can provide van service for David."

"And how about for me too?" I asked, just to make sure that I was included.

"Um," she hesitated, "you want to go too?"

"Debra, he's not even four months old!" I pointed out, squashing a twinge of self-doubt that I might be being unreasonable. "I can't send him by himself."

"Oh," she said, as it seemed to have just registered that the idea of three-month-old David traveling alone was somewhat preposterous. "I'll have to call you back."

After another conference with her supervisor, she apologetically informed: "The best we can do is provide you and David with transportation during his evaluation period for the first week . . ., because if you go too, you'd need a van with a wheelchair lift. That would cost sixty dollars round-trip, where if David were just transported by regular school bus, it would only cost twelve."

"Well, then what's the use of going for the evaluation?" I asked in only mild disgust (the policy wasn't her fault). "You may be able to appeal because of the circumstances." Reluctantly, I agreed to have her set up the transportation for David's appointment.

We coordinated the appointment around David's feeding and napping schedule. Our pickup was ten-thirty so that we'd be at the school by eleven. Carrie, our permanent replacement for Chavallah, was just getting David's car seat out of our van as I sat on the sidewalk with David in my lap when a rickety school bus pulled up. My stomach muscles tightened as the driver stepped out. He was a skinny, raggedy-looking man with stringy gray hair and a day's growth of beard on his weathered face.

Out of habit, I swallowed my reservations and greeted him. "Hi, I'm Denise and this is David."

He nodded.

"And your name is . . . ?" I prompted.

"Paul," he answered curtly after clearing his throat, then turned to Carrie who clambered over with the car seat. "You going with her?"

"No. She isn't," I answered quickly, attempting to set him straight that he should be talking to me, not to my nondisabled housekeeper.

"Oh, okay."

He began unlatching the doors to the lift. "They gave me this old bus today, so the ride might be a little bumpy."

I grimaced, remembering those bucking bronco school bus rides. I pressed my lips tightly together as I rolled myself onto the lift. The driver locked my brakes and pressed the "up" switch on the controls. The metal platform protested with alarming rattles and creaks as it was raised to the level of the bus floor.

The driver hopped up, indicating that I should back in to the wheel locks beside the hump of the rear wheel of the bus (I was definitely in for a bumpy ride). Kneeling down to fasten my wheelchair in place, the driver took off his wire-rimmed sunglasses. I caught a glimpse of his bloodshot eyes and thought I smelled the faint odor of alcohol. Some things never change.

The driver walked to the front of the bus and motioned to Carrie to bring David in. She carried him up the steps in his carseat and strapped him into the worn brown vinyl seat in front of me, with his back to me. She looked at me warily with her timid gray eyes while making sure he was secured.

"You sure you're going to be all right?" she mumbled. *No, I wasn't,* I answered myself, but felt I didn't have any real choice. "Listen," I said to her, "if we're not back in a couple of hours, call Neil."

I stroked the top of David's head as the doors cranked shut to reassure him against the strange noises, and to remind myself where we were. I kept trying to swallow what felt like green slime in my throat, fighting back the memories—the long history—of not being in control, being taken to places I didn't want to go, and having to make "the best of it" in order to survive in a society where I was always a disability, never a person. *This was Highway 580, in California, and I'm David's mother,* I told myself, not The East River Drive, three thousand miles away. Yet I had traveled that ugly Drive for so many more years, and I've racked up so many more painful memories spanning the years of my childhood.

Childhood. A very young childhood. I was three and a half. They fitted me with long-legged metal braces (up to my hipbone) and wooden crutches and told my mother that it would best if I were admitted into the hospital to get me "up on my feet." "Only for a few months," the doctor said—the same doctor who likened me to a vegetable twelve years later. My mother would be "allowed to visit me for two hours on Wednesday afternoons" and, of course, she could take me home for weekends—if she wanted. And so, after we came home from a summer in Rockaway, when I was three and a half, I went into the Pediatric Rehabilitation Ward at Bellevue Hospital in Manhattan. The best route from the Bronx was along the East River Drive.

My mother took me to be admitted on a dismal Monday morning during the worst hurricane storm of the season. The rain flooded the Drive. Traffic backed up. Headlights and taillights inched their way along the dark, angry East River. I hoped we would have to turn back, but it was only rain, not snow.

Bellevue Hospital: a massive red brick (the color of an armory), pseudomedieval monstrosity with an interior of green walls and black checkerboard polished floors. Cold slippery floors that adhered to my clammy knees and my tear-streaked cheek as I lay on them kicking and screaming, begging my mother not to leave. But they persuaded her to go: "She'll calm down after you go," they said. My mother looked at me, her eyes filled with an apologetic pleading. She had to listen to them. They were the experts. At three and a half, I'd have to understand. . . . The sad thing was, I did.

Harsh voices hissed and threatened with grown-up reasoning and shaming. "Don't act like a baby. . . . She'll visit onWednesday. . . . Oh, stop it, right now!" They sat me up on a bench. Stern hands roughly wiped my face. I swallowed my sobs as hard as I could, yet some escaped, shuddering through my body. "Now, come on, stop this!" *I was trying, trying.* Oh, it wasn't a good morning for them!

I slept in a crib between Stephanie and Maria. We eyed each other through our bars. Maria had dark, curly hair, a cast on both legs up to her waist, and a grandmother who didn't speak English. Blonde Stephanie didn't have legs or arms—just a few clawlike fingers protruding from one shoulder—a misshapen nose, and no grandmother, mother, or any other family. She lived at the hospital and I remember hearing, even though I was so young, that they had found her as an infant, in a garbage can. *Yes, I remember at three and a half.*

I didn't know that what I felt at the time was called fear. I just knew it would be better for me if I cooperated. The nurses and aides liked it better if you cooperated. The physical therapists liked it better if you cooperated. The doctors liked it better if you cooperated. *(Now that I think about it, perhaps that was the beginning of my lifelong battle with constipation!)* They called my speech "unintelligible" (only understood by my immediate family and people with patience), so I learned, at three and a half, to survive on my smile, my wits, and my spelling.

"I want soda," I garbled, finally getting the attention of a nurse's aide. We were outside in the courtyard one not-too-chilly autumn day for someone's birthday party.

"What d'ya want, little girl?" she asked impatiently. Not many of the staff bothered learning patients' names, and I had just interrupted a conversation she was having with a male orderly.

"I want s-o-d-a." I looked up into her face as I spoke and then pointed to the bottle of Hoffman cola standing on the table a few feet away.

Her eyes grew wide. She called the nurse over. "Miss Crush, Miss Crush, you gotta come hear this. This little one knows how to spell!"

Miss Crush, the only nurse at Bellevue with curly red hair, freckles, and a warm compassionate smile, strode over to me. Her crisp white uniform practically crackled as she knelt down. Her green eyes flickered when I repeated, "I want s-o-d-a." She couldn't wait to tell my mother. . . . And my mother, of course, beamed with surprised pride; she didn't know that it was her "difficult" six-year-old daughter, Shelley, who was teaching me, her insufferable baby sister, how to spell.

That episode seemed to establish my reputation as "the little genius" not only on the Pediatric Ward, but also at home. The only person with sense not to buy it was Shelley, but I wasn't about to give myself away, for now the hospital staff started being nice to me. They even remembered my name.

However, it still didn't help my Sunday night panic when my uncle Joey would drive me back for another week's stay at Bellevue. My stomach would quiver as I sat with my mother in the back seat of the car. It rumbled when my uncle turned on the motor, and, as if on cue, my tears began just as we reached the underpass of the UN at 45th Street. The lamplights of the Drive blurred through my tears. I sniffled. My father, sitting in the front seat (he was too `high-strung' to get behind the wheel of a car), glanced back and, inept with words of comfort, wisecracked: "Uh-oh, here come the waterworks."

"Neisie, please don't start," my mother pleaded, but by the time we got off the Drive at 23rd Street, I was in hysterics. Images that I had no words for—green walls, immobile Maria, abandoned Stephanie—loomed in my head.

I mastered crutch-walking in three weeks, instead of a few months, with the help of green and yellow ribbons tied onto my crutches and shoes so I would remember which foot to move after each crutch. Every three months (six months when I got older) I had to appear at the outpatient clinic so the doctors could check my progress and the brace man could adjust my braces as I grew. Every three months as we rode along the Drive, I silently held on to a terror that only disappeared once we were on our way home.

The yellow and fuchsia ice plants bloomed among the green ivy and oak trees along the highway. A sign of spring on a rare fog-free morning in the Bay Area. *This was definitely not the East River Drive.*

My hand rested on the back of David's carseat as my index and middle finger played with his fine copper hair. We jolted with every rumble and grumble of the lurching bus. We rolled over some bumps that caused us to be elevated inches in the air. Each time, David was startled and clenched his fists. I could see the blue ring of his Binky pacifier bob up and down as I faintly heard him ferociously sucking it above the rattling of the bus. I wanted to cry for him; this wasn't right.

We turned off the highway and onto Foothill Boulevard. This wasn't the way Neil had driven us a few weeks ago for our initial meeting at the school. The straggle-haired driver leaned forward, turning his head left and right to catch glimpses of street signs. He had no idea where we were. Periodically, he looked into his rearview mirror and, though his eyes were shaded by sunglasses, I sensed questioning looks from them—wondering if I knew the way, debating whether it was worth asking me since he wasn't sure if he would understand me, or if I would even be credible. I'd been this route of other people's skepticism so many times before.

I seethed with resentment and waited for the rattling to dull as we stopped at a red light. "Turn right on 35th and follow it to the BART Station, then make a left. It'll be about half a mile from there," I shouted each word carefully from the back of the bus.

He nodded and followed my directions. Ten minutes later, he pulled into the disabled parking spot in front of Whitten School. "First I'll help you off and then I'll give the baby to you," he said, in a tone free of previous condescension or anxiety that it held before, as he started walking toward me.

"Are you going to take us home?" I asked when David was safely in my lap.

"I'm not scheduled to," he replied. "So let me take out the carseat."

Here we go again—a different driver, another round. He followed me through the lime green hallways that led to the PT room and set the carseat against the wall on the black and green checkered floor. Before he left, he wished me a good day.

The room was a double-sized schoolroom with several rectangular mirrors spaced along the walls. One corner had a set of wooden steps that went nowhere—they were used to practice step-walking. Parallel bars spanned across three mirrors between the two doorways, and gray vinyl-coated mats lay along the opposite wall. Three examining tables stood at the far end of the room, each about three feet apart. It might have been larger, but nonetheless, it was almost a clone of the PT room I had spent hours in as a child at P.S. 85—right down to the faintly prevalent smell of ammonia disinfectant.

David's therapist, Becky, whom we met at a preliminary interview two weeks ago, strode over to us in her pink sweater, gray slacks, and white Nikes. Her welcome smile brought me out of my previous state of anxiety.

"He's ready to go," I said.

I watched her get on her knees with him and finish up the examination that she had started last time. David cooed and gurgled as she tossed him around like all the others had done before her. Becky cooed and gurgled back. Finally, before the thirty-minute period was up, she jiggled him on her lap with some stretching exercises and rolled him around on a yellow beach ball. At first, not knowing what to make of it, David opened his eyes a little wider and his jaw dropped. His forehead creased with wrinkles of perplexity—a look I was surprised to see on a four-month-old. Then he relaxed and smiled, as if he consciously decided he was safe. He was, I thought, such a remarkable baby!

When the session ended, Becky helped settle David once again in my lap. She carried the carseat while we wended our way down the corridor and turned the sharp corner of the L-shaped one-story building.

The double doors beyond the school's entrance, which I hadn't noticed before, opened onto another half of the corridor. Children roamed in the hallway. Children on crutches wearing protective helmets. Children in manual wheelchairs struggling to push themselves. Children on their way to lunch or to the bathroom.

Nausea rose slowly from my stomach. Whitten, this place, was a segregated school, where some "experts" had decided there was no place for such children in mainstream education or recreation. In all respects, nothing had changed since my grammar school days—although our little HC (Health Class) Unit was located in the basement of a public school, beyond the double doors of the gymnasium. We, too, were "sheltered" from the mainstream, hardly ever seeing our nondisabled counterparts except during fire drills; we had our own entrance. To avoid being trampled (or so it was reasoned) by the "regular" kids, our rickety school buses—staffed mostly by grumpy drivers and sourpussed matrons—delivered us to school a half an hour before the nine o'clock school bell and picked us up a half an hour before the three o'clock recess bell. I often wondered, when I heard the voices of those "regular" kids echo from the gymnasium (during their lunch hour or music class), who was being sheltered from whom. Didn't anyone expect that one day we, the little `cripplettes' of the fifties and sixties would grow up to have to deal with other people's stares and discomfort? But then again, who'd have thought we would go to work, get married and, most improbable of all, raise children?

I realized, too, as I watched the children at Whitten, that I was internally wrestling with my own "cripophobia"—my own discomfort with, and fear of, disabled individuals. It was something that embarrassed me—it wasn't politically correct—but "cripophobia" is a demon that most of us, disabled or not, learn from the time we're very young because, in our world, it may be okay to be different, but not too different.

It used to please my mother whenever my teacher would remark on how "normal" I looked sitting quietly at my desk, not like the other CP kids who couldn't focus their eyes, or kept their arms bent out at 45 degree angles, or forgot to keep their mouths closed and swallow their abundant saliva. I sat at my desk attentively, my braced feet on the floor, and never allowed more than one drop of drool to escape my lips. I, too, wanted to keep up the momentary fallacy that, as it was often phrased, "there looked like nothing was wrong with me." If I ever lapsed in my pretense, I would be reminded: "Denise, put your hands in your lap and sit up straight," Miss Sheehan prompted at two in the afternoon when my energy waned (after being up since six in the morning). At home, after an even longer day, my mother nagged, "Neisie, honey, wipe your mouth and swallow. You don't want anybody to cup your chin and say what a pretty little girl you are, and then go 'blech' when you drool over their hand."

I didn't fault their intentions to enhance my awareness of myself and besides, I wanted to look 'good,' too. Yet now I see that it was all done at the expense of my own self-acceptance; it negated the value of my having a disability, as well as devaluing my disabled peers. I became so self-conscious: I wouldn't even smile for photographs because when I did, I made funny faces. As my mother put it, "It looks like you have CP."

When I saw those kids in Whitten's hallway, slumped over, drooling, adorned with equipment that looked like something out of an industrial catalog, a desperate inner voice tried to assure me, "I'm not like them. . . . ," even though, at times, my arms do flail and I drool too. As much as I wanted to belong to the rest of society, I would always be set apart from it either by my choosing or by somebody elses. I just wished that I had learned at an earlier age that I shouldn't have struggled to "overcome my disability"; it was a ridiculous battle to wage, fighting to defeat a very integral part of who I am. It has taken me too long to learn that I could smile for the camera, as the disapproving voice in my head grows fainter and fainter. . . . Perhaps for David, it's a voice he'll never hear.

Becky left David and me to wait in the warmth of the afternoon sun. Ten minutes passed. Fifteen. Then twenty. Most drivers ran late, I assured myself: *They'll be here, Neisie, have a little faith.* Yet, in my gut,

I had a stark feeling that David and I had been forgotten.

At forty-five minutes, I went back inside to find Becky. She called the van company and returned with an answer I didn't want but expected to hear: "They didn't know they were supposed to take you home. They said they'll send someone as soon as they could. It may take another hour."

And they had expected me to send David by himself!

I wished I were a bull—an angry, raging bull.

I controlled myself. I had enough diapers and bottles to last the afternoon ("Always take extra," Kate had advised). I soothed David to sleep. When the bus driver arrived an hour later, I calmly told her where we lived, even though she first asked Becky.

Once we were home, I settled David in his crib and then called Neil. He wasn't there. I left a voice message.

"It's two P.M. We just got home. We're not going back!"

Chapter Ten

An Ice Cream Cone

There wasn't much of an adjustment for me to make in loving a three-month-old baby boy. Every morning I'd watch him sleep so peacefully beside me—his smooth pale brow and almost paper-thin eyelids still marked by fading "stork bites" and his pink lips softly closed, innocent of demand or judgment. Being unable to resist temptation, but not wanting to disturb David's slumber, I carefully braced the heel of my left hand on the bed right below his chin in order to stroke his round silky cheek with my index finger. I felt his warm shallow breath on my cupped palm. My stomach quivered. In love? Definitely!

Adjusting to the world around David and me was quite another story.

For me, most of the time, life had been a constant series of daily personal chores, which always began with getting up in the morning. I had my routine so well established before David came—a regimen that could last anywhere from one to two hours, depending on whether I ate enough prunes the night before, or if it was shower day when it might take forever to dry off in my steamy bedroom, or if I had a tight muscle in my neck, which made dressing myself more cumbersome than it could be on some days. Having cerebral palsy always made things a little more complicated. On a good day, if I were fairly rested and relaxed, getting dressed could take fifteen minutes. On other days, I might have trouble: my hands and my bra hooks could play their own game of tag, my socks could get snagged on my toenails and cling to every wrinkle on the bottom of my feet, and my elastic waist slacks would not amply stretch while I tried to hike them up before I lost my balance.

Neil seemed to greet the day with more zest: a zest he credited to his parents, Holocaust survivors who had seen enough death in their lives to treasure and guard every moment of wakefulness. While Neil was just as susceptible as I was to good days and bad days, he paid as little attention to them as possible. At six in the morning, a stuck zipper on his shirt might evoke muttered curses from his lips, but since he had no time to deal with it, he'd just rip it apart so he could get it off and put on another one.

And, at the risk of sounding sexist, his cool, smooth skin—having fewer curves and folds—dried off more efficiently, he didn't wear a bra, and he had no rear end at all. His clothes slid on with less effort, even though he grunted and snorted every time he tightened his tie and got on his knees to tuck his shirt into his jockey shorts (a tip on neatness he still claims was the best thing he ever learned from me), pull up his pants, and fasten them.

But except for changing David's diaper, giving him a bottle, and putting David in bed with me before he left for work, Neil's daily routine really didn't change. Mine did, enormously! Suddenly, I was responsible for another human being, which took more physical and emotional energy than I ever dreamed possible. No one could have ever prepared me for the depths of motherhood—a daily spectrum of euphoria, isolation, despair, dependence, contentedness, frustration, and, at day's end, complete and utter exhaustion.

Accepting this new little being into my life was simple and easy, but with that acceptance I was hurled into the throes of anxiety. Suddenly, I was supposed be an adult—something I was never taught, but always told, to be. Suddenly, I was supposed to tell somebody how I wanted things done in my home. I didn't do very well with Chavallah. I was uncomfortable in the role of employer, just as my mother had been. I remember her having difficulty telling the cleaning woman, who came to our house once every two weeks, how she wanted things done. When the woman left at the end of the day, my mother would be "aggravated" because she didn't vacuum behind the couch, there were streaks on the windows, and the faucets didn't shine the way they did when my mother cleaned them. But she never said a word to the woman the next time, as if she felt guilty for imposing her standard of cleaning on someone else, especially since her own chronic backache prevented her from doing her own heavy housework.

I knew that same aggravation. I felt it fill my gut, like a massive blob, and bubble under my skin: a mixture of frustration, resentment, and self-loathing. My mother's image formed so clearly in my mind; her purplish lips whitened as she struggled to contain the boiling emotion seeping out through the thickened tone of her voice. Her aggravation was a way of life for her, and I can't help wondering how much of that aggravation, over the years, contributed to her death because it ate her up inside. And though I try so hard to handle situations differently, I've been disturbed by those destructive feelings I seem to share with her. Now that I face the same role as she had, those similarities in our feelings scare me even more.

My new weekday routine began at seven-fifteen when the radio would go off. I got up, slid David more to the middle of the bed, and placed pillows around him (not too close to risk smothering him), in case it was the day for him to start rolling over. With a reluctant sigh, I forced myself to leave the bedroom to begin my mundane routine. On most mornings, I was dressed—except for socks and loafers—by the time I heard Carrie's shallow knock on the front door before she used the key to let herself in.

Neil and I hired Carrie about a month after Chavallah moved out. Fortunately, there had been no rush to find somebody new since we had Lydia and a ten-day visit from my sister with her oldest son, eight-year-old Larry, which coincided with a visit from Jackie, Neil's friend from his days at Hofstra. I was grateful for the reprieve of searching for, we hoped, a better replacement, even though living in a small, two-bedroom house with three extra people didn't do that much for my stress reduction. Neil's mother wanted to come out, too (I suppose she was curious), but he managed to put her off; Neil told her that we would be going back east in June, and she could see her grandson then. Boy, was I relieved!

Neil and I knew we had made a mistake hiring Chavallah and we didn't trust ourselves not to repeat it. We asked Neil's boss, Aetna, to help us in our search for a replacement. I felt a little guilty asking someone else for help; after all, as an independent living counselor, I used to insist that my clients hire their attendants on their own. I could afford to be very politically correct back then.

Carrie had been one of the first callers that Aetna had screened. She was in her late twenties, divorced twice, had an eight-year-old son who lived with her first husband and his wife. She seemed timid to me, wearing a loose-fitting jumper that hid her shape and glasses that seemed too big for her small moon-shaped face and turned-up

nose. But she seemed comfortable talking with us. Neil had no difficulty getting Carrie into a conversation—then again, Neil could get
anyone into a conversation (when he wanted to). She even laughed at
his jokes at the right time.

Neil liked her immediately. I had reservations, of course.

According to her resume, she was never at a job for very long—
six months at the most. She had raised her son as a single mother
while she did child care and house cleaning, she explained, but when
he was a little older she remarried. Then she went back to school after
her second divorce but had to drop out because of money. Within the
last year, she recovered from leg surgery—a result of a ski injury—
and decided that Gavin should live with his father until she became
financially secure. At the present time, she was working as a receptionist in a veterinary office, but her income barely covered rent.

She seemed delighted and very enthusiastic about working for
us. She had been adopted, too, she told us—as well as her sister and
brother—but her parents had been very secretive about it. In fact, she
and both her siblings now had a rather distant relationship with her
parents.

My antennae were up during the whole two-hour interview. Two
marriages, two divorces, and an eight-year-old kid by age twenty-
eight. Strained family ties. *Was she stable enough? Was she harboring
some deep-seated hostility that she would take out on us? Most of all, could
I trust her not to kidnap my baby?*

Unless I had more faith in crystal balls, I knew I couldn't expect
those questions to be answered in a way that would satisfy my fears.
So I had to look on the practical side. Carrie's references checked out:
she was prompt, efficient, and hardworking, good with babies and
young children. I liked the way she was with David—I heard her
sweetly cooing at him while she changed his diaper during the interview. After I mulled it around in my mind, and considered the fact
that Aetna wasn't being inundated with prospective candidates, I
decided we should take a chance on Carrie. She seemed like a lost
soul with a good heart. Maybe it would do her as much good to
become part of our home, too. I felt I could trust her, as much as I
could trust any stranger to help me care for my baby. And Carrie,
unlike her infamous predecessor, Chavallah, wasn't pushy!

David would usually just be waking up as Carrie opened the
front door. I'd be with him, having crawled back on the bed to catch
his first smile of the day. It always took me a moment to find my

voice to call out a greeting to Carrie.

Talk about lost souls, I never quite knew what to do with myself when Carrie came in the morning. She knew what she had to do—give David a bath, feed him breakfast, make bottles for the day, clean up. I didn't want to hover over her or interrupt her work by getting into long conversations (though she didn't seem to mind). I wondered, though, about my role as David's mother: Would he learn that he had to rely on someone else? Would he think less of me as his mother if I weren't always part of the picture? I tried to counter my arguments with the analogy of the working mother who had to totally rely on au pairs and child care. *It was the same,* wasn't it? . . . Yet every day, around eleven, when it was time for Carrie to leave, I realized that my analogy was bogus: a working mother could solely care for the physical needs of her child without too much bother. For me, many of those physical needs took the time and energy of a five-mile uphill run.

It had not been in our agreement that Carrie be available for diaper changes during her time off in the afternoon, although I had hoped that she'd be the kind of person I would feel comfortable asking if I knew she was around. But she seemed so guarded and reluctant to offer any of her time, and I always felt as if I would be imposing. My fear of her resentment and my knowledge that our finances were already being stretched to the limit prevented me seeing any possibility of renegotiating our agreement even for an extra ten minutes. But the problem wasn't just time. The major dilemma was the unpredictability of when, during the long five hours of the afternoon, David would need a clean diaper.

David's diaper still took me so long to change. It was easy enough to slide the diaper out from under him when it was just soaked with urine, but a "dump" had to be more carefully removed and cleaned up. It required at least four or five wet wipes whenever I did it—Neil often teased me about getting out a magnifying glass; I was almost phobic about diaper rash, knowing it would necessitate more diaper changes during the day. But I didn't mind that part at all—it gave me a time of intimacy with my son while I cleaned off his tender bottom and felt the cool softness of his young skin. It was such a loving task for me and often as I did it, I'd recall those mornings when my mother would sit on my bed, take one foot at a time from under the warm cover and, as it rested in her lap (sole side up), she'd slip on my cotton sock.

Yet David's new diaper wasn't easy to put on. I had to prepare for the procedure so methodically: I unfolded the new Pamper even before I took off the old. I peeled back the closed tapes—starting them with the corner of my thumbnail and then taking them between my thumb and forefinger—holding my breath with determination not to scrunch up each adhesive tab causing it to stick to itself. I placed the diaper aside until I was ready to slide it under David's bottom; that was easy enough to do, rocking David from one side to the next while I maneuvered the diaper to precisely where it should be.

But then it was time to tape, to hold each one of the two corners down and fold those adhesive tabs over the little Sesame Street characters along the waistband. I'd do the side I thought I had more control over first (the left side facing me), as I held the corner steady with my left hand so that my right hand could grasp it from my left one to hold it in position. The then freed, more coordinated fingers of my left hand groped carefully for the tape to anchor it to the waistband. "One down and one to go," the thought would float through my head before I went on to conquer the second side. Only quite often I'd find that I would have to go back to the first side because I hadn't left enough of a corner to tape on the right side. Sometimes after I'd finish I decided that the diaper was too loose, or too tight, or too low, or too high, or that the tapes were rubbing on David's skin, and so the diaper needed to be adjusted. Sometimes the tapes would lose their adhesive, and I'd have to start all over again with a new diaper.

It wasn't uncommon for a diaper change to take me up to forty minutes, but through it all—the jostling and jiggling, my sweating and absentminded drooling—David cooed or sucked his pacifier, played with his fingers or his rattle. Intermittently, I'd stop my labor and talk to him. He'd smile and blabber back. His patience made my effort possible. And when it was over—the diaper snugly on (more or less), the sleeper zipped, and our energy exhausted—I'd turn him on his stomach and rub his back. He'd sleep for two hours!

David and I spent most of our afternoons on a two-inch-thick, four foot by six foot foam mat that lay on the hardwood floor in our bright daylit living room. The mat was my idea. When I had been at Kate's in St. Louis, David and I spent our time spread out on thick blankets in the dark, carpeted den. On my knees I was able to feed, burp, diaper, and cradle him. Kate determined that all I needed to be self-sufficient with David was a bed! I didn't want to ruin her fantasy, but if I had to spend day after day in my small, dark bedroom, shades drawn so that passersby couldn't see in, I'd become as restless as a caged alley cat.

"I want the mat over by the couch," I directed the day Neil and Jackie came home from the foam shop.

"I don't want it there. It sticks out too far in the middle of the floor," he announced. "It won't look neat."

"But I thought if it were over against the couch I'll be able to get David up and into my lap." I explained, after planning the whole thing out in my head. Since the distance from the mat to my lap would be too far for me to lift fifteen pounds of baby, I reasoned that I could first lift David a foot and a half onto the couch, roll right up to it, and then scoot him safely up the remaining distance onto my knees.

"It'll look too messy!" He stared at me grimly.

I pressed my lips together and clenched my teeth. He stared at me with a grave, stone face.

"I'm not staying in that bedroom all day." I argued.

No response: *Another head for Mount Rushmore.*

"Neil," my sister intervened. "Come here and feel it. It's very light. You should have no trouble pushing it back against the wall when you want to."

Still slumped and looking wounded in his wheelchair—his usual position when it came to arguing with me—Neil rolled up to the mat to test my sister's suggestion. It was indeed valid. He was satisfied again.

That was all that mattered to him: neatness! Not my feelings, not how I would manage with David by myself during the day. I twinged with resentment, but said nothing. It wouldn't make any difference. I knew from the four years we had been together, there were certain things about me that Neil just didn't want to understand.

The joy of having David eased some of my feelings of isolation during those long hours of the afternoon, but I constantly had to remind myself, as I sat in the house, that I wasn't the same young girl who was stuck in an inaccessible Bronx apartment, that my life wasn't empty and desperate. In fact, it was quite the opposite.

Everything just took so much energy, including making plans. I would, on occasion, have spurts of *oomph* and make phone calls, invite friends over, but most of them worked during the day, and being a writer, I had always been somewhat of a loner. I was almost overwhelmed at the thought of trying to join a play group or a mothers' group with strangers who had inaccessible houses or lived outside of "rolling distance." Fortunately, some woman I knew just had a baby, too, and decided to get a mothers' group together made up of artistic women. Diane asked if I was interested. We had, for the most part, a core group of four. We met once a week for a couple of hours. It still didn't get David and me out of the house much because of accessibility: they came to us.

As the weather grew warmer, I was determined to venture out alone with David—providing I could get him into and out of his Kacoon. I took Megan Kirschbaum up on her offer to call her if I needed help in figuring out how to do things when David and I were on our own. As it turned out, I already had the idea; I just needed someone around to give me moral support.

I started out with the Kacoon spread open on the bed with David lying nearby. Megan stood beside me. "Could you hand me a pillow? I need it to line the bottom of the Kacoon. Otherwise David gets swallowed up by the material."

Megan walked to the head of the bed to get the pillow. "Denise, have you tried another type of baby carrier?" She asked.

"I've looked at them, but they all had straps, or snaps, or ties." I said.

"Well, there's Velcro. Wouldn't that help?" she suggested. "This just seems like a lot of work."

"I know, but I really like the Kacoon," I said defensively. "I'm afraid that with a front carrier my chin would knock into his head. He's very long, you know."

She didn't press the point further. She picked up a pillow and brought it to me. I tucked it down into the purple folds of the Kacoon. Then I reached for David, grabbing the middle of his terry-cloth sleeper, and lifted him onto the rectangular pillow. Leaning my body as far over him as I could, I put my head and left arm through the wide Kacoon strap and, bracing his body with mine, I pulled him onto my lap. He was safely cradled against me, close to my heart.

"Oh, I see now," Megan voiced. "That's a real nice position for both of you, isn't it?"

"Mm-hmm," I nodded, feeling rather pleased with myself. "I can feed him a bottle like this, and he can nap too."

With a little less effort, I was able to get David out of the sling.

In my family, doing anything more than necessary had always been a hassle. My mother suffered chronic back pain and bouts with phlebitis from poor circulation. My father worked long days. "I-just-sat-down-wait-till-I-get-up" droned like a mantra in response to many requests. No one had any extra energy—even my sister, who was barely three years older than me. She actually shamed me into drinking coffee without sugar ("Only babies drink it that way"), because she didn't want to be bothered putting the sugar in and stirring it, and then having to wash an extra spoon.

David, I determined, was never going to be burdened with that kind of guilt or self-consciousness. No matter how difficult, I'd take him out for walks at least twice a week or more. He'd usually fall asleep, which meant I could stop and have a mocha at a neighborhood cafe. Other patrons would nod and smile. On the street, when I glanced at people coming toward us, I often caught a look of amazed joy on their faces when they saw us (so different than those disdainful stares or pitying "tsks" I got in my youth). One day, I was even stopped by an elderly man about my father's age.

"Excuse me, I know I'm staring," he offered apologetically, "and I don't mean to; I've certainly seen a wheelchair before, and I've certainly seen a baby before. But I've never seen the two of them together! You've just made my day. Thank you."

I beamed at him as we passed. Then I cooed down at David. "And he certainly made ours. Didn't he?"

I rolled down the streets with David snugly cradled in his Kacoon against the warmth of my chest. It wasn't easy getting him into that thing, but it was certainly worth it!

After our transportation fiasco to Whitten for physical therapy, our Regional Center caseworker, Debra, thought that CCS (California Children's Services) could be `persuaded' to provide us with home therapy visits; in the long run, it would be more cost-effective. That meant David had to be evaluated again. This time by CCS's medical director.

Dr. Molinar, having spent just a few minutes examining David, announced to a group of onlooking staff, "I don't see any overt spasticity in this baby. He muscle tone is good. He exhibits a slight tension in his legs, but," she shook her head, "what I'm seeing here doesn't warrant therapy."

Neil, who had taken the morning off, gurgled smugly all the way home. He couldn't wait to report to Dr. Parker at David's monthly well-baby checkup a few days later. Dr. Parker, however, still insisted on physical therapy. "I just can't ignore David's medical background, even though, in the end, I'll probably be eating crow."

Neil's resolve was no match for Ann Parker's earnest charm. She offered her help with CCS, but Neil and I decided to go the private route. Our health insurance would probably cover 70 percent to 80 percent of the cost, and being able to choose was worth the price.

Twice a week, David's physical therapist, Hildred Yost, came to the house to work with him. Hildred was a private physical therapist whose name we had gotten from my friend who worked at Stanford. She looked, of course, nothing like I'd pictured a Hildred Yost to look like—a similar version of Miss Stern, (my squarish, bland physical therapist, whom I had for years in P.S. 85), but with an Eastern European accent. One day I'd learn to curb my writer's imagination!

Appearing usually in a flairy blue denim skirt, white man-tailored blouse, and a rainbow-colored scarf tied loosely around her neck, she had to bend her silvery gray head slightly to fit through our doorway; our built-up ramp platform had shaved a few inches off of the door sill—tall people had to duck to enter.

Hildred would come in the late morning after David was fed and bathed. Sometimes she'd bring an orange beach ball and perch David on top, rolling him gently from side to side in order to loosen his sturdy shoulder and neck muscles. I'd be in charge of holding up his Mickey Mouse doll, slightly off to one side so that David would stretch to grab it. David didn't seem to mind at all—once in a while he'd whimper, only to be quickly soothed by his pacifier and Hildred's easy rendition of *Here We Go Looby-loo*. Every now and then I felt a tingle of envy, wishing that I had had a Hildred Yost when I was young. And she even changed David's diaper before she left.

I wished that the other issue involving Regional Center, respite care, could have been resolved as easily as physical therapy. I knew, though, from my conversation with Debra, I was in for more *tsurris*. It was the same story—they'd provide respite care, home health care, through a vendorized agency (licensed by the state), which trained its own workers. Under Regional Center guidelines, we were authorized to have four hours of respite care a week.

I had no choice, beforehand, as to who could come into my home and take care of my baby. Moreover, if I adhered to the principal purpose of respite care, I was supposed leave my baby with a stranger while I went out and had a good time.

I requested a worker for weekend mornings, thinking that it would help to have someone competent come in to keep David's morning routine on track, to make bottles to keep in the fridge through the weekend, and to do a never empty basket of baby laundry.

Yes, it would have helped—*if they had been competent*. Out of a parade of home health care workers, there were only two fitting that qualification. Most were so inept that I didn't dare take my eyes off them for a moment for fear that David might end up headfirst in his bathwater. These woman in their white uniforms, who were supposedly trained to care for children with disabilities, looked quite dumbstruck when Neil or I greeted them at the door. Instead of having a two-hour respite, I spent two hours cloaked in a heavy mantle of anxiety and dread every Saturday and Sunday morning.

What made it even worse was that while I spent those two hours making sure that even the bottle caps were screwed on right so the milk wouldn't leak out, Neil would just sit slumped down in his chair at the dining table with a scowl on his face for the *whole* two hours. When I asked what was wrong, his response was, "Nothing. I'm tired." *I knew he was tired!* After working almost ten hours a day during the week, Neil was the one who changed David's diaper at night and in the early morning. He voluntarily got up with David when he fussed during the night (several times over one two-week period), because I "took care of him all day." Yet I read more into his silence than fatigue. It looked like withdrawal to me, and I took it very personally.

There had always been a strong bond between Neil and me; the connection had been there from the very beginning of our relationship. I had more than a clue on our first date when he poured out his intimate hopes and dreams to me. He talked freely, letting go of his practiced convention of drawing people out to help them feel at ease. It wasn't that the private Neil was so different than the public one (he still had a rather Pollyannaish view of life), but he was so much more real, so much more human.

I had sat listening to his resonant, gravelly voice, not worrying about whether he liked me or not, or whether I liked him—it seemed as if we already knew that. He was a man who was very much a part of the world—a rational idealist. He wore a suit and tie and worked twelve hours a day in the corporate world, and yet he had dreams—

becoming a vice president, getting a Ph.D., adopting a child. I needed someone like him, who believed in dreams, and he needed someone like me—to worry about the details. We knew, too, each other's struggles and appreciations of experiencing life with having cerebral palsy—getting past first impressions, playing verbal aerobics with our speech, and orgasming over sugar cubes. Sometimes, no words needed to be spoken. Even in the midst of our disagreements, we could realize how, in the context of our lives, those conflicts were irrelevant. The common spark between us couldn't stayed buried for too long.

We had been discussing his former marriage one warm Sunday in mid-October along the pier of Jack London Square, after our first brunch together.

"So, weren't you angry at her for having the affair?"

"No, just hurt," he answered, before admitting, "Well, I was angry at my friend for having the affair with her."

His anger seemed a bit misplaced. "But she had a part in it, too!" I reiterated.

However, he had no intention of blaming his ex-wife for much of anything. He told me that he would have stuck it out if she had wanted a reconciliation, even though he'd been unhappy before then. He even admitted his marriage had been a mistake. "But when you get married, you stay married," he affirmed.

I found myself getting emotional. "You would have stayed in it no matter how you felt?"

"Yes . . . You look upset," he said to me.

I struggled to find the words to explain. I just had this feeling, this intuition, that I was going to be the one to pay for the emotions he couldn't yet access—the anger that he determinedly buried—if our relationship became more involved.

He waited for my answer as I mutely searched for words. Yet I knew I couldn't tell him in any words he would understand.

The pleasant tone of a stranger interrupted our tortured silence. "Excuse me, my wife and I were wondering if we could buy the two of you an ice cream cone?"

Neil and I snatched a glance at each other before we looked up at the elderly man, who was smiling so sincerely. Our words came out only seconds apart. "No, thank you."

Still smiling congenially, he accepted our answer. After bidding us a nice day, the man and his wife strolled off.

Neil's bemused expression mirrored my own. An ease fell between us. There was no pressure to react, console, or placate as there might have been had we been with someone else—someone nondisabled, or even someone without a speech impairment—who could have readily expressed sarcasm, anger, indignation; our own feeling might have easily become mixed up with someone else's. But here we were in the moment. Neither of us read the man's gesture as pitying or condescending. It was just a beautiful day, the man and his wife saw the two of us as enjoying it, and that made him feel good— good enough to offer to buy us an ice cream cone. Both Neil and I chose to perceive it as just an act of kindness.

A mischievous look crept into Neil's face. *"Could you hold an ice cream cone?"*

"Un-uh!" I shook my head. *"Could you?"*

"Naw," he responded with an easy shrug. Then deep wrinkles creased his freckled nose. "Too bad he didn't offer to buy a steak dinner. I might have taken him up on it!"

"Neil! You're terrible!" I said, and pretended to be appalled, but a playful glimmer remained with us for a long time afterward.

Yet at other times when I would share my feelings with Neil, expecting his support and comfort, he'd be as understanding as a dead fish. It shocked me, too, since he showed other people so much compassion, even though once they had gone he'd roll his eyes.

Once, during our first year of marriage, I had come home from work feeling extremely vulnerable. I was the coordinator of a project and had to write a manual for its completion. After writing a draft of the introduction, I had shown it to my boss. It was waiting on my desk for me a few days later—no comments, just red pencil marks and squiggly arrows everywhere.

"All that work I put into it, too." I lamented over dinner that night.

"So . . . ?

I looked at Neil. "He just ripped it apart."

"So, you'll fix it," Neil said dispassionately. "It's not the end of the world. . . ."

"Don't you understand? I worked hard on it."

Neil played some chords on his invisible violin before asking, "Are you PMS?"

I angrily ignored his question. "Didn't you ever hear of constructive criticism? It seems to me he could have found something good about it."

"Hogwash!" The retort flowed from his mouth more clearly and easily than his name. "You know, you're just being a crippled baby!"

I stormed into our bedroom and slammed the door shut. Every once in a while, when I'd think of a good comeback, I'd open the door, yell out the words, and slam it shut again. He groaned back, "I'm not the enemy," but I wasn't so sure! I sometimes felt that Neil expected me to have as thick a skin as he did. He had a great desire for life to be simple, and feelings complicated it—especially mine!

So, while our inept respite worker scurried around and I rolled close at her heels, Neil slouched at the dining room table. I avoided his stares. Maybe this time we were both being "crippled babies": despising the situation and ourselves for not taking a stand.

Then suddenly, as soon as the worker left, the same man who had sat lifelessly defeated, claiming exhaustion only moments early, became a whirlwind of determination. Neil, who had always been driven by a need to occupy every waking moment, dragged us around to every park and children's activity he could find. It didn't make any difference to Neil that David slept through everything, or that it took a great deal of energy to pack up, get in the van, land and secure David into his carseat. We'd be gone from early afternoon until seven or eight in the evening. The lateness in returning depended upon which one of our friends we would catch at home to feed David—*Have Gerber's, will travel.*

It irritated me that Neil could choose what he did and didn't want to deal with! It was easy for him to focus his energy on David, the child he had been waiting for all his life, and avoid the aggravation. Perhaps he thought that I expected him to fix things; I didn't (well, maybe if he came out of a lamp). I just wanted him to *be there*, not retreating into his shell buried deep in the sand. The stress and strain of having our lives changed so quickly in recent months had made us both so vulnerable. We receded in our patterns: he was in denial; I was aggravated.

What we needed was some stranger to offer us an ice cream cone, but we were too tired and too overwhelmed to go out to Jack London Square.

Chapter Eleven

Mother Overload

There was little doubt in my mind that David was made for us and we were made for David. The three of us belonged together. What other baby would delight in being precariously swung in the air by the sturdily woven threads of his sleeper whenever his parents transferred him from one surface to another; or guide my unsteady finger to his mouth to suck off a wad of baby food on my fingertip, since Dr. Parker had put five-month-old David on solids three times a day and no one else was around to feed him lunch? (I cheated when my arm tired; I gave him a bottle.) And the best thing of all, he was a great sleeper. He slept through my entire morning wake-up routine and took two-hour naps twice a day (maybe he was exhausted too).

After a few months, when my adrenaline subsided, I was able to think about writing again. Within the six months prior to Colleen's life-altering phone call, I had gotten one story published in *Across the Generations* (a California literary anthology), and I had done a book review (on request) for the *San Francisco Chronicle*, receiving my first $100 as a writer. The anthology had come in early November, but the *Chronicle* piece—although accepted in January—wasn't printed until February 15, three days before my impending visit to St. Louis. The thrill of having my work appear in one of the largest circulated daily newspapers in California paled against my anxiety over traveling almost two thousand miles to see an infant who might very well become my son. I never got to relish those two brief moments of glory. Fate stepped in, perhaps, to prevent my ego from inflating.

With David's two-hour naps during our long afternoons, I forced myself to make a concerted effort to write. I had, like most writers I knew, an ongoing struggle with myself when it came to sitting down at the computer. Words, thoughts, beginnings, endings could swim in my head from my first fuzzy threads of wakefulness in the morning to my last ribbon of consciousness at night. Yet when I finally had the time to "work," I could argue with so many "good" reasons to put it off—lie down and rest, make some phone calls, relax and watch a soap opera, eat lunch. Thankfully, my self-discipline won out over half the time and, once I started, I forgot how hungry, or tired, or isolated I was. I felt productive for two hours.

Writing, however, does not have many tangible rewards. It isn't measurable: "How many pages did you write today?" Neil would ask eagerly when I told him I wrote that day. "When will the story be finished?" another friend would ask. I didn't know how to answer. Other writers knew volume had little to do with writing, but now I had no time to meet with other writers. No time to sit and talk over coffee at the Hudson Bay Cafe. I had to drop out of my women's writing group—which had met at my house while Neil good-naturedly shut himself up in our bedroom or in what used to be the den; I was too tired at seven o'clock even every other Monday to get out of the house and be dragged up somebody's stairs.

I *was* tired. Not just from physical exhaustion but the anxiety of having to cope with constant change. There was something new or difficult to deal with practically every day. I found myself faced with a bad bout of diaper rash (from a sulfur infection), ear infections, and inadequate help. I met the first two with resolved determination. I gently applied topical salve to David's blistering tush before every diaper change. I poured the right amount of amoxicillin into the medicine spoon as I held it steadily between my thighs, then poured that into the little medicine baby bottle (capping it with a nipple), and let David suck it down, which he fortunately did without any fuss.

Inadequate help, though, proved my albatross. It weighed so heavily upon my shoulders. I resented having to wait for Carrie to return from her excursions or for an always delayed Lydia (she still cleaned house) to relieve me of the demands of mothering. It was hard to feel what I felt about the strain and isolation of motherhood and, at the same time, to cherish David so much. Day after day wore into one another, month after month. I tried desperately to keep it together, but one day I fell apart.

It was a sunny spring day in May. The kind of day for sitting around, the air heavy, like an invisible lead apron. I didn't feel peppy enough to take David out; a muscle in my leg had begun bothering me a few days before. It wasn't a writing day either—although I did try. As a matter of fact, it was also a Friday; yet another unrelenting weekend before me. Well, at least Lydia was coming in the midafternoon to clean.

Since I expected Lydia at three-thirty, I had told Carrie that she had time to get back by five. So, with an extra hour off, she decided to go window shopping at a mall—an almost two-hour BART and bus ride away. ("There's a little juice bar where they make the best fresh fruit Smoothie I've ever tasted," she said.)

I had changed David's diaper early in the afternoon before his nap. I hadn't done such a good job; he was soaked when he woke up. It was around three then. I couldn't leave him in wet clothes for a half hour, and I figured by the time I'd get everything peeled off, Lydia would arrive. Only she didn't.

Ten minutes to pull out a dry towel from our overstuffed linen closet (David soaked through the cotton coverlet on the foam pad); fifteen to unzip his sleeper and slip out his legs *and arms*; another five to unfold the baby wipes and wash him down. Finally, I was ready for the clean, dry diaper. *Where was she . . . ? Should I wait a few minutes . . . ? But he's due for a bottle. More milk, more pee. Well, I'll go warm it up; David's starting to grunt. Maybe by that time . . .*

I got off my bony, floor-worn knees (I crept a lot as a child and ruined my kneecaps) and into my wheelchair again. I took a bottle out of the fridge, warmed it up for forty-four arbitrary seconds, and went back to David, whose disconcerting grunts had turned into impatient squawks. I slid down onto the mat and stuck the nipple in David's mouth, then proceeded with the diaper.

I finished diapering at 4:00. The bottle was empty at 4:05. I burped him. At 4:20, I smelled an unmistakable odor: David pooped. *Still no sign of Lydia.* No muffled swish of a car pulling up in front. I even got back up in my wheelchair to look out the bay window, as if my eyes could magnetically draw her into sight. At 4:30, still alone with David, and feeling miserable, I call my very pregnant neighbor Jo Anne. By the time she walked the twenty-yard diagonal from her corner to mine, I succumbed to hysterics.

"I can't do this! I can't do this," I muttered over and over. Somehow, I was on the floor by the front door, just rocking and wailing, when she came in. "I'm not cut out to be a mother. It's too, too much for me. Too, too much."

Jo Anne knelt down and put her arm around me. Her voice soothed. "Neisie, it's okay. You're okay."

"No, I can't even change a diaper," I wailed. "I'm so alone. Carrie galavants off to a mall. Lydia's supposed be here an hour ago. I just sit and wait, that's all I do. Sit and wait."

"Neisie, we all go through this," she assured. "Here, let's get you up on a chair."

She scooted over the dining room chair near the computer table, since my wheelchair was over by the mat. When I settled in it, Jo Anne went for the tissues in my bedroom. She returned with a wad, which I immediately buried my wet face in. I blew my nose and sniffed back my tears, trying not to get any on the billowing folds of Jo Anne's striped maternity dress.

I sighed, exhaling a mixture of relief and sadness, as though a pressure valve within me had been loosened to let off the steam that had built up over the last few months. *Why did it always have to come down to hysterics?* I heaved another sigh just as I heard Lydia's perky little knocks on the door.

"What's wrong?" she asked when she saw me as soon as Jo Anne opened the door. The concern in her voice irritated me more.

"Where were you?" I snapped. "You said you'd be here over an hour ago!"

"I was working out on a boat in the marina. It docked back later than I thought it would," Lydia replied. "Did anything happen? Is David all right?"

I felt my tears well again, thinking that my answer would sound so foolish, so unreasonable. I couldn't bring myself to tell her, so I just said weakly, "No. Nothing happened."

"Well, I'd better get cracking," she piped.

I sniffed. "Oh, before you start, could you change David? He pooped."

With Lydia dispatched and humming, I turned to Jo Anne and shrugged my shoulders helplessly.

"You know, Neisie, when Jerusa was first born, there were days when I thought I'd go bonkers . . . "

I nodded. My sister had once told me that when she had taken her Lamaze class, her instructor warned there'd be days when they'd feel like throwing the baby out the window, and they needed to call someone right away—even grab a stranger! Though I didn't fear that I'd harm David, I had just felt so inadequate; David deserved a mother who could cradle him in her arms, rock him to sleep, and diaper him in five seconds.

"Sometimes, Jo Anne, I think," I swallowed hard, "that maybe it was a mistake." As soon I said it I wanted to take it back. *How could adopting David ever be a mistake?*

"Oh, for Pete's sake!" Jo Anne only cussed—she had gone to finishing school. "You would never have done it if you didn't know you could."

"But Neil was the one who was so passionate. Maybe I just got so caught up —"

"Neisie, you are no shrinking violet." I laughed at the way she put it. "And you knew better than Neil that it wasn't going to be easy."

She was right.

Yet it wasn't just the physical and emotional pressures but the psychological ones as well. I knew our families were waiting, watching. In their hearts, they wanted us to succeed; in their minds, they seriously doubted our ability. They voiced worries and gave trivial advice, but they couldn't extend their faith in us or offer words of encouragement. I already had enough anxieties of my own. It didn't help me to hear Neil repeat a conversation he had with his mother right after we hired Carrie: "Why is her son living with his father?" she had questioned. "Something isn't right that he isn't living with his mother." My sister also annoyed me; she always had some esoteric advice: "Collect the teddy bear logos on the Pampers boxes and send them in to get nice toys." Yet when I had asked her to help me figure out how to get David in the Kacoon during her visit, she put it off until `later'; she liked strolling David in his stroller whenever we went for walks. `Later,' of course, never came.

Neil had the ability to distance himself: "My brother said something very interesting today," Neil related of the phone call that had taken place earlier in his day. "He said that this is the first time in my life that if I fail, I'll really screw up."

I could feel my muscles tighten.

Neil continued easily, "I've always been ready to get in there and do it—you know, starting the computer program, going after the job I wanted, getting married—but this is a whole other thing. If this doesn't work, I'll blow it royally!"

I restrained myself—we had company that evening; Karen and John were over for a rather unceremonious celebration of my thirty-seventh birthday. I just commented through my clenched jaw, "That's a very negative way to put it."

"Why?" The logical, detached question, of course!

"He's not given you much credit for who you are. Having a baby is not something you look at in terms of putting another notch on your belt," I replied heatedly and then let it drop.

I felt the heaviness of those comments weigh me down, along with my own doubts and the pressure of my own motherhood. I'd been dragging this load around for months. No wonder I had finally cracked.

By the time I had a chance to talk to Neil that evening, the whole episode seemed so anticlimactic. It was hard to express the intensity of what I had felt only hours ago to a man who lived in the moment. I wished, sometimes, I could be more like him, wrapped up in the excitement and ecstasy of having a new baby, but I couldn't.

"I want to go back and see Jose for a few weeks," I said, deciding that my outburst had been a sign for me to get help. "He's only doing short-term therapy now, anyway. I'd like to go for a month, just until our trip to Washington. Could we afford it?"

Neil nodded. He knew I was anxious about the trip—our families would be there. I thought, perhaps, that Jose could help me work through some of my feelings about Neil's mother and brother but, after my first session, I realized that it was too complicated. Much of what I felt was tied to my own insecurities. Jose's advice to me for the trip: "Try not to have expectations. Stay neutral!" That was, of course, easier said than done.

Chapter Twelve
Family Value

Neil's brother, who lived just outside of D.C., had borrowed a lift-equipped van from work to meet the four of us (Carrie included) at the airport and drive us to the hotel. Connie, his fiancée, and his mother, who had flown up from Florida, were with him. They came on board to greet us while we waited for our wheelchairs; we were the only passengers left on the plane.

Neil sat by the aisle so I was farther away from them. His mother stretched over to lightly brush my cheek with her lips and his brother hugged me gingerly. Both brothers made the introductions for Connie, Carrie, and of course, David.

"He's kinda cute," Steve commented.

"He's a big boy," Neil's mother remarked.

David looked around him as Carrie held him in her arms. He was pale and tired. None of the strangers paid him much attention; the usual airline chaos involving our wheelchairs immediately took precedence. It may have also relieved the awkwardness of the moment, allowing Neil's brother—in some effort to *do* something—to pace in and out of the cabin in his Bermuda shorts and sandals, to check on the whereabouts of the motorized chairs. Carrie, in the meantime, standing in the aisle next to our seats with David, kept having to duck out of the way; Neil's mother bustled back and forth searching the overhead compartments for our carry-on luggage, her large, white handbag swinging on her arm quite close to Carrie and David's heads.

Neil quickly started a conversation with Connie, who sat on the arm of the seat across from him with one long, suntanned leg crossed over the other; he asked about her work, his usual ice-breaking topic.

It was also his way of easing the strain, or rather, avoiding the painful awareness that, at the moment, his position, as well as mine, was quite helpless.

For Neil and me (and probably most disabled people), there were always moments of helplessness scattered throughout our lives; they come with the territory. On good days, we shrug at them, even laugh them off. On bad days, we may curse them and indulge ourselves in sarcastic self-pity. We know, however, that those moments will pass, that they in no way mean that we are helpless or dependent. Only, around family, our helplessness in such situations intensifies, magnifies, conjuring up memories for them and for us of being dependent children. Once again, we need to be `taken care of' and `done for.'

Our families have been there to see our struggle to dress ourselves, feed ourselves, move away, but they don't really know how we function in everyday life. They only get periodic glimpses of our autonomy when they come out for whirlwind visits or when we go to conferences in their part of the country. We never visit their homes, either, since they all live up insurmountable steps; not exactly welcome mats to two people using motorized wheelchairs—considered to be heavy, troublesome pieces of equipment that can track dirt onto carpets and chip paint off doorway frames.

Neil's chair arrived, and then mine. Unfortunately, his didn't work. I could detect that "here we go again" feeling in the air. Steve, with Neil's guidance, reconnected all the plugs that the airline disconnected to make sure the wheelchair wouldn't blow up. I was luckier—my chair connections were too inaccessible for anyone to bother reaching: only one plug had to be reconnected.

We collected our baggage while Steve and Connie brought the van around. By the time we trudged outside with our load, Steve had the van lift lowered.

"Here Steve, could you hold David?" Neil had had David on his lap from the time his wheelchair started working, but he didn't want David to ride up with him on the lift; it was unfamiliar machinery.

"Un-uh, I'm not getting pooped on," his brother refused.

I bit my tongue and breathed deeply, reminding myself to "stay neutral," to keep my sense of humor. *After all, he is a bachelor,* I thought, trying to keep down the counterarguments: *He's a thirty-three-year-old doctor of virology. He works with bacteria all day! And he's afraid of baby poop?!!*

Neil's mother handed Steve her armload, and matter-of-factly took the baby from Neil.

The darkness of evening spread upon the city as Steve drove us to our hotel.

"We'll stay for a little while," he announced as we entered the room, most of it taken up by two queen-sized beds. He strode over to the brocade loveseat wedged in the corner and sat down, stretching out his legs on the small coffee table. He made himself quite at home. Connie took the seat beside him. Steve folded his hands behind his dark head and yawned. "I was up early today and I have to be at the lab at six-thirty tomorrow."

He wasn't the only one who had a long day, but I guess he just didn't notice.

Neil parked close to them on the other side of the coffee table. "How about you, Connie? Do you go to work with Steve?" She was his lab assistant.

It was always work!

"No, I teach aerobics in the morning," she answered.

She looked like the aerobics type!

I had crawled up on the bed, since there was no room for me anywhere else, and Neil's mother had placed David on the bed, too. He was contentedly sucking his pacifier as she took off his thin blanket, revealing his bare arms and legs; it was warm in the room.

It was also time for inspection.

"Tell me, Denise," she began, as she peered down at him through thick glasses. "Where's the cerebral palsy? I don't see it."

"Well, his arms and legs are a little tight," I answered, choosing simple words so that she'd understand me.

She looked at me briefly when I spoke, then again looked down at David. Her head tilted only slightly; her short, thick form stood erect; her expression remained impassive. David's eyes searched her face, and I thought I saw the flicker of a smile on her lips, but she caught herself in time.

A cold shiver went through me. *Why couldn't she say how beautiful he was . . . , or something kind? What was wrong with these people? Would it kill any of them to pay a little attention to the new member of the family?* They had shown David the same disinterest I felt they had always shown me. Even Neil showed more attentiveness to his brother's sleek, honey-haired fiancee than to his wife and son!

I swallowed my hurt and disappointment. "You know, David could use a new diaper. Do you want to change him?"

Carrie had gone to put her luggage in the adjoining room and I wouldn't have felt comfortable changing David myself in front of this audience. (Neil, most likely, felt the same way.) I thought, also, that asking a grandmother to change her grandson's diaper would, in some way, ease the strain: Wasn't it a typical thing for a grandma to do?

"No," she said hesitantly. "No, I wouldn't know how. Let the girl do it when she comes back."

She walked away.

Tears stung my eyes. This baby that I looked down upon, who hardly whimpered during our daylong travel, whose blue eyes incredibly drank in everything around him, had been such a precious gift to us, yet they couldn't see it! I bent over David, cooed, and kissed his cheek. "I love you," I murmured. "Yes, I do."

"You know, D-D-David's f-f-foster mother will be here tomorrow," I heard Neil stammer.

"Uh, why is she coming?" his mother asked in a suspicious tone. "She's checking the baby?"

"No, Ma," Neil groaned with mild exasperation. "They stay at their farm in North Carolina for the summer. She's driving up just to see us."

"She can't take the baby away?"

"No, Ma," Neil reassured.

Steve stood up, stretching out his hairy, sinewy arms and legs. "Well, we should be going," he announced and squeezed past Neil. He stopped at the foot of the bed and glanced down at David. "You know . . . , he's a very good-looking baby."

It's about time someone noticed!

"So, Denise," his brown eyes strayed from David to me, "everything going okay with you? Doing any teaching?"

"A few lectures here and there, but I haven't done anything lately," I answered evenly, quickly adding, "I did design a display for the annual Disability Awareness Day in San Francisco. I've been doing some writing, too." My words felt so empty.

"Anyhow," Neil slipped in before his brother and I might have discussed anything else, "what time is Eta arriving tomorrow?"

"Her plane lands at noon, but she's meeting a friend to go shopping. You know our jet-setting sister, Eta," Steve turned to his big brother and said with a little laugh.

Tomorrow, Steve figured, he'd bring his mother by around noon when Neil's meeting would break for lunch. He would come back with Eta and Connie at five. Then we'd decide what we were doing for dinner. With those arrangements made, we all said good-night.

"Well, that went okay!" Neil spoke the sentence as soon as the door closed, in a tone that made me wish that I could have enough coordination to hurl a lamp across the room.

"What planet are you on?!" I shouted. "Never mind how they ignored me, but the way they treated David . . . , like he had *the plague!*"

With an outstretched arm and a voice filled with restrained anger, he warned, "Denise, don't start!"

I took a deep breath into my sinking chest; I had lost Neil already. It was just what I had feared, just what seemed to happen every time we were around his family. We stopped being husband and wife or even friends and partners. Suddenly, I became a stranger to him, feeling as if he didn't want me around. In other circumstances, I had no doubt that I could trust Neil with my life—that if we were both drowning and only one of us could be saved, he would forfeit his own life. Yet when it came to his family, I was on my own; Neil couldn't share his lifesaver.

Even worse, the conflict between my understanding, my feelings, and my guilt tore me apart. I knew that what had just occurred was only the product of years and years of Jacobson family dynamics. How could I have been so arrogant to expect that Neil's family could shrug off all those years of struggle in their relationship with him to accept him as a man, husband, and father? Then me, as his wife? And most of all, David, as the son Neil now *chose* to raise, knowing that he might have a disability? I could understand that this meal could be hard for them to swallow, let alone digest.

Who could fault them for their reactions to us? Neil's mother, after surviving not only the atrocities of the Lodz ghetto and Auschwitz but the postwar death of a newborn son, had focused so much of her life on raising Neil. How could she understand Neil's choices, which would undoubtedly make his life more difficult? She couldn't just accept this little being, this tiny foreigner—David—as a part of her family without making her own assessment, before she slowly abandoned her shield, sword, and even, possibly, her armor (though, paradoxically, she reacted almost protectively when she feared Kate could take David away).

And what about Steve—a man who grew up in the shadow of his

disabled brother—refusing to hold his nephew even for a moment? From the time Steve was a small child, he had been told that he was born to grow up and take care of Neil. Quite a covenant for a child. And though that reality will probably never come to pass, the emotion for Steve must still exist somewhere inside of him. The guilt, hurt, and anger hung between both brothers like a dusty velvet drapery.

And Neil's sister, Eta, an interior decorator who had carved out a life for herself so removed from the painful memories of her mother's? Her visits with Neil and me were always graciously short, sweet (a few hours stopover from one destination to another), and yet so distant, as if she were afraid we would demand more of her than she was prepared to give.

It seemed so ironic. I've gone into classes full of students from kindergartners to medical residents, from therapists to pharmacists. Their bodies tense; their eyes shift when I roll into the room. I'm fully aware that, at that moment, most of them would rather be somewhere else. I feel a little uncomfortable, but I begin speaking, after a deep swallow. I choose words I can say clearly: "For the first few minutes you may not understand me too well, because, in case you haven't noticed, I talk differently than most of you. Some blame it on my cerebral palsy. Others claim it's my New York accent."

Their laughter, immediately following, tells me that I've broken through the barrier of their fear and discomfort. In acknowledging my speech imperfection, I've put the unspeakable out on the table; I've tapped into their thoughts and feelings. By the end of the session, not only have they learned something about people with disabilities, they've learned something about themselves.

But those are strangers. I have no history with them. Within a fairly short time I've transformed myself—in their eyes—from an object of pity into someone as human as they are. My detachment from them facilitated my ability to teach.

It's different with family. They're not there to learn; they know all they want to know about disability. They don't want an attitude readjustment, either, though they might need one badly. It's scary for them to have their old values and beliefs challenged, but unfortunately, for Neil's family especially, that's exactly what he and I have done, and seem to keep doing.

Sadly, it still didn't make the pain of their actions any easier for me to bear. I got ready for bed in silence, scrunched in between the tightly tucked in sheets, and after what seemed like hours, fell asleep facing the wall. I hoped things would get a little better tomorrow, when Kate and my father arrived.

My father arrived in the lavish hotel lobby at midmorning just as Carrie, David, and I came out of the restaurant from a late breakfast. The airport shuttle had dropped him off at our hotel although he was staying at a less expensive one down the block. He looked cute, wearing his little beige cap and cotton sports jacket over his plaid shirt, which was tucked into print pants. But he had aged since I last saw him. His jet black hair, which I had always pictured him still having, had long since turned yellowish white. His neck had disappeared, swallowed up by rounded shoulders. He hadn't fit the image of the thin, wiry man that I remembered in years, but each time I saw him, I was overcome with a beat or two of sadness when I faced the reality that he was old. I was glad to see him.

He greeted me with a warm hug and kiss; I breathed in the same scent of Old Spice that I did as a little girl. My father shook hands with Carrie when I introduced them, and peered down at David in his stroller.

"Why, hello," my dad chuckled as he bent closer to David. David stared at his grandfather with his usual wide-eyed curiosity. My dad turned to me with a delighted grin. "You know, Neisie, he's very cute," he said. Then with a curled forefinger, he jostled David's marshmallow cheek. David laughed.

Only seconds later, Kate and two of her daughters appeared. Not realizing my father had just arrived, she made a beeline for David. "Excuse me," she said to my dad, as she bent over the stroller to pick up my baby, "but you've had him long enough! It's my turn now." When she learned, however, that he had arrived only moments earlier, she profusely apologized. My hard-of-hearing, sometimes socially spaced-out father wasn't put out—though he looked a bit awestruck, but once I explained Kate's presence, he seemed delighted to make her acquaintance. (He was impressed that she had driven so far to see us.)

It went quite differently with Kate and Neil's mother. At first, my mother-in-law was polite—wary, of course, but polite—as she tried prying Kate for details about "how `the baby' was when he was born." Kate clammed up. "Neil and Denise know more more than I do; I never read the medical report." Neil's mother persisted: "But, I mean, how did he seem to you?" Kate glanced at me before she answered, "Like a wonderful baby!" Failing to gain Kate's confidence, Neil's mother retreated into silence and waited for her son to get out of his meeting for lunch.

Deciding the hotel restaurant was too expensive, we had brought back food from a nearby hamburger take-out joint and ate in the hotel lobby. Over crumpled wrappers, we made plans for the afternoon: Carrie and Kate's older daughter, Nan, would go off sightseeing, and the rest of us, my father, Kate, eight-year-old Andrea, David, and I would walk to Capitol Mall. Neil had to go back to his meeting. His mother, though, claiming she was still tired from her trip from Florida, chose to take a nap in our hotel room.

My father and I ended up eating dinner alone that evening. It was my doing, though I hadn't expected it to turn out that way. We were to have all gone out together, Neil and his family, my father and myself. Kate had excused herself and Andrea from what she thought would be a family function. I hadn't given Carrie a specific time to return from sightseeing because I assumed we would take David along with all of us when we went out for dinner, as we did when we were at home.

"What time will your assistant be back to watch David?" Eta asked, sitting leisurely in the club chair in her white designer jumpsuit with pastel trim, surrounded by department store shopping bags.

"I'm not sure," I answered timidly, feeling self-conscious, too, in my worn-out everyday clothes. "I thought we could take David with us."

"Oh, but you wouldn't want to take him to a restaurant, would you?" Her voice held concern, but I couldn't tell for whom.

Suddenly, it sounded like a bad idea.

Neil didn't say anything. He just sat slumped in his suit and tie. I suggested we split up for dinner. No one protested.

It was decided that my father and I would go out first and Neil and his family would stay with David until Carrie or I returned. We made no plans to meet up, even if Carrie came back.

I sat in the cafeteria-style restaurant and picked at my dried-out roast beef.

My father, looking up between bites of his turkey dinner, noticed. "Neisie, you're not eating. What's the matter?

I shook my head and gave my shoulders a forlorn shrug. I answered with a little girl's sadness. "They don't like me. They're not very kind."

"I know," he said (they had barely said hello to him when my father, David, and I came back from our afternoon with Kate). He waved his hand. "Neisie, don't let it bother you. You're better than they are, honey. They're not nice people. You don't need them."

He was trying to make me feel better, and that comforted me. But it wasn't that simple. It wasn't a question of being better than them. They weren't horrible people. And most of all, *I did need them.*

I wanted a family who would include me, who would appreciate and value my experiences—something even my own family had trouble doing. To my father, I was still a little girl, not able to zip up my jacket when I tried doing it myself. He grabbed the opening from my hands, saying the same old line—"Here Neisie, let me do that. I could do it quicker."

Even my sister Shelley couldn't fully understand the significance of valuing a disability and how it could relate to self-esteem and self-worth. I could see how she struggled with it in her own family.

My sister and her husband arrived with their children, eight-year-old Larry and almost four-year-old Seth, on Friday. By then, Neil's mother and sister had left D.C.; so did my father and Kate. We changed our hotel to a less expensive one in a seedier part of town since, after Neil's conference was over, his expenses were no longer covered by his sponsor. The second hotel would also be more afford-able for Shelley and Jack. We had rooms across from one another at the end of the hallway and kept our doors open.

Shelley had come into our room and sat down on the bed. Neil and I were settling in to our cramped new space, half the size of the other hotel room. David napped on the other double bed.

"Oy, I need a break," my sister sighed. "They're driving me nuts."

"How come?" I asked, looking away from the opened window. The hot, sticky air was full of summer city noises—honking cars, muffled voices, periodic shouts, and an occasional shattering of glass.

"Oh, Larry got this watch kit out of a cereal box and Jack's having trouble putting it together," she answered, pushing up the frames of her glasses. "Larry's getting annoyed with him, and Seth's butting in. It's a circus in there!"

"Mommy, Mommy." Seth came running through the opened door and requested my sister's return to their room.

I was surprised when I heard him speak; I knew his hearing was impaired—". . . a moderate to severe hearing loss," Shelley had told me, "but he can hear without his hearing aids and his speech is clear." Yet his speech droned in a monotone with drawn-out vowels and over-emphasized, or sometimes unpronounced, consonants.

Maybe she'd been around me too long.

Seth's disability was diagnosed about a year and a half ago. Yet whenever Shelley and Jack talked about it, they never used the word *deaf,* or even *disabled* for that matter. From time to time, I'd mention teaching him sign language and, when Shelley and Larry came to visit us back in April, I had introduced her to my friend Mary, who ran a preschool program for deaf and hard-of-hearing children. Mary explained the benefits of "total communication" for hearing impaired and deaf children; it also helped to develop social skills and appropriate behavior. Shelley seemed open to it, even though Jack, she said, was resistant; the doctors and audiologist in New York told them that Seth would do fine with spoken language. I supposed they all wanted Seth to "fit in" with the mainstream, and sign language would make him "stand out"(just as my wheelchair had made my disability more "obvious"). Never mind that having sign language as a skill might lessen Seth's frustration about communicating, or enable him to be more autonomous. "Besides, I don't think I'd be able to learn sign language," my sister had confided to me. "I'd never remember."

Now Seth, repeating his request, took his mother's hand from her lap and started pulling.

"Seth, I'll be there in a minute!" Mustering her energy, she raised her voice and enunciated slowly.

"No-no-no-no!" He shook his brown head furiously. "Now!"

My sister stood up, saying to Neil and me, "He doesn't leave me alone; he's very clingy," before Seth dragged her out of the room.

Neil and I spoke no words, but exchanged knowing glances. We both had been dependent upon our mothers, not just physically but emotionally as well. They had been the buffers between us and the outside world. In their presence, we never had to speak for ourselves; they spoke for us, they felt for us, and they knew what was best for us. Having our mothers as interpreters and shields made life so comforting, but it prevented others from seeing us as self-sufficient. We remained children long after our childhood was over.

In fact, both Neil and I lapsed into childhood passivity all too often—relinquishing our power and our presence to nondisabled people. It was almost second nature for us to become followers, to let others decide what to do, where to go, when to do it. By ourselves we took care of our son, but we gave over his care as soon as some other willing, nondisabled soul was around. Certainly, it was easier and, as usual, it made sense. But it bothered me, perhaps not in terms of our physical capability, but rather, our emotional inconsistency.

During that week, whenever we went out walking and Carrie pushed David in his stroller (which Neil always insisted on doing himself at home), Neil rolled far ahead, focusing his attention on the others in the group who set the pace. He never looked to see where we were, even in the darkness of evening on our way back from dinner through the raunchy neighborhood of our hotel. I was angry at him for neglecting us, but I was more upset with myself.

How could I be so affected by other people's behavior toward me? Just a remark or disapproving look could start turning my wheels of insecurity. I argued with myself: it shouldn't have made any difference if I were in Berkeley, Washington, or Kalamazoo, or if I were with friends, family, or strangers. I was David's mother! I would always be David's mother! But I worried that, as David grew up, he'd begin to see how easy it was for other people to usurp my authority and responsibility. I knew I would have little control over how people reacted, but it was my behavior that concerned me. I wanted him to know that he could count on me.

Maybe I was being too hard on myself. No parent is perfect. People are human; they're allowed to make mistakes. Yet the nature of our family was different than most. The issues and situations that Neil, David, and I were going to face in our future, invariably, would take on an added dimension. I just wanted my son to know that, no matter what, I'd be there when he needed me. My biggest obstacle: I had to convince myself of it first.

If nothing else, that week served to remind me of the pain and hurt that have burdened Neil and me since we were children. Our families had never been able to accept the concept of disability as anything less than a cross to bear, a misfortune that one must "make the best of." Sadly, the rift it caused between our families and us seemed impossible to mend now that we were grown.

Neil and I had struggled long and hard to acknowledge our disability as part of ourselves. Only then did we begin to feel equal with the rest of society and comfortable with who we were. We realized that our cerebral palsy was an intricate part of us and our strengths and weaknesses, adding its own importance to our life experiences. We learned, through the years, that we didn't need to apologize for our wheelchairs, or feel ashamed about how we looked. Moreover, we weren't responsible for how other people felt about us. Now we would teach what we had learned to David. Unlike his parents, who grew up questioning what importance their lives had, David would always know that, whether or not he had a disability, his life was of great value.

Chapter Thirteen

Getting Used to Change

Right before our trip to D.C., David had begun to roll over from his stomach to his back. He'd also started propping himself up on his arms to see what the world had to offer. He didn't have much room left to grow in the port-a-crib in our bedroom. Indeed, when we returned home at the end of June, I declared that it was time for David to use his crib in his own room at night. (Neil took the separation the hardest.)

In August, his eighth month, David raised himself on all fours—ferociously sucking his pacifier—and crept off the foam mat as I watched from my wheelchair. I had been expecting it—he had been scooting around the house for a month or so on his stomach. In fact, I had metal hooks and eyes put on the bedroom doors and a gate across the kitchen entrance to keep him out of trouble. The roadblocks may have impeded my access to those rooms but it was well worth it; I wouldn't have to worry about not being able to get to him fast enough when I was alone with him during the day.

"He's crawling," I reported to Hildred, David's physical therapist, on her first visit of the week. (I didn't really need to tell her; he had crept his way to the door to greet her.)

"Well, then this is probably my last visit," she replied.

I had never realized that Hildred had had a goal in mind for David; she worked with him to relax and strengthen his muscles in what I thought of as more of an ancillary role. Until I heard Hildred's response, I hadn't considered David's crawling as anything more than the accomplishment of a natural stage of a baby's development. Neither had Neil. Our reaction to watching David thump around on his hands and knees (looking back at us every few feet for assurance) was one of simple delight and amusement. It was as if Neil and I had decided—both on our own—that whatever David's prognosis, it was virtually irrelevant: if he had a disability, it was okay, if he didn't have one, that was okay, too. We had no expectations other than knowing he was, for us, the most wonderful baby in the world. We had also adopted a wait-and-see attitude, since Dr. Parker never made any proclamation that, just because David could crawl, he didn't have cerebral palsy. Rather, David's ability to crawl just meant that David crawled.

David's new mobility and development constantly amazed me. He crawled around on the hardwood floors exploring corners and table legs and the chrome on my wheelchair. He rolled his ball from the dining room through the living room to the entranceway of the house, laughing at it when it picked up speed and got away from him. I watched him, usually from a spot on the mat, ready to spring in case something happened. One day, it did; he bumped his head on a protruding corner of the archway between the dining and living room. He wailed. I jumped into my chair with unusual speed, switched on the motor, and turned toward him. Yet before I could roll the very short distance to him, David crept over to me. He used the chrome bars of my wheelchair to pull himself into a standing position so that I could grab him under his arms. As I lifted, he climbed into my lap for comfort. *No one had ever taught him how to do that,* although no doubt he had seen me get into my chair that way countless times. *But he was barely eight months old!*

By the beginning of September, I began realizing that, for possibly the next five years of my life, change and chaos would be the status quo. I longed desperately for stability, but it seemed to be beyond my control. In July, Carrie had given me two weeks' notice. Without any forewarning she announced to me one morning, over a batch of formula, that she was taking another job as a companion for an elderly woman who lived on a vast estate. I felt so betrayed, not only because I befriended her—consoling her heartbreaking renditions of the injustices put upon her and her son by her ex-husband—but because the day she had borrowed the van to take "a drive in the country" had been (as I later figured out) the day of her interview.

To replace Carrie we hired a morning and a late afternoon/early evening attendant. I thought that an attendant, rather than a child care employee, would be easier to train to my way of doing things—and maybe I'd feel more in control. I had also had it with live-in help;

it might be better not to rely on just one person, even if it meant I would have to deal with two more personalities. The rate of turnover for attendants, though, was high. About every four months we needed to hired a new morning or evening attendant since, for most people, attendant work is an interim career—supplemental income while they're going to school, or building up their massage business, or earning extra money to save for a six-month sojourn to Europe. And with every new employee (most unfamiliar with baby care) I had to start from square one:

"Rinse off the nipples and the collars when you take them out of the dishwasher to make sure the soap is off . . .

"Test the bottles to make sure they don't leak . . .

"Make sure his diaper is up high enough in front; boys tend to pee over the top . . ."

Most of the women who worked with us understood that I wasn't being nitpicky—that a soap-filmed bottle nipple could cause diarrhea, that a leaky bottle, as well as a leaky diaper, meant David might need a change of clothes during the long afternoon or at night. Yet some didn't understand no matter how patient I tried to be. Ironically, those were the same women who freely gave me unsolicited advice on baby care based solely on the expertise of being politically correct.

With an air of self-righteousness they'd suggest to me how much healthier for David it would be if I fed him cooked, ground-up food instead of the store-bought variety: "A lot of parents prefer it, you know." Almost every time they handled a Pamper, they'd feel obligated to remind me in words, and later with disdainful looks, that it wasn't biodegradable.

As if I didn't have enough to worry about!

Many nights, when I told Neil some of the highlights of my day, my own voice swelled with the fullness of frustration. I could hear my mother's words mingle with my own, frothing forth like the rush of a river cascading down a set of great falls. I wondered if he heard that fullness in my voice.

"Frisbee was over a half hour late again this morning," I reported on a situation that had become chronic during the last week, ever since she had quit her early morning job.

"Did you say anything?"

"Yeah. And you know what she told me?" The white waves were approaching the falls' edge. "She reasoned that it wasn't so important for her to get here on time since we never had anywhere to go."

My dilemma with Frisbee (her childhood nickname that she only physically outgrew) was that the later she came, the later she stayed. While I resented her blatant disregard for my wishes, I could count on her sticking around to feed David lunch. I had less clarity, too, about our relationship; it blurred into informality; Frisbee would volunteer to drive us on outings where she had an interest in going, or build a sukkah in the backyard for Sukkoth (the Jewish holiday of harvest). Yet David's unbiodegradable Pamper leaked whenever Frisbee diapered him.

"Well," Neil sighed a tired sigh. "As the saying goes: you gotta take the good with the bad."

But how much good is worth how much bad? I grappled with that question daily as I also came to the realization that I needed more child care. It had been on my mind recently as David became more active. He squirmed and wiggled during those long diaper changes after he gave up his pacifier (he finally figured out there was no milk in it). I didn't even have Hildred's visits to look forward to anymore; she had always left David with a clean, snugly fitting diaper. And one afternoon, when I went in to check on him at nap time, I found nine-month-old David perched on top of the five-foot-high shelf attachment to his crib with a big, proud smile on his face. For both our sakes I swallowed my panic. I went over to him and stood up. He knew enough to turn around and inch himself down feet first and, while bracing my short five-foot-two body against the crib, I guided him with a calm voice and assuring hand on his back. Once he was down on his mattress, he giggled with delight, and I couldn't help but share his joy as my muscles relaxed with relief.

It was time, I thought, for someone else to keep David occupied. I just didn't have enough energy!

"If only we could afford more child care," I mumbled one evening to Neil as we sat at the dining table. My tired head rested on my arm.

Neil slouched. "I wish I could ask for a raise."

I lifted my head up. *A raise? Of course! My father used to ask for a raise when he couldn't make ends meet.* Wrinkling my brow, I asked, "Why can't you?"

"Corporate protocol," he answered with a shrug. "It's not acceptable. No one does it!"

"But you're highly valued in the bank. I'm sure if you talked to them—"

"No one does it!" He reiterated with irritation.

"But you give so much to that place," I persisted. "They rely on you. You've worked round-the-clock without overtime or comp time. Don't you realize how much you're worth to them?

"So?" he stared defiantly at me. "That's my job. I do what they expect. They pay me a good salary."

"Right. Good for a family that doesn't have crip-related expenses."

We had had this argument so many times. Once I even accused him of being a closet Republican, which, in his amusement, he didn't bother to deny. I also suspected that in his little corporate world, his disability faded into the walls of those prefabbed, carpeted cubicles. Asking for a raise, no matter how innocuous it seemed, might feel to him as if he were giving his disability unwarranted attention.

Suddenly, I was mad! All these months, I had struggled with my guilt about not earning an income. I had struggled to assert myself not only in my own home but among our families. And what did *he* do? Nothing! He took refuge at work. Unlike Neil, I had no refuge.

"Neil," I looked evenly at him. "You're a wimp!"

His lips tightened. His arm twitched. His green-brown eyes bore coldly on me: how dare I accuse him—a man who'd achieved so much, a man seen so benevolently by family, friends, and colleagues, a man who took pride in avoiding adversity? I had called him a wimp; I hit him below the belt!

I didn't think calling him a wimp was all that terrible; certainly not as bad as when he called me a crippled baby. I thought, in fact, that what his brother had implied to him a few months ago, about Neil's possible failing at fatherhood, was much more of an insult! Neil, however, was so adept at intellectualizing the camouflaged criticism from his family, that I suppose being called a wimp was too much of a direct blow.

Within seconds he erected his invisible, impenetrable, stone fortress; I refused to attempt to break it down with an apology. A deep gloom hung over him (and the house) all evening. By bedtime, I thought he had sulked long enough.

I used the line he always used on me when I was angry. "Remember Freida and Joe's advice—never go to bed mad." The advice (from a couple we knew who were married forty-five years) didn't work on Neil (it rarely worked on me), although he didn't pull away during the night when I draped my arm across his almost hair-less chest and mumbled that I loved him.

He had no usual parting words of "Good-bye Bubbie, have a good (`good' flowed out more easily than `nice') day," the next morning. By the time I got up, I felt a blob of guilt floating in my stomach. I decided I'd call him whenever Frisbee left—eleven-thirty or twelve.

At ten-thirty the phone rang. I picked it up and immediately heard Neil's unmistakable cackle. I could hardly wait for the words.

"I got it!" he stated excitedly, and then cackled again. "An' you know what else . . . ? I didn't even have to ask."

He had gone into his new boss's office (his division had had a reorganization) and before Neil could stammer past "I-I-I n-n-n-need," she finished the sentence, "a raise."

"I can't believe it!" He told me. "It was so easy!"

Neil grinned at me sheepishly all evening; his look was worth a thousand apologies. Oddly enough, over the years, Neil has grown to embrace the concept of himself as a wimp and freely admits, in certain situations, he is, without any excuse, exactly *that—a wimp!*

It took a few months to actually have the request for a raise go through proper channels and get approved. We celebrated it along with the arrival of December 19—David's first birthday and Neil's thirty-fourth.

The most poignant moment of all those months took place on a late Saturday morning, two weeks after the birthday celebration. Neil and I had been watching David coast along the furniture for some months, and we suspected that it wouldn't be long before he could walk. Sure enough, ten days after his birthday, he took several wobbly, tentative steps without holding on. His steps were timid and cautious, as he shifted his weight with each step and held his little bent arms out in the air for balance. Curiously, it reminded me of my own attempts at walking without support. I could almost feel what David experienced as he teetered and tottered on his uncertain limbs, trying to find out whether or not he could trust them.

On the fourth day, Saturday, however, as Neil and I watched from the dining room table, David stood up and, with a sudden sure-footed stride that neither Neil or I could have ever fathomed, walked toward us with a delightful giggle. Neil and I glanced at each other, swallowing perhaps the long-forgotten, hidden tears of our own childhood, and smiled with wonder at our remarkable little boy.

Chapter Fourteen
From One Childhood to Another

Despite all the stresses and strains I went through adjusting to motherhood, I also discovered a world of childhood I had never known before. David insisted I become a participant in his play, and as exhausted as I was in the evenings, I willingly complied.

I started out watching David roll his plastic balls with twirling butterflies and bobbing ducks inside them from the throne of my wheelchair. Soon, though, I couldn't bear the distance between us; the sight of his purposeful movement and curious wonder pulled me down onto the blue carpet in his room amidst building blocks, Duplos, and a multicolored hodgepodge of stuffed animals and things with wheels. I had to get closer no matter how much my bent legs—that I'd reposition every so often—would ache afterward.

David welcomed me down to his level with a big grin. He often offered me blocks or a truck, or best of all, a warm snuggle as he crawled his way into a comfortable crook of my body. We looked at picture books and Mother Goose rhymes. He liked when I sang them or made up my own lyrics about David, of course!

Neil would pass by, groan at the mess, and remark, "I didn't get you a baby; I got you a playmate!"

I'd smile at him with delight while David tugged at my sweater for me to get on all fours, indicating that he wanted a horsie ride. Once I got on my hands and knees, David pulled himself on top of me and straddled across my back. Since he was quite a solid little boy, I couldn't carry him very far, and besides, my worn-out kneecaps prevented me from creeping on the bare hardwood floors. So instead, I'd rock him back and forth, jostling him from side to side as he stretched my sweater to the next size. The sound of his deep laughs touched my ears and tickled my heart.

I had spent the better part of my childhood as an observer watching other children play—excluded by the all too often myopic view of a nondisabled world (unwilling to modify a round hole to fit a square peg), as well as the physical limitations of my own disability both out of doors and inside. I was not allowed the mobility of a wheelchair to even join in a game of tag because of my mother's fear that I'd become too dependent on it, and besides, we lived up two flights of stairs. Ginny Dolls (Barbie's forebearers) frustrated me with all their buttons, buckles, and bows, and board games—like Monopoly—had too many bills, cards, and little thingamabobs to handle. My only chances to join in came on rainy days, when the women neighbors played mah jongg at our house. My mother commanded my sister and the other kids, as they ran off to play dress-up in the bedroom, to include me. I'd follow them on my hands and knees—clumping down on the hard linoleum floor and the thin woolen carpet—ignoring the black and blue marks and the rug burns I got along the way.

"You can be the evil stepmother or the wicked witch," one of them would yell when I reached the threshold, and then throw one of my mother's ugliest house dresses at me.

"Why can't I be the princess?" I asked in protest. "I'm always the evil stepmother."

"Tough! You don't like it, we won't let you play."

"And don't go tattling to Mommy," my sister added.

Fighting back my tears, I struggled into the dress. They had the upper hand. Even if I told my mother, it wouldn't help. "You have to understand, Neisie," she'd say, "kids are cruel."

I crept after them as they tried to get away from the `mean old witch.' I couldn't keep up with them as they clunked off in my mother's high heels and rhinestone jewelry; my legs kept getting caught in the stupid old house dress. Soon, a muscle in the back of my neck would go into one quick, familiar spasm, in protest of all my tensely driven motion. The cramp jerked my head back, lasting no more than a second or two, but the pain was so deep that it sent shivers up through my head and down my spine. I sat there by myself until the pain subsided back into the dull headache, which had begun sometime earlier. I interrupted my mother's game to ask for aspirin, then I'd lie down. Dress-up time was over anyway; the kids were dancing to 45s.

Then there were those dreadful every other Saturdays at the

Carolians, where hard-pressed parents sent their handicapped children for recreation. The Carolians was a pet project of the New York Philanthropic League, a group of wealthy ladies devoted to bringing some happiness to those unfortunate handicapped children. Run by Sue Samuels, a spinsterish, energetic woman with a slight limp (from a bout with polio), the Carolians—also known as the Rainbow Clubhouse—offered children from kindergarten through high school something to do on Saturdays and a break for their parents.

No matter how I protested, I always found myself squeezed into some volunteer's car or station wagon for a trip down to the tenement neighborhood of the West Side. My stomach rumbled as my mother or father waved good-bye, entrusting me to some do-gooder stranger who wouldn't recognize me even four hours later when it was time to go home; they put identifying number tags (the personal touch!) on our coats as soon as we arrived there to make sure we went home in the right vehicle.

Someone usually carried me inside, stood me up on my crutches, and then left me amidst a sea of other children, not knowing that in order to feel safe I needed a person to walk behind me. I attempted to tell them but the echoing din drowned me out. So, with my aluminum, rubber-tipped crutches under the armpits of my bulky winter coat, I hobbled my way across the slippery linoleum floor to the old creaking elevator. It didn't really matter which activity I was placed in, just as long as I made it there (hugging the wall most of the way). Besides, by the time I got to where I was supposed to be going—for the first half hour, at least—I was too tired to care.

I guess I was supposed to have fun and to learn to be with people. Except this was somebody else's definition of fun: playing checkers or making clay ashtrays—just the thing for a kid like me (who spent hours trying to buckle her braces) to enjoy. Most of the time I sat with kids who had no spark in their eyes at all, but so few of the counselors ever noticed our eyes. They only knew us by disabilities, and some disabilities were more acceptable than others.

If anyone had asked me what I would have liked to do, I don't think I would have had the guts to tell them. I wanted to be in dramatics, to get a chance to be someone else . . . to be a star! Yet I was aware of an unspoken sanction. No one had to tell me why only the kids with polio joined the drama club. Once in awhile, a kid with spina bifida would slip through—if he or she looked like a polio. Only rarely would a child who had cerebral palsy be up on the stage of that drafty auditorium, in a minor role without a speaking part—a subject of unspoken condescension. The message was clear: we were too ugly to be seen or heard (except during a telethon to evoke pity and guilt in order to raise money). That was the reality, according to Carolian gospel, that went along with the "fun." And I wasn't the only one who learned it; every other kid learned it too.

"Did you have a good time?" my mother would ask when I came home.

I'd shrug off her question, having no idea what to answer. If I said no, how could I have explained why? I was only nine or ten. It would only sound as though I was complaining. "Mommy, could I have some aspirin? I have a headache," I'd reply instead. It was true, too, and much easier for my mother to understand that kind of pain than the pain of prejudice.

David was still too young to know about prejudice, or to even care. He was too busy learning about tumbling blocks and how Mommy could put his Lego train together. It didn't matter how long it took. In fact, my slowness seemed to help him grasp the concept of how to do it, for very often, when he'd attempt to do it by himself the next time, he'd succeed. His attitude about his success was very matter-of-fact; he responded to my cheers with a momentary glance as if he wondered what the big deal was about since, if Mommy could do it, he could do it too!

So this was what being young was about. I let David lead me, realizing that my experience at child's play had been very limited—Neil's too (he was also a survivor of the Carolians). It made me wonder how much we had missed during our childhood, how much was taken away. How much of our difficulty in decision making stemmed from the play and experiences Neil and I didn't have as children?

Our childhood had been so circumscribed—the therapy, the education, even the recreation. There had always been a plan from a therapist, a teacher, a camp counselor, and we were expected to go along. Now, in our adulthood, both Neil and I had trouble when we found unplanned time on our hands. It almost paralyzed us on weekends when we had no plans. I would sulk, not having any idea of what I wanted to do, and Neil would work on the computer. Quite often I felt that we just wasted Saturdays and Sundays away.

While Neil read books on infant and child development, I experienced it; I was determined to learn about David from David. I sensed that what I was discovering from David I would never have found in any books.

It fascinated me to watch David develop. At nine months old, he could operate the van lift, pushing the switches in correct sequence to open the doors, unfold and then lower the lift (those simple mechanics flustered most nondisabled adults). Settled snugly in Neil's lap on the lift's platform, David raised them both up by pressing another small lever forward. He knew how to reverse the lever to make the lift go down, *at nine months old.*

More intriguing, however, was witnessing the development of David's own intuitiveness; though sometimes the results unsettled me.

I can remember one weekend morning when David was nine or ten months old. We still had a respite worker—Toni—a delightful, assuring woman who made my weekends something to look forward to (until we lost her to a well-deserved promotion). As soon as Neil let her in, she strode through the house, wearing her deep red sweatshirt and matching sweatpants, into the kitchen and put on a pot of coffee for the three of us.

Toni knew the routine—David's laundry in the machine, breakfast for everyone (with or without Regional Center approval), laundry in the dryer, cleanup, David's bath and dressing, making the bottles, folding and putting away laundry. She did it all in two hours with minutes to chat and minutes to spare.

I had settled in the kitchen, chatting with her while she made up a batch of formula. When she started filling the bottles, I automatically stopped in midsentence to remind, "Don't forget to—"

"—Make sure they don't leak," she finished my sentence, eyeing me with dark knowing eyes. "Denise, how long have I been doing this?"

"A while," I smirked sheepishly. "But a lot of people have worked here a while and every now and then—"

"Well, I'm not those other people," Toni refuted playfully. "The bottles I make will not leak." But she lowered her voice and mumbled, "Now watch, the next time I come back she'll tell me one of these damned bottles leaked. *Then I'll really have hell to pay.*"

I concurred with a knowing smile.

We heard the melodic bell tones of a hard plastic ball as it rolled from the hardwood dining room floor onto the kitchen linoleum. I could see it out of the corner of my eye. David wasn't far behind on all fours, playing his version of "soccer" with it. He giggled gleeful every time his palm inadvertently pushed the ball away. He scooted after it and reached out to touch it with one hand, but he miscalculated the pressure he put on the ball; it rolled away much quicker than he expected it to roll. He lost his balance and flopped on his face. Stunned momentarily, he sat himself up and, more angry than hurt, started to cry.

Before Toni or I could make a move, David, still in tears, got on his hands and knees. I leaned forward ready to pick him up, but he crept the few feet past me and stopped at Toni's white sneakered feet and red pant legs. He held his arms up to her.

She picked him up and held him in those strong arms of hers. He sat high up looking down on the counter, the stove, and me—a view he didn't get to see very often. He sniffed back his tears while his eyes searched my face intently.

"Are you okay?" I questioned in a soothing voice as I tried to hide my hurt when I looked up in his face. I rolled to them and began stroking David's little bare foot. "You're all right; it's okay," I reassured.

Not more than a minute later, David calmed down. Toni put him in my lap. An awkward silence hung between the respite worker and me.

Determined not to let my wound fester (as I had done with so many wounds in the past), I gave it air. "Well, David sure knew where he wanted to go. I thought I had a few years before he'd rush into the arms of another woman."

"I feel terrible!" Toni groaned. "I can't believe he did that."

The two of us commiserated about it until Toni finished making the bottles. I tried to make her feel better. It only made sense that David would go to her; Toni's arms were stronger, safer, and higher than mine. David knew they would take him farther away from the danger—that was a fact of life.

After a few moments, David squirmed out of my lap and returned to the ball, as if nothing had happened. Yet something did happen—for from that time on, when he cried and he needed comfort—no matter how close he was to stronger, safer, higher arms—he always came to me. It caused me to wonder if David had sensed my feelings that morning, if he had somehow instinctively known how to reassure me. It seemed incredible that David could be so intuitive, and yet I had certainly felt so open to him. I was learning such wonderful things from him. I was learning to be a mother, forcing myself to give him his own choices even now when he was so young. I gained his allegiance as my reward.

There was no question that David accepted Neil and me as his parents. Unfortunately, I kept worrying about the view other people might take. We still had to appear in court to have a judge sign the final adoption papers. I couldn't help feeling as if we were on probation.

David's status as an "at risk" infant (because of the symptoms he'd shown after his birth) certainly put us in more contact with people in authority—social workers, doctors, therapists—than other adoptive parents. Most of those professionals were very open to us, treating us with the respect that had been so unusual for either us or our parents to receive when we were growing up. I would often anticipate probing questions that stemmed more from judgmental presumptions than healthy curiosity. At every well-baby checkup, I expected (more so than Neil) to be criticized for inadequate baby care. Just the slightest appearance of the blemish from a diaper rash, or an obvious scratch or bruise on David, near to the time of a visit to Dr. Parker's office, put me on the defensive.

It had been the day of one scheduled appointment, in fact, when, right before we left the house, David fell, scraping a significant half-inch gash down his barely inch-long nose on, of all things, Neil's wheelchair. I was sure we'd be accused of neglect, abuse, or incompetence.

My nails dug deep into my palms as we waited for Dr. Parker's entrance into the small, white examining room where a portrait of a hippopotamus family hung on one wall. She opened the door with her usual buoyant energy, greeting Neil and me warmly as David sat playing with a Busy Box on the floor.

"Well," she said as she caught sight of David's face as soon as he turned toward her. My breath caught in my throat. Dr. Parker looked around at us. "I'm glad to see you're not overprotecting him!"

Realizing that Dr. Parker, as well as others, was on our side, I started to relax a little more. Yet tension still hovered around us, not only because the adoption wasn't final—the court appearance was just a few months away—but since November, a custody case had hit the media. It had, at the same time, nothing, yet everything, to do with us:

Chapter Fifteen
Omens and Signs

The phone rang.

"Denise? Are you okay?"

I recognized the smooth voice with the Australian accent immediately. It was Barbara, the social worker from AASK assigned as our case worker until David's adoption became final. Oddly, her words sounded edged with concern.

"I'm fine, Barbara," I assured her.

"Where's David?"

"He's taking a nap in his crib," I answered somewhat uneasily. "Why? What's going on?"

I heard her exhale. "I'm so relieved! I was getting ready to go to work and had the TV on when I heard on one of those news updates that a disabled couple in the Bay Area had their baby taken away. They gave no details. I was afraid it might be you."

I switched on the TV as soon as I hung up the phone to watch the midday news. There was some time left before the program would air. I went to check on David.

The heavy cotton curtain shielded most of his room from the bright autumn sunlight, although some direct daylight peeked through the midsection crevice. I slowly rolled into the middle of the room so I could swing a 90 degree angle to be right up against the bars of the crib. David was such a sound sleeper and so used to the hum of my wheelchair (it probably even lulled him to sleep) that I never worried about waking him up. He knew when he had enough sleep.

He slept in his long-sleeved teddy bear shirt and blue Osh Kosh overalls (he was going to the babysitter's this afternoon and could wear clothing with snaps). His face was turned to the back wall of the crib as he lay on his stomach. His hair, now long enough to cover the strawberry birthmark at the base of his skull, looked so yellow even in the shaded room, yet in photographs it still came out red. In sunlight, though, each strand had its own distinct color; I would notice it as he sat in his carseat while we drove in the van. Some strands held the colors of autumn wheat, some shimmered with a coppery bronze, and others flamed like the sun at sunrise, noon, and sunset. *This child was beautiful inside and out.* If he were ever taken from me . . . I couldn't bear the thought!

Tiffany Callo's story made news for several weeks. Tiffany, who had cerebral palsy, lived in San Jose, about seventy-five miles south of Berkeley. She shared a home with Tony, who was disabled with juvenile arthritis. They received public assistance. Those were the facts. The details in the news reports, however, sounded sketchy: one gave Tiffany's age as nineteen; another, twenty-four. One report said that her child—a few months younger than David—was taken away by the county because Tony was abusive to Tiffany and their attendants. In fact, one attendant announced during an interview that Tony had hidden Tiffany's birth control pills and Tiffany was pregnant again. The issue, it seemed, concerned abuse, not disability—at least that's what I wanted to believe.

I didn't want to believe that a state had the right to take away a baby from his mother because she had CP. I didn't want to believe that they would rather spend hundreds of dollars a month to keep a baby in foster care rather than spend a good deal less a month to provide the mother with support services so that the baby could stay at home. I didn't want to believe that just seventy-five miles away from progressive Berkeley, with its Center for Independent Living (the founding organization of the independent living movement worldwide) and Through the Looking Glass (developing techniques and adaptive devices for disabled parents to care for their babies), Tiffany Callo was going to lose custody of her first child, and probably her second, because she was disabled and poor.

Disability, however, was indeed the issue, for even when she and Tony separated a few weeks later, the baby remained in foster care. Social Services insisted that Tiffany needed to have a 24-hour-a-day attendant for the baby, but they refused to pay for one since her baby was not disabled.

People in the local disabled community had given our name to the press; reporters called Neil and me requesting interviews. We declined. We were nervous; our adoption of David still had to be finalized, *in court*. Neil and I didn't want to draw any unnecessary attention to the three of us.

I wished I could have spoken up for Tiffany, although she had many other well-versed disabled women advocates speaking out for her. None of them had cerebral palsy, and though our circumstances differed, our common denominator of having significant cerebral palsy made society see us in much the same way.

Tiffany Callo's life had been so unlike mine. I had spent my childhood at home living with my parents and older sister. Tiffany spent most of her childhood in foster homes. When she turned eighteen, she got public assistance benefits and looked for her own apartment—something I didn't have the guts to do until I was twenty-eight. She met Tony and moved in with him.

Yet I knew too well the prejudices she faced growing up. I remembered reading old articles and chapters on cerebral palsy during my college days, texts written by prominent psychologists and physicians who were considered "experts" in the field. The literature claimed that most cerebral palsied "patients" tended to appear falsely mature and were likely to be extremely self-centered. They all made it sound as if those behaviors were inherent characteristics of the disability, rather than the results of the way children and adults with cerebral palsy were socialized and psychologically pressured to understand and accept the labels and limits that others place upon them. The writers of this literature gave little exploration into the sociological dynamics of how most children and adults with CP were treated; perhaps if they had, they would have made the connection between the behavior of a child who is seen as self-centered and the fact that the child is someone always being "given to" with no expectation from anyone to "give back" in any way. Even though those texts are forty years old, those ideas have never been challenged. That mentality still existed.

Cerebral palsy is a complex disability to understand and an uncomfortable one to look at: it's easy to dismiss a person with uncoordinated limbs and muscles and labored speech as someone who's not physically or mentally capable of achieving any form of success, especially when this view is fueled by archaic and biased thought and literature. In this society, where judgments are too quickly determined by first impressions, those of us who have cerebral palsy are faced, over and over again, with a burden of proving that there's so much more to us than meets the eye.

Tiffany Callo's case was set to be heard sometime in June, after she was given a battery of tests to determine if she were "fit" to be a mother. The media's attention ebbed during the winter months, although they did report the birth of her second child, Jesse, in January, who was immediately put into foster care with his brother. Tiffany was allowed to see them once a week for a few hours.

In February, Barbara called again, this time with good news. Our court date for the finalization of David's adoption had been set for March 30, exactly one year and ten days after he came home. We could bring whomever we liked along.

I was awake before dawn that morning with a thousand thoughts racing through my head while I lay in bed. What would I wear? I hadn't put on a dress in so long. The few things in my closet were so old. Not that they wouldn't fit; I hardly ate anything to make me gain weight. Oh, why didn't I think of this days ago? What's David going to wear? I should've bought him a new outfit. We have to make a good impression. *It's a court appearance—with a judge!* Oh, no, I didn't think to ask Barbara what's going to happen. Wait, she said the clerk would call us forward and the judge would ask us some questions and her some questions. Then he'd sign the adoption papers. She said this was just a formality.

That's what Debbie Kaplan, a friend, had said too. She and Ralph went before the same judge, Judge Bancroft—the judge for adoptions—last year, when they adopted Desmond. "Judge Bancroft is wonderful," Debbie oozed.

Sure, I thought, but neither Debbie nor Ralph has cerebral palsy. They both have spinal cord injuries; their upper limbs move with coordination and their speech is clear. Who knows how the judge will react when he sees Neil, me, and David? *Beauty and the Beasts* may be his first thought. Even the most intelligent people succumb to the ignorance of prejudice.

Daylight began to raise the curtain of darkness outside the window. I braced myself for the morning chill and threw off the comforter just as Neil's radio alarm went off.

"Coffee," he mumbled, before I even settled in my wheelchair.

I grunted agreeably. "Will you come feed Aries before you take a shower?" I had showered the night before and didn't want to chance spilling cat food juice all over myself which I invariably did when I popped the top of the can. Neil was better at it; he held the can at arm's length so the vacuum-packed smelly contents wouldn't spray him. I was much better at making coffee.

Although jittery from nervous anticipation and not enough sleep, I went about my usual morning routine and drank my coffee anyway. My stomach rumbled as I gulped it down and ate a few bites of a plain doughnut. Mild waves of nausea passed over me. I gagged and took deep breaths until they subsided; I wasn't willing to let an inherent nervous trait from my father overcome me!

An hour and a half later, wearing a blue cotton pinstriped dress with enough buttons down the front to make up for all the years I avoided any clothes with buttons (I used Neil's buttonhook), I greeted Melissa at the front door.

"Come on in," I said. "David's still asleep, of course!"

David's sleeping habits had barely changed since his infancy—except he rarely woke up anymore during the night or took a morning nap. He slept until eight-thirty or nine in the morning—just perfect for me—but I was already worrying how I would get him up when he started school.

Melissa followed me into David's room. She'd been working for us since we let Frisbee go a few months ago after her lateness almost caused us to miss an appointment with Dr. Parker. David liked Melissa with her long blonde braid. They had almost the same coloring; they looked like they could be blood-related.

I slid the crib gate opened and rested my chin on the mattress. "Oh, David," I cajoled softly. "It's time to get up. Melissa's here."

I touched the palm of his curled hand. He swallowed. Lazily, his eyes focused on my face through half-open lids. As always, I smiled at him. "Good morning, Cupcake." His mouth widened to reveal tiny white teeth, returning an even brighter smile with magical joy.

After laying out David's clothes, his teddy bear shirt with blue denim pants complete with suspenders, I left David in Melissa's capable hands and went to check on Neil in the kitchen. I found him slumped in his chair with his head resting on his chest. Not a good sign.

"How's the coffee?" I asked.

He shrugged. His extended right arm twitched; he was nervous.

"Are you all right?" *How could I have asked such a dumb question?*

He gave me the response I expected—his head moved an eighth of an inch for a barely perceptible "no."

"Do you want me to call Janet and Anda to meet us here instead of at the courthouse so Janet could drive the van?"

For moral support, we had invited the couple to go with us, along with another good friend, Robin, who was bringing along her two-year-old niece, Allison. I would have asked more friends, too, except it was a weekday—most of them were at work. At first, I thought we had asked too many people, but facing Neil now, I knew we needed all the support we could get. He didn't even answer my question.

"I'll go call Janet," I volunteered.

"No!" He growled.

With all my restraint, I held back the urge to let him have it. He wasn't in this alone! If he was that nervous, he shouldn't be driving; it would affect his coordination. We could have an accident. But as I looked at the harsh creases in his face, I knew arguing would only make matters worse. I didn't want to argue today. I had to have faith that he knew his capability even in his present state. If I couldn't trust Neil, who could I trust?

A half hour later, Melissa had David fed, dressed, and ready to go. In his usual manner, Neil flipped his charcoal gray suit jacket over his head and went to brush his thinning hair. I slipped on a yellow cardigan as Melissa packed up my backpack with the essentials—diapers, bottles, another set of just-in-case clothes, and David's jacket that he didn't need to wear. It was a beautiful, early spring morning warmed by the rays of a bright sun with the faint smell of newly blossoming flowers in the air.

Melissa settled David into his carseat while Neil put the key into the ignition—on his first try. A good sign. He started the motor.

"Wave `bye-bye' to Melissa, David," I coached as she waved at him. He turned to me. I showed him the gesture. Facing the window again, he opened and shut his hand before we sped away—off to the courthouse.

To get to Family Court of the Oakland County Courthouse, we had to go in the entrance of the Municipal Court building across the street, take an elevator to the basement, go through the tunnel in the basement of the county courthouse, and take another elevator up to the floor where they held Family Court. Luckily, Neil and I knew the way; each of us had served on jury duty years ago.

Our group of friends greeted us outside the closed courtroom door. We were early. We had to wait ten minutes before an official opened the oak-paneled doors.

My mouth was dry as I settled myself up in front of the first row of stationary seats. David toddled among the rows behind me with his friend, Allison. Robin kept her eye on both. Janet and Anda stood nearby talking to each other while Barbara, our case worker, rummaged through her briefcase for the appropriate file. The clerk called Neil up to her box to verify some information. I saw him struggling to answer.

"Excuse me," the clerk called over for attention. I poked Janet to turn to her. "Could you tell me what he's saying?"

I felt my tears well. This was not starting out the right way. *A bad omen?* Anda gently squeezed my shoulder to reassure me while Janet went to the clerk's station. We waited a minute longer for them to finish. Janet, as she walked toward us, gave a nod that everything was okay. Neil, however, did not look happy.

Now we just had to wait.

When I looked around to check on David, I saw more adults wandering in with children much older than David and Allison. I realized that, until then, I had given no thought to where I was or to what else must go on here—custody cases, child abuse hearings, the whole gamut of family affairs. As I panned the rows of seats, noticing the expressions on those other faces, I felt a mixture of compassion, guilt, and relief because I wasn't in their places. I spotted David and Allison chasing one another through that seating section, giggling with laughter.

"The matter of adoption: Neil and Denise Jacobson," the clerk announced, at last, in a thin voice that was hard to hear. "Come this way, please."

Confusion erupted over our little group. There had been no call to order, nor any appearance of a judge, just the barely audible voice of the clerk who had needed help understanding Neil. It took several moments of scrambling before the members of our entourage headed in the right direction—*passing right by Neil and me.* Robin even picked up David and started to carry him off.

"Wait! Wait!" Neil's desperate roar brought the procession to a halt. *"I want David!"* And only when David sat snugly in father's lap did we proceed to Judge Bancroft's chambers.

The judge, wearing a dark blue pinstriped suit, greeted us at the entrance to his small, cramped chambers. A benevolent looking man with wisps of gray combing through his curly black hair and beard, he stood at a comfortable enough height for Neil and me to look up at him without straining our necks. He extended his hand, smiling warmly, as Barbara introduced the principal players of this event.

"C-C-Can our friends join us?" Neil managed to ask.

"Surely," he replied. Taking note of how many there were, he gestured to a brown leather couch next to the window and two other empty chairs adjacent to it. He then placed a straight-back chair in front of his desk, but off to one side of it, for Barbara, leaving enough room beside her for Neil and me to park our wheelchairs.

Before taking his high-back seat of authority behind his desk, he went over to open his closet in a corner of the small, dark office. He bent down and pulled out something I couldn't yet see. As he closed the closet door, Janet asked permission to take pictures. He turned to look at Neil and me. "Only if I get to pose with the three of you after the signing."

Oh good, he intended to sign!

Neil and I nodded as we watched him walk back to the desk. My stomach still rumbled. Everything seemed to be happening in slow motion. I reached over for David's hand, but he was more interested in playing with his suspenders than touching his mother's clammy palm. He only looked up when Judge Bancroft placed a little windup merry-go-round music box on the corner of his desk. It held his attention for all of a moment; two-year-old Allison was much more impressed than my sixteen-month-old son. *Oy vey! I hoped the judge wouldn't think it was our fault that David's behavior was antisocial.*

After the merry-go-round, the judge *still* wasn't ready to open the folder on his desk. Next he pulled out a package of balloons from a bottom drawer of his desk and handed a few to Robin "for later."

"Now," he said finally after he adjusted his seat to his desk. He folded his large hands on the folder in front of him. He looked directly at us. "I am required to ask you one question before we begin."

He paused. Suddenly, he seemed so serious.

Uh-oh, here it comes. He's probably heard of Tiffany Callo too.

I crossed my feet to keep them still. The sweat dripped down my back. From the corner of my eye, I saw Neil's twitching arm. I noticed drops of moisture on his forehead. We were thinking the same thought. We knew what the judge would ask: Did we think we'd be able to . . . ?

"Do you still want to go through with this adoption?"

Stunned, Neil and I glanced at each other. It certainly wasn't the question we had expected. Why, how could anyone have asked that looking at those round pink cheeks and magnetic blue eyes? We looked back at Judge Bancroft, only to realize that we had yet to give him our answer.

"*Yes!*" Neil and I said in unusually loud harmony, and then repeated it more calmly. "Yes!"

A smile graced the judge's friendly face. He opened the folder and started flipping easily through the pages while he chatted about how much he liked presiding over adoptions.

Just sign the papers, sign the papers, I silently urged, chewing my lips, *before you retire.*

Barbara handed over the Interstate Compact and David's birth certificate at the judge's request. He skimmed both documents.

"Everything looks fine," the judge said approvingly, reaching, at last, for his ballpoint pen.

I caught my breath. My eyes followed that pen from the time Judge Bancroft took it from its desk-set holder and first touched the adoption decree with its fine point until he crossed the `t' in Bancroft. I breathed again while he added the date.

Then it was our turn to sign. I was first, since David still occupied Neil's arms. Judge Bancroft stood up and brought the document around to me. He waited patiently while I adjusted the document and myself to the right juxtaposition. I took the pen he offered, consciously trying to keep my excess movements from going haywire in the wake of my excitement. With tears blurring my vision, I signed my name more or less on the line. When I finished, I exchanged the pen for David so that Neil could sign.

Janet took pictures through the whole signing ceremony, and I had to contain myself a while longer as the judge posed with the three of us just as we had agreed to do. Afterward, Neil and I thanked Judge Bancroft. He shook our hands again while the others in our group prepared to exit.

I headed for the door as soon as it opened. Neil followed at my wheels. Judge Bancroft called after us, "I hope to see you soon with the next one!"

In the hallway outside the courtroom, our faces wet with tears and our words constricted in our throats, Neil and I hugged each other as David squirmed in between. What he really wanted, his parents both knew, was his bottle. Neil started to reach into his backpack, but I had one tucked inside my wheelchair. I reached behind me and pulled it out. David took quick possession, put it in his mouth, and leaned his head against my chest. I placed my hand gently on his rounded stomach while Neil's hand rested just above David's knees. Janet snapped the picture.

It was over; a relief for both Neil and me. We would go home, put the papers in our file, and answer the phone calls of congratulations and *mazel tov* from our friends and family. We had been so lucky, unlike Tiffany Callo who, a few months later, in the face of a long, drawn out court battle, would decide to relinquish custody of her two children. The court would promise that her children would stay together; later Social Services would renege on that promise, sending the children to live separately in homes that were hundreds of miles apart.

Neil and I certainly had cause to celebrate, but we also knew that our little ceremony with Judge Bancroft was just a rite of passage, a sign of a beginning rather than an ending. Neil, David, and I would go home together; Neil would be with me as we raised David. Tiffany, had she won custody of her children, would have had to raise them alone, in a world that still knew little about, and expected even less from, people with cerebral palsy.

Chapter Sixteen
A Toddler's Step Away

Neil basked in the glory that David needed and wanted him the way no one ever did before. Many nights, when Neil got home, worn out from a full day's work, David would run into his big, open arms for a bear-crushing hug. Neil, making boisterous sounds, would awkwardly swoop a giggling David up to his lap. David, paying no attention to what anatomical areas his strong little hands and legs nudged and prodded on Neil's body, squirmed and fidgeted until he settled himself in the crook of Neil's arm. Neil would drape his forearm across his son's legs; they both looked so comfortable and relaxed. Then Neil and his son whizzed off, heading for one of the bedrooms. I stayed behind to close the front door and watch them disappear, savoring the sight of the back of David's small blond head slightly bobbing up and down on his father's protective arm.

Like his own father, Neil envisioned himself as the man who came home after a hard day's work to entertain his adoring child. He'd do things just to make David laugh: speed up when David was about to hop on the back of his wheelchair, hold an object just out of reach for David to grasp at, or tickle him. None of it frustrated David. In fact, he loved running after Neil and eventually caught up (when Neil purposely slowed down); he teased Neil in good-natured reciprocity; and David appeared to thoroughly relish being tickled by Neil. Of course Neil's tickles were a combination of pokes and squeezes, but administered to the right spots, they produced joyous laughter just the same.

I was glad that Neil could bring levity to David's new stage of toddlerhood but, once again, I started out quite apprehensive. Faced with David's new sense of autonomy and an eagerness to explore his world, I, the perennial worrier, had visions of David running off in crowded stores, up stairs, and off sidewalks.

Neil and I watched David with awe in the playground, where the play structures sat in a very safe but wheelchair inaccessible bed of sand. With a surefooted stride, so uncharacteristic of a toddler, he would walk over to some parent pushing another child on a swing. He would glance back at Neil or me for consent, tug gently at the adult to get attention, and point to an empty swing saying "Push." He loved to go high, and when the parent gave us a look of skepticism, we'd nod approval. After he had enough, he'd say a thank you (I often prompted) and go on to what Neil and I dubbed "the killer slide." Half a story high with several twists and turns, it was designed to thrill daring six- and seven-year-olds. The first time David tackled that slide, he was about three and, luckily, I wasn't there.

"I almost had a heart attack the first three times he did it," Neil said when they came home. He described how David climbed up the ladder so cautiously and then controlled his slide down by gliding his hands along the side guards. "After about the third or fourth time, he really got good. Then every time he hit the sand, he'd laugh hysterically. . . . I got a kick out of it."

David's judgment, though, astounded me the most; it often seemed far more advanced than his years. Whatever it was that had made him try "the killer slide," had stopped him from running into a street when we were out for walks, or taking off in any direction inside stores and supermarkets. Harried mothers often approached me to ask how I managed to train David to stay within sight while they chased their kids up and down the aisles. I didn't have an answer. Somehow, David just seemed to know both his parents' limits and his own.

For perhaps the first time in my life, I was the center of someone's world: not as a burden, but as a protector. Suddenly, I found myself the mother I had often dreamed about becoming, an improbable dream, I had thought. David had thrust me into my now cherished role, one that demanded use of all my resources and strengths.

Yet David had also become my teacher. He offered me lessons involving patience and trust. The first, patience, I had known well on a physical level but sorely lacked on an emotional one; I discovered that the whole experience of loving and raising a child is a long exercise in emotional patience, with many tests to take. The second, trust, was a more complicated lesson to learn. Not only did I have to learn to trust David — in fact, that was the easy part — but I had to learn to trust myself. That trust, my instinct and intuition, which would prove so crucial in mothering a child, had been buried within me for such a long time.

I had been so accustomed, over my long, perhaps drawn-out years of childhood, to bury or ignore the powerful voices of my own inner thoughts and feelings. The effects of my having cerebral palsy had placed a strain on my family because of the help I needed. I often felt imprisoned by the emotional tension resulting from that strain, conflicted by both my feelings and those of my family. Yet, as a child, I couldn't really understand the complexity of what I was feeling or why I felt it. Moreover, I didn't want to cause any further discomfort to anyone. One thing was always clear: I had to be nice—I was in no position to risk abandonment. I could not afford to express my sadness, pain, and anger. Yet, every now and then, I had a tantrum to let out those emotions that I otherwise tightly controlled: I could be the spoiled brat who wanted her own way, an easy explanation for everyone concerned.

Through the years, I had been slowly trying to find a way to express my own truth. I was getting better at recognizing my own feelings but I still had difficulty giving voice to them. I often struggled to convince myself that I had a right to be heard and, more important, that I had something worth saying. Before David, however, the choice of speaking out or not was at my own expense. Now that would no longer be true; another human being depended upon my actions.

I expected that having a child would force me into situations in which I had very little to go on except for my instinct and intuition. It came down to an issue of trust and believing myself capable of protecting my son, knowing, at times, I would have to say the things that needed to be said and do the things that needed to be done in difficult circumstances. As David's world grew bigger, my instinct and intuition also told me that those situations were just a toddler's step away.

Neil and I started David in a nursery school program when he was almost two. We thought he needed more activity than his neighborhood babysitter could provide. Our search for a wheelchair-accessible, neighborhood day care led us to a private, inaccessible, licensed home day care—more than a mile away. But the woman, Jean Shetland, seemed nice—restrained, but nice—and even willing to arrange for David to be picked up and dropped off by some of the other parents. It might not have been the ideal place, but we thought David would be well cared for and safe. So we ignored little passing condescending remarks and incidents.

"I'm so glad that David's in our program," Jean said to us on the evening when Neil and I let ourselves be hauled up the steps by parents we didn't know to attend a parent gathering; both of us struggled with our emotions to feel as though we belonged. Neil and I glanced at each other as we sat immobilized and uncomfortable on a sunken sofa listening to Jean preen, "I feel like I'm doing my part for the community!"

I bit my lip. *Tokens are for subways!*

In all the months David went to Jean's, I came face to face again with the inadequacy I had felt as a dependent child fearing that I asked for too much. I depended on mothers I didn't know to drive him, and they sometimes forgot. The first time it happened, Chris, Jean's assistant, offered to come get David, but apparently on the way over she had second thoughts.

"We can't do this every day," this twenty-something-year-old scolded me in the living room of my home. "It's the only time I will be able to do this."

In automatic reflex, I apologized for the inconvenience, profusely, before they left. A few minutes afterward, my anger bloomed. How dare that little twerp admonish me! I hadn't asked her to come. She volunteered. What was I supposed to do, turn her down and try to find a friend who wasn't busy to drive him? Guilt began seeping through; maybe I was partly at fault for letting her come. She was only trying to be helpful. Even so, what right did she have to treat me like a little girl, and why did I feel like one?

By the time I talked to Jean later that morning, my feelings succumbed to watered down rationality. I explained that I had had no expectation when I called that either she or Chris had any responsibility to pick up David, that Chris had made the wrong assumption, and that I thought her lecture was inappropriate. I was very rational, very polite, and, in the end, very resentful in betraying my own feelings of how Chris had made me feel.

"I fell right into the trap," I told Neil that night when we were by ourselves. I pressed my lips together and shook my head with disdain. "I had the feeling her offer to pick up David would backfire, and it did."

"Bubbie, I give you a lot of credit," my husband responded.

I looked at him. "Why?"

"Because you have to put up with this crap and stupidity," he answered. "That's why I work at a bank. I don't have to put up with stuff like that. If people can't deal with me, they get fired. It's their problem, not mine."

I remembered Neil once telling of the time at work when he called the computer operation division and a new employee made fun of him and then hung up. Neil called back twice. The same thing happened. Fifteen minutes later, Neil put in a personal appearance down at computer operations, to the surprise of the supervisor and the new employee. The supervisor wanted to fire the *schlump*, but after seeing the young guy's pained reaction, Neil knew he was suffering enough for his mistake; he would never hang up on Neil again.

The bank was Neil's haven. He was liked and respected. He provided a service and filled a role. Everything was so clear cut and well defined. Real life wasn't like that; it was full of ignorance and fallibility, and short on insight and resolution.

I appreciated Neil's words to me that night, but I wished I could have gotten a little more of his physical presence!

To further complicate the situation at school, David, according to Jean, was not adapting as well as the other children. He seemed unresponsive to her, "spacy." He ignored her when she called his name. "I even tried to sound like you," she confided (as if the way Neil and I pronounced "David" was so unrecognizable, or that David had never heard anyone else say his name). The real problem, however, according to her, was that he appeared "unsocial." The other kids interacted with each other. Twenty-three-month-old David contentedly played by himself. It concerned Jean that David would leave his eleven other schoolmates singing songs at circle time to play quietly with a toy car.

"David's been getting chronic ear infections," I told Jean. Within a two-and-a-half-month period, he had two colds and four ear infections. (I was getting quite good at pouring bubble gum flavored amoxicillin and subsequent antibiotics into the medicine spoon.) While other children ran high fevers, displayed crankiness, cried, or showed obvious signs of pain or discomfort, David's illness wasn't easy to detect. In fact, I eventually learned that I could gauge David's health more by how I reacted to him; for instance, if I found myself irritated at him because his normal behavior seemed slightly more intense—restlessness in falling asleep, poor appetite, a little more uncooperative—I'd begin to suspect that he might be sick. Sometimes, it took me a few days to recognize the symptoms. I tried to explain it to her; I didn't think she believed me.

How could my experience of David be so different than Jean's? At home he was such a self-sufficient little guy. He could get his own bottle from the refrigerator but took it only with permission. He took his own bowl for cereal (our unbreakable dishes were at the right height). He spoke his limited vocabulary very clearly but preferred showing rather than telling. And he thought a lot; he figured out how to use his little stepping stool to get something out of his reach. Once, as I struggled with the cellophane on a seemingly easy-to-open package, he stood nearby repeating the word "fork" several times. When I eyed him with a puzzled look, he toddled into the kitchen, where I heard him unlatch the safety latch of the silverware drawer. David returned and handed me the fork. I finally got it—he had seen me open my prunes as well as other packages and boxes by piercing them with a fork prong.

My intuition told me that David didn't belong at Jean's. I felt she had made certain false assumptions and resented accommodating us; her feelings colored the way she saw David. I worried that he was becoming her scapegoat, that her attitude toward our disability prevented her from appreciating David. I feared she would blame him and ostracize him; the other children would pick up on the way she'd treat him. David would become an outcast by the time he was two.

On the other hand, maybe Jean's observations had validity. Perhaps Neil was right that I was being overdramatic; he rolled his eyes at my "outcast" scenario. It was, after all, only home day care. She had a good reputation (we had checked it out) and a waiting list of children. We were lucky David got in.

I spoke to Dr. Berberich (one of Dr. Parker's office partners—she was in Boston on her two-year sabbatical). He assured me that there was nothing to indicate a delay in David's development. Yet our visits with him were often so short, I wondered about the accuracy of his assessment.

Not sure who to listen to (everyone had opinions), I put in a long-distance call to Dr. Parker. She gave two suggestions—to go back to see the neuro-developmental specialist who had examined David in his infancy, and to take David for a speech and language evaluation.

I didn't particularly want to go back to that specialist. He had examined David at four months old and found no developmental delay at that time. But as comfortable as he seemed to be handling David, he was equally uncomfortable talking with Neil and me. It was as if it had never occurred to him that the children he treated would eventually grow up and might be like us. I had to admit, however, that it probably made more sense to see Dr. Mankie again before we saw anyone else.

Neil took off work to go with us, but the scheduled appointment interfered with David's nap time. I worried that he would be irritable, which would affect his behavior. And indeed, David proved very uncooperative with the doctor's young assistant as she tried to entice him with colored cubes, a bottle with a raisin inside, and a ball.

Sometime later, the casually dressed, balding doctor entered the crowded little room. He leaned against the examining table that David sat on, where the items the assistant brought in still lay. Paying no attention to David, the specialist asked Neil and me for background information. The tenseness of the situation understandably affected the flow and clarity of our speech, but he appeared to comprehend what we had said. I noticed that while he listened, his hand absently began playing with the cubes on the table. David took an interest. It didn't take long for David to become fully engaged with the tasks at hand. I was impressed: at least Dr. Mankie knew what to do with children.

We received a copy of the report sent to Dr. Berberich. It concluded that David had no "neurological deficit and is of normal intelligence." It suggested, but with uncertainty, that he appeared "to have a mild speech delay"; my son did not say one of the thirty to forty words that I had told the doctor was in his vocabulary. *Not one word!* The report described David as being "very inquisitive about toys . . . exploited their mechanical features . . . sometimes ingeniously," but not "particularly animated or pleased by people around him including his parents." Dr. Mankie raised concerns about David's disinterest in his surroundings, but he indicated that "some of this can be attributed to the behavior of an independent two-year-old."

He reassured us, as he stated at the end of the report, that David was developing pretty "normally." In that respect, I felt relieved. The tone of the report, however, revealed his skepticism regarding Neil's and my abilities as parents. He wrote, "Because of limitations in communication, we (he used the plural pronoun throughout the report) were not quite sure if we got a well-rounded picture of David's relationship with his parents. We also weren't certain of how well they were able to manage in terms of safety issues in the home with an active and energetic toddler." I didn't blame him for his skepticism; I blamed him for his disrespect.

"I knew he was not the person that you should have asked about ideas for getting David into his carseat," I said as Neil finished reading the report. Lately, we had found we had to bribe David with a bottle to get him to climb into it. Neil thought Dr. Mankie might have better suggestions; he didn't. "So, Neil, what do you think?"

"We ought to invite him over," Neil responded thoughtfully.

"What? Are you crazy?" I lashed out. "This man implies that we aren't fit to be parents; he assumes that we're raising David in a kiddie den of iniquity. He hasn't the vaguest idea of what we're capable of or what our home is like. He thinks we're a couple of stupid cripples who want to play house. . . . And you want to invite him over?!"

But I shouldn't have been surprised. Neil rarely emoted. He problem-solved. He couldn't understand how that letter made me feel so discounted. After the care I painstakingly took to make sure David was safe but not overprotected: my ears always alert for sounds in the bathroom, in the kitchen, in every room I wasn't in. At the playground I watched for potential accidents; no one would be able to accuse me of neglect. Neil took a more relaxed approach, but I watched and listened, fully aware that I compensated for what I thought I lacked in speed and physical ability.

I looked at my husband as I wondered, once again, where he put the hurt. "Well," I said, switching to a more immediate subject. "What are we going to do about Jean's?"

"David seems to be all right about going," Neil, sitting in his usual slumped-down, disinterested posture, replied.

"Just because he isn't kicking and screaming before he goes doesn't mean he's okay," I interjected. "Maybe he's trying to tell us something by getting all those ear infections."

My inference struck him as too metaphysical; Neil rolled his eyes. This conversation wasn't getting us anywhere. It was tempting to just let the situation slide. What harm could come of it? David was still under two—one of the youngest children in Jean's program. Maybe he just needed time to get used to it. Maybe Jean needed time to get used to him. Maybe Neil was right. Then again, maybe I was right and David needed an advocate!

I decided to go observe this "distracted" behavior Jean was so concerned about. I brought my friend Janet along for moral support, physical support (to help me up Jean's steps on my own terms), and to bear witness.

When we arrived, the children were inside playing with instruments. David smiled at us briefly and then continued experimenting with the sound of the little toy piano. The other kids wandered over to the sunken sofa where I sat, curious to know why I walked and talked "that way." Cerebral palsy is hard to explain to two- and three-year-olds.

"My muscles aren't steady," I answered and turned my head in another direction. I didn't feel up to "show and tell." The kids soon found other things more interesting.

I watched my son playing so intently, deep in concentration with whatever toy he picked out and explored: a Japanese instrument, a yellow dump truck, a hand puppet. Jean rang a tiny bell and in a singsong voice called the children into the kitchen for a midmorning snack. Eleven toddlers squeezed around a small low table, sitting on their knees, for juice and crackers. Jean, in that same tone, had to call David twice by name to get his attention. But when he went to put his toy back on the shelf where it belonged, Janet spoke his name with the same softness (but without the singsong) Jean had used; David turned to Janet immediately.

I noticed that, unlike his peers, David didn't chatter or even speak. If he wanted more snack, he'd lift his bowl. If he wanted more juice, he'd lift his cup. He had trouble, too, staying on his knees, as did one or two of the other children in Jean's tightly run regimen.

In the basement of the house Jean had shelves and shelves of toys, which the children had access to after their snack.

"David is only interested in a few," she informed Janet and me with concern as we went around through the gate to the back of the house. "He seems to only like toys with wheels."

"Well, he's had a lot of experience with wheels," Janet pointed out.

On my own once again in my wheelchair, I rambled around on the concrete portion of the patio in the backyard watching David at play. He especially liked the orange and yellow car he rolled in, but after awhile, he joined a few of the other tots who were jumping and romping on the large grassy patch of yard. Minutes later, Jean approached them.

"Who wants to play a game?" she asked.

"Me, me, me!" most of them shouted back.

She wanted them to each take a white, lightweight lawn chair from a stack, line them up in a row, and sit on them. She took one for herself and placed it ten feet away, facing what was to be the line, and sat down waiting for the children to be ready. That is, all but David. He was in his seat before she was in hers. While she sat directing his peers, David, with his hands in his lap, sat swinging his legs and looking around. Of course, by the time everyone settled in their places about ten minutes later, he was bored, and so he walked away toward the sandbox.

The thick fog of anxiety and doubt I had been living in for the past two and a half months began lifting. Jean wanted control. David, because of who he was, which included being our son, happened to be an "independent two-year-old" and wonderfully sure of himself. Jean would never appreciate him.

Jean used her little bell and singsong voice again to gather the kids for circle time. David joined his group, crossing his legs to sit down on the hard surface of the patio. It was mid-December, the season for jolly Christmas songs. Jean even had her assistant (a substitute for the day) pass out bells to the children for a rendition of "Jingle Bells."

"I used to do some celebration for Chanukah," Jean explained to Janet and me while the bells made the rounds. "That was when I was dating a Jewish man. I'm not up on the Jewish holidays that much anymore."

Janet and I exchanged looks.

"Jingle bells, jingle bells, jingle all the way . . ."

David and another little boy eased themselves quietly out of the circle and went off in different directions. David headed for the orange car.

"I'll get them," the assistant said as she leaped up. She went after the other boy first, retrieved him, and sat him back down. Then she started for my son.

"Oh, don't even bother with David," Jean said flatly, then went to her singing.

Tears stung my eyes. He wasn't even two and she wrote him off already. Right in front of the other children. I know they were only toddlers, but even kids that young pick up nuances and innuendos. And she was a teacher—a role model—sending out a clear message of intolerance without having any awareness of what she was doing.

I didn't even confront Jean, afraid that in my highly emotional state I'd be inarticulate in content and unclear in my words. Besides, it was neither the time nor the place.

Knowing Neil considered me overly anxious and overly critical, I deferred telling him anything when he got home from work. "Ask Janet," I said.

He smiled with whimsy; he thought I played coy. After dinner, he called Janet. I got on the extension.

"So, what's the bottom line?" he asked after they talked for awhile.

"The bottom line is," she said without hesitation, "you've gotta get him out of there."

"Well, that's very clear," he stated. "I like that!"

David never went back to Jean's. He came down with a bad ear infection right before the winter break.

I listened to Neil's end of his final conversation with Jean. It sounded very cordial. "We think it's better not to have him stay," Neil said. Jean seemed to agree.

But the anger remained with me. It had taken me three months to get David out of a miserable situation—because I had tried being rational instead of trusting my instinct.

To let off some steam a few weeks later, I wrote Dr. Mankie a two-page single-spaced letter disputing some of his biased assumptions. It took me days to compose it and peck it out on the computer. In response, he wrote three short paragraphs reiterating that he had given his professional opinion and turned down my invitation to visit our home to discuss his reservations further. We were welcome, he stated, to talk with him "on the phone" (a preposterous response since he couldn't even understand us in person!).

I may not have gotten the satisfaction I wanted from him, but as I looked back over the last three months of grappling with my own indecision, I started to realize that what other people thought or said wasn't as important as I was brought up to believe. Of course, I had known it intellectually, but belief often lags behind knowledge. I understood much better now. David had to come first! I had to trust that I knew what was best for him. He had to know that he could count on me.

Chapter Seventeen

The Seeds of Trust

It was going to be a long day. I had my routine mammogram scheduled for ten o'clock, which meant that I had to wake up half an hour earlier, at six, so I could shower, dress, and be all finished with myself before I went in to wake David to get him ready by 8:45. I'd drop him at his preschool, hopefully by nine, then travel a mile by wheelchair to the ten o'clock appointment. If I were lucky, I'd be out by noon, grab lunch along the way, and go home to do some writing before I picked up David at 2:45 to take him to his language therapy appointment with Amy—more than another mile away in the other direction.

Waking up my son was not a task I looked forward to, for although he smiled as soon as his eyes opened, it often took a good ten minutes to raise him out of his deep slumber and start him on the road to dressing, eating, brushing, and finally, preschool. Over the last two years, I developed a whole repertoire of tactics to keep David on track, which included cajoling, playing beat the clock, offering rewards, threatening time-outs, dressing him by myself with his cooperation. None of them ever worked for more than a week at time: it all depended on the stage of development David was going through that week.

By 8:50, running our usual five minutes behind, David wriggled into the jacket that Grandma Guta (Neil's mother) had brought him on her last visit and hopped on the built-in platform on the back of my wheelchair. I grabbed his Mickey Mouse lunchbox as David's small hands tightened around my chair handles. We creaked through the door slowly so I could pull the door shut behind by tugging on the old belt tied to the doorknob.

"Goooo," my little charioteer ordered after I carefully descended our switchback ramp.

Off we whizzed into the sunny, mild mid-September morning, down three tree-lined streets with uneven sidewalks and across two parking lots to get to the little white building with blue trim and six steps to the door. I checked my watch. It was only three minutes after nine—the front door was still open.

David hugged me good-bye with his strong little arms, took his lunchbox, and climbed the stairs. I made sure he was safely inside before I sighed a somewhat exhausted sigh. At least, I'd have a little extra time to stop for a mocha and a bagel before my next task; it would take me less than twenty minutes to cover a mile.

I had scheduled my mammogram at the same place I had my first one, two years ago—a small laboratory and X-ray unit located on the second floor of the building that also housed the office of David's pediatrician. Even with taking my time at the cafe, I arrived ten minutes early. The receptionist retrieved my records from the computer. All I had to do was sign the permission form. I sat in the waiting area thumbing through an old *Time* magazine until I heard my name. I looked up at the white-coated technician—a different woman than last time.

"Oh, you're in a wheelchair," she frowned. "This might be a problem. Can you stand up?"

Not for a mammogram. I knew I couldn't stand up, hold still, and have my breast squished all at once. "But can't you lower the machine? That's the way it was done last time."

They had just gotten a brand new, updated model, she explained. It took faster X rays. It just didn't lower enough for a woman in a wheelchair. "Wait here just a minute. I'll be right back," she said and disappeared before I could get another word out.

Without consulting me, she made an appointment for my mammogram to be done across the street at the hospital at one o'clock. I was irritated, but I didn't want to kill another day. Since I was already there, I just had to kill almost three hours.

So I stopped up on the third floor and said hello to Ellie, the receptionist, and Judy, the pediatric social worker. Next, I browsed around the new metaphysical bookstore, a furniture store, and a toy store, then found my way to a spot outside the toddler park to read. Feeling the warmth of the strong noon sun, I took off my jacket and settled down with the morning paper. But the air smelled so sweet and the sound of the children's distant voices made my mind wander off in no particular direction. I was surprised when I checked my watch and found it time to go.

Following the other lab tech's directions, I wended my way through the hospital corridors and several sets of double doors until I saw the sign reading Pathology Lab/Mammography. I pushed open the heavy door and rolled up to the glass window. The short woman in the lab coat peered down at me. She had been expecting me, she said. She called me "darling." Not a good sign.

I didn't feel up to asserting myself. It was already afternoon. My energy was waning; I had been up early, the air had made me sleepy, and I hadn't eaten lunch yet. So I just followed her directions, listened to her muttering about how difficult it was to get me in the right position, and endured each "darling" by grinding my teeth and blinking back hot tears of rage and humiliation. *Next time, I would bring a friend along!*

"Bye, darling," I snapped, tearing out of the room when the ordeal was over. I just missed ramming the wall.

I zipped through the hospital and out onto the streets. My watch read almost two o'clock. If I hurried, I could grab a frozen yogurt before I had to pick David up at 2:45; the yogurt place was a block from the preschool. Frozen yogurt was not my favorite snack—a little too messy to eat with a tiny plastic teaspoon—but at least it was more substantial than a doughnut from the bakery.

I waited at the bottom of the steps, watching as other mothers or fathers helped their children collect their assorted artwork, lunchboxes, and jackets. They scooted past me on the way down. Some children said "bye" to me, some didn't. Most just wanted to get out of school, having enough of structure and rules for one day—even if it was only preschool. David, however, dawdled. By the time Kim, the head teacher, helped David gather his things, it was almost three. We had just half an hour to get to Amy's office.

For just about a year and a half, David and I had been making the twice-a-week trek, up and down fairly steep, twisted, and turning, and often broken, sidewalks to Faltz's Associates, Speech and Language—*I try not to cringe*—Pathologists. I could have chosen to take him someplace closer and more accessible (Amy's brown-shingled office had steps) for language therapy, but I liked Piedmont Avenue with its boutiques and cafes. I always had something to do while David spent a laborious half an hour with a very conscientious taskmaster. More important, Amy was comfortable with my disability.

Amy Faltz first evaluated David when he was a little over two years old. I had called her several months after the nursery school fiasco. I only had a feeling that something might not be kosher, even though friends and neighbors, including David's very chatty and experienced new babysitter, Louise, tried to assure me that David was just a slow talker. He didn't seem to understand some of the things two-year-olds generally begin to understand—concepts of time, for example. "You can have ice cream after you eat your dinner," is a way most parents start teaching their toddler time sequences—cause and effect. David gave no sign of his desire to have ice cream unless he saw it right in front of him. Unlike children his age who start pestering their parents in the supermarket and toy stores with "I want that," David never peeped. "You're lucky," people would say when I mentioned my observation, but I couldn't help feeling that this behavior was inconsistent with the ebullience David otherwise displayed. And for a child who giggled and laughed during his play with others, he rarely acknowledged anyone's arrival or departure, including "Mommy" or "Daddy."

Amy concluded after the evaluation that David displayed good skills for language development, but he seemed to lag a few months behind other children his age. Rather than intervene with therapy immediately, Amy preferred to wait and see. She recommended monitoring his progress within the next three to five months.

Five months flew by so quickly. Amy and I spoke on the phone. David seemed to be speaking more, I told her. He still didn't chatter, but he never struck me as the chattering type. I was glad about that—kids who incessantly jabbered drove me nuts! We scheduled another phone check in September. It didn't take place; Amy went on a six-month sabbatical to be with the baby she and her husband had adopted. Besides, David seemed to be doing well.

I let myself be assured for the time being. Neil and I had practically breezed through David's second year, braced at any time for the "terrible twos." They never came. David had spent a contented nine months of his second year with Louise and two other tots in the mornings. I brought him home for his two-hour nap and then we usually went out somewhere shopping or to the park. He got along with other kids, sharing his toys or theirs, and gave up the things he played with upon request. However, he wasn't always aware of a request, especially at the playground where words could be muffled by other noises in the open air. Then trouble would occur when a child or mother attempted to wrench the toy from David which would incite him into his defiant, stubborn mode. I'd be only feet away, but couldn't get to them (in the sand) to intervene. I could only watch as it happened, and comfort David when it was all over.

That September, David started the Montessori preschool.

Gena Lawrence and Jan Gardener, the school's codirectors, unlike Jean Shetland, appreciated the differences of each child in their program. They found David's unassuming independence quite remarkable. At the first parent-teacher conference in November, they praised David's self-sufficiency and his hand-eye coordination; he liked to work in the kitchen, measuring and pouring different substances—water, sand, salt—from one container to another. It didn't surprise me; at home, he insisted on pouring his own medicine now (under my hawkish eye). They mentioned David's reserve in verbalizing, keeping to himself, and appearing to have a little trouble understanding the rules, but "some children take longer to adjust," they reassured.

David's third year proved much more of a challenge. The almost "tranquil twos" turned into the "traumatic threes" very shortly after David's third birthday. He became more daring and defiant. He climbed over furniture, misbehaved at meals, broke things he wasn't supposed to touch, but unlike his peers, he displayed little understanding of the consequences. He was still small enough for me to pick up (he didn't even run away) and put in a chair for time-out, like they did at school, but it was obvious that he didn't know it was a consequence or the reason for it.

"Mommy said eat dinner," I told him one evening.

"Bottle," David said, pointing to the kitchen.

We still hadn't weaned him. The bottle was convenient for all of us; it still got David into his carseat and quieted him down at night. (Kate assured me whenever we spoke on the phone that I had nothing to worry about: "I never saw a high school kid with a baby bottle.")

"David, eat dinner!" I repeated firmly.

"Bottle," he repeated.

"No," I shook my head.

My dinner was getting cold. Neil just sat there. It went on for ten minutes longer before David pushed his plate away, into my drink. My iced tea poured onto the table and dribbled to the floor.

"David, that was bad," I scolded. I went to his seat, pulled him onto my lap without any resistance from him, and took him over to the white chair in the living room. "That's a time-out."

He sat there docilely looking around for something interesting to watch. I went to him after a few minutes and tried to explain. "You made the iced tea spill. That's why you got time-out."

He responded with a blank stare. He didn't understand. I hugged him.

"Mom . . . bottle?" he asked after our embrace.

I looked into the blue eyes beseeching me. I nodded.

I felt a sense of failure. I didn't want him to grow into an unruly kid, and Neil just sat there as he usually did. He couldn't bear seeing David cry or be unhappy. He rarely disciplined David for anything, except when he scribbled on Neil's important papers, or when David would hit or bite—which he was doing more of at school.

I knew about hitting and biting: signs of frustrations when the words wouldn't come and the anger swelled inside. I knew it all too well as the only way, it seemed, to be heard. I called Amy.

This time, Amy evaluated David at his preschool using more for-malized tests, since he was older. This time the language delay appeared very evident. Amy put words to my observations when she interpreted the test results. The report described David's difficulty with "receptive" language. David could understand simple sen-tences: "What is this?" and "Get the ball." More abstract questions stymied him: "What do you do with a book?" or "How did you get to school today?"—though he could have readily answered if he had been asked whether he rode to school with Mommy or Daddy. David's struggle to "process" language explained why he often seemed to misinterpret his interactions with others—sometimes he'd respond with such belligerence to comments like "May I hold your cup for you while you're getting into your seat?" He wasn't able to recognize the politeness in someone's voice or the smile on a person's face to cue him in on the intent of the offer. In his "expressive" lan-guage skills, David appeared to be "one year below his age level." Although he pronounced words extremely well and his sentences were grammatically correct, David rarely spoke spontaneously or volunteered information the way other three-year-olds were apt to do. Very often, if you talked to David about apples, he'd bring up zebras.

Why? What caused it? Is this the slight "abnormality" that

showed up in the CAT scan during David's first few weeks of life?

Amy shrugged her shoulders in response to my questions. "I really can't tell you. How we explain it, in simple terms, is that there's something loose in the wiring."

She wanted to start David in language therapy immediately. That was well over a year ago, and he has shown steady improvement. He got along better in school; he even had a best friend, Nathan, or Nate the Great, as he liked to be called (after a boy detective in a children's book). At times, David's language delay was hardly noticeable and people would question the need for therapy. Neil and I both found it very complicated to explain. "It's good for the economy," Neil would offer his pat reply; I'd just wait until they asked David about apples and he responded with zebras. Then I'd nod, "That's why."

On level ground, David could ride on the back of my wheelchair. Still, he had a fondness for my lap, claiming that his hands got too sweaty to hold on to my wheelchair handles after awhile or his legs got too tired. It also felt safer to have him on my lap when we traveled over hilly terrain: I could see what he was doing instead of having to check behind me periodically to make sure he was still there. More than a few times I caught David out of the corner of my eye silently playing "Look, Ma, no hands," as I whizzed along a sidewalk.

I loved having David on my lap, too. The weight of his body grounded me—his nearness like a down comforter wrapped around my heart. The view of his golden hair upon his tan, strong yet fragile neck delighted me even at the end of a long day. And to my ears, "The Wheels on the Bus" was the most beautiful song in the world when David sang it in his soothing voice, soft as velvet as we rolled along. *This time of our lives wouldn't last for long.*

On the way to Amy's we stopped to admire some of the flowery front yards that graced the narrow residential side streets I chose for our path to Piedmont. David liked the one with the towering sunflowers.

"Mom." He pointed as we came upon them. "That one's dead!"

I saw the sunflower's drooping face, its center turning brown. "Aw, that's very sad, David."

I started explaining that the seeds of sunflowers can be dried and eaten, but he interrupted, "Why did it die?"

"Flowers only live a short time."

"When I grow up my flowers will live forever," he stated. "I have special power."

I looked at his profile, wondering how I should respond. I decided not to. I agreed with him.

We approached the last steep hill. I stopped to scoot farther back in my wheelchair before we descended. My lower back ached from the stress and strain of the long day.

"David," I said, my mouth close to his ear so he would hear me as we neared the traffic of Piedmont. "I know I told you that I'd come in and watch you work with Amy today, but how about if I do it next time?"

"No, Mommy," he turned his head to look at me and answered. "Come today."

I looked at the innocence of his round face, the smattering of freckles across his little nose and flushed cheeks, the coppery lashes that outlined his eyes. David never asked for much. How could I refuse?

Amy met me at the bottom of the eight narrow steps and took my right arm. We had the routine down; we did it every few weeks. Leaving my wheelchair parked below, we trudged up the stairs and through a tiny alcove to Amy's office. David, leading the way, carried my oversized wallet. Out of breath, sweat dripping down my back, and not a moment too soon, I plopped down in an armchair next to the lamp in the small, cozy office to watch my son struggle through his half-hour therapy session with Amy.

Until Amy, I had never heard of a diagnosis called "language delay." It had more to do with the internal process of speech, the way thoughts and messages are received and expressed, rather than the mechanics of breath control and sound. Of course, I was all too familiar with the latter. I struggled through speech therapy during eight years of grammar school, three times a week—four if another kid was absent. I had to sit in front of the large rectangular mirror making faces at myself during warm-up exercises. Fastidious Mrs. Bobrick, my therapist, had me take deep breaths and hold each vowel sound as long as I could—she timed me with a stopwatch. The next exercise was worse. She held a candied tongue depressor an inch or so from my lips and made me try to reach it with my uncooperative tongue—above, below, right side and left. Sometimes, she stuck peanut butter on the roof of my mouth and I had to push it off with the tip of my tongue; I cheated with my finger when she wasn't looking. I hated peanut butter!

But Mrs. Bobrick never let up. She drilled me on `l' sounds, and `s' sounds, and those horrible `th,' `ks,' and `sh' combinations, most of which I mastered while making contorted faces.

David and Amy sat on little plastic chairs at a white David-sized table just a few feet from me. Amy brought out the two-by-three-inch cards with pairs of objects on each.

"David, what's this?" Amy asked.

"A pail and shovel," David answered easily.

"Good, David." Then came the hard part. "Where would you use them?"

David put his elbows on the table and cupped his chin in his hands. Amy reminded him to sit up straight. He listened, placing his hands back on the table ledge. It was three-thirty in the afternoon. He was tired. I empathized.

After the paired cards, she took out sets of story-sequence cards involving different activities. ("Sequencing is a prerequisite for abstract thinking," Amy once explained.) David had to put the cards in the order of which activity would come first: getting dressed, waking up, going to school, or eating breakfast. There were five sets. Some he got quickly, some he didn't. Amy had to hint.

David had the most trouble with the last activity, the story cards. They were boring looking black-and-white photographs of children and adults doing various things. In one they were making a birthday cake. In another they were having a picnic.

"What kind of cake are they baking, David?" Amy asked.

David stared at the picture for a good thirty seconds before he answered. "They bought it at the store."

I felt the hard weight of a jagged stone slab upon my chest. *Why did he need to know about making a stupid cake anyhow? So what if he couldn't tell what was going on? He wasn't even interested.*

His eyes wandered around the room. He'd had a long day. Couldn't Amy see that?

Yet he wouldn't always be around people who would patiently play "twenty questions" with him to find out what he was talking about. Neil and I wouldn't always be there to interpret and explain for him, or prompt him. And Amy had only thirty minutes at a time. She took her work and our hard-earned money very seriously. It was just so difficult for me to watch David struggle, but I had to; I was his mother.

David perked up at the next picture Amy showed him. His

favorite—a drawing this time of a silly-looking witch on a broomstick in a room of a house. Everything was topsy-turvy. With a smile and more than a few giggles, David told Amy what ridiculous things the witch had done. "She put the sink upside down and the table on the wall."

"Good, David. What room is it?"

"Kitchen," he answered.

I felt better.

David helped Amy put the cards away and played with the miniature garage in the final minutes of the session. Even then she continued to keep him talking; children with language delays tend not to vocalize during play like their peers. At last, Amy brought out a tin box with stickers. David chose one. It was time to go.

Just a few more blocks was the foremost thought on my mind as I saw the corner of 51st Street and Broadway up ahead. My back ached badly now and David, sitting on my lap at this hour of the late afternoon, felt as heavy as the forty pounds he weighed. In fact, I didn't know how much longer I'd be able to make the twice-a-week trek, up and down those steep hills. I had a two-week reprieve; next week was the start of the High Holy Days, and Amy had a conference to go to the week after.

We passed the entrance to Grand Auto and neared the rounded corner of Broadway and 51st. It was not one of my favorite crossings. Traffic came from all directions. Lights and arrows changed at the blink of an eye. Cars breezed through the narrow right turnoff between the curb cut and the triangular island that I had to reach before crossing the wide thoroughfares of either Broadway or 51st.

David had stopped singing. He bent over the right armrest of my chair watching the wheels go round. The motion had fascinated him ever since he was a baby. He seemed to be leaning a little farther over than usual, and I thought about saying something, but the right turn lane was clearing. I saw our opportunity to make the first leg of that precarious crossing.

I started, only to be stopped—just as we made it to the edge of the island—by the piercing shrieks of my son. He sprang upright. I was ready to scold him for doing whatever it was he knew he shouldn't be doing while we were in the midst of crossing the street, until I saw the drops of blood dripping down on the sleeve of my pink jacket, my tan pants, and my chrome footrests. He held up the middle finger of his right hand. It was drenched with blood.

Instinctively my palm pressed forward on the joystick so we would be clear of traffic. My wheelchair squealed laboriously up the curb cut and then rested. I ignored the ominous squeal and examined David's finger to see if it was still all there, knowing that if it wasn't, I'd have to start looking for a little piece of finger, too. The wound was pretty deep but the fingertip was still there, joint and all.

"It's gonna be okay, David," I tried to soothe above his hysterical cry. His tongue quivered as tears rolled down his soft round cheeks. Our bodies may have been physically separate, yet his pain wrenched my heart. I swallowed my own tears. "You'll be fine. You'll be fine."

On the corner we had just come from, I spotted a young girl wearing the plaid uniform of St. Theresa's high school. She was on her way over.

"We can go back in there and wash it off," she suggested, nodding in the direction of Grand Auto.

My wheelchair inched back across the street, barely making it up the curb, but the girl didn't realize I was having trouble. "Here," she said, taking David by the hand, "I'll take him in."

The entrance was only ten feet away. I coaxed him to go with her and, very unlike him, he went without protest—his finger must have hurt very badly for him to have gone with a stranger, or perhaps he trusted my permission to go.

As I watched them disappear inside the glass doors, I suddenly questioned my decision: should I have let him go with that girl? That wasn't the only way into or out of that building—what if she took off with him out the side exit? Half of me panicked as I desperately rolled my disabled wheelchair toward the double doors. Half of me scolded back, *"Neisie, have a little faith!"*

There seemed to be very little forward power on the right side of my wheelchair. I had to back up the slight incline of the doorway. Once I got on the flat vinyl surface, I was able to turn and approach one of two bored looking women at the checkout counter.

"Where's the little boy?" I asked.

"Huh?"

I repeated. "Where's the little boy?"

"She wants to know where the little boy is," her coworker translated.

"Oh . . . They took him to the bathroom," she answered her peer.

"Where is it?" I demanded.

She turned back to me in a manner belying no awareness at all of my irritation. "Oh, follow me."

She disappeared between the aisle of car gizmos and white-walled tires. I creaked after her, having the first chance to glimpse down over the right side of the wheelchair. I was relieved when I saw what was wrong. The quarter-inch rubber drive belt had come off its track, which ran from the rear wheel around the pulley attached to the right motor in front. It would be a cinch to fix, especially at Grand Auto!

"I don't think she could get back into the bathroom," I heard somebody say as I neared a freestanding counter a few feet from the side door. "He'll be right out, anyway."

So, she didn't take off with him! I breathed with relief, already thinking about whether I should take David home, call the doctor, and find someone to drive us there; or I could whiz us straight down College Avenue to the office a little less than two miles away, in just about the same amount of time. First, however, I needed to have my drive belt realigned or we wouldn't be going anywhere.

There was a man standing behind the counter wearing a short-sleeved white shirt and dark blue tie. He looked as though he might be the manager, since all the other men passing by me were in dark gray mechanics' uniforms. I opened my mouth to speak as soon as he glanced down at me, but not a second later, he averted his eyes, looking helpfully into those of a standing customer who had just approached.

Gritting my teeth, I swallowed and waited for him to finish. When he did, he started to turn away—just as I had expected.

"Sir. Sir. *SIR*," I persisted louder and louder until, when others started looking, he could no longer ignore me. "I need some help with my wheelchair."

I pointed to the drive belt. He barely bent down to give it a look before calling over a man in overalls. Then he walked back behind the counter, leaving me to explain what needed to be done on my wheelchair to a very intimidated auto mechanic. (*So much for faith!*) In the midst of my struggle to explain, David came out of the bathroom. His howling grew louder as he approached. I heard voices talking to him, trying to console him.

"Your finger will be all right, son. "

"They'll be here soon. They'll make it all better."

"They" sounded ominous, but at that moment I was too involved to even ask who *they* were. David, his injured finger wrapped in a brown paper towel, stepped up on my footrests, straddled my left leg, and settled into my lap. Tears streamed down his cheeks. I wanted to comfort him, yet his cries were interrupting my attempt at directing the two auto mechanics now working on getting the quarter-inch drive belt back in place. It was so simple. I had watched it being done so many times before at the wheelchair repair shop. I had told friends how to do it when I had belt trouble at home. But now with David sobbing on my lap, a small crowd fussing over him, and baffled repairmen flanking my wheelchair, I couldn't remember whether the belt should be slipped around the back wheel or front pulley first.

If only David would be quiet, I could reason it out with them. I fought the urge to yell at him the way my parents—not having many other coping skills—would have yelled at me when I was in hysterics. I just wanted my wheelchair working again, so that we could get out of there . . . , before "they" came. Unfortunately, both happened at the same time.

The same woman clerk led the two paramedics to us. The blond-haired one squatted down in front of David. The bearded dark-haired one with glasses stood beside him, hands on hips.

"She his mother?" the bearded one asked.

Who the hell else would I be?

Someone answered yes.

"What's his name?" the one who squatted asked.

"David," I replied, as I glimpsed quickly at his name tag, catching only his first name—Kevin—since David's head obstructed my view of his last.

"David, can I see your finger?"

"No!" David howled through tears.

"David, honey, you need to show him your finger," I coaxed in a deliberately calm voice.

"It hurts to touch," David sniffed.

"I know," I said, "but right now, he just wants to look at it."

David looked at me with swollen, watery eyes, then put out his wrapped finger. The paramedic unwrapped it with slow gentleness.

"Looks pretty bad," he said, looking up his partner. "I want to clean it off to get a better look."

"No!" my son screamed, jerking away his finger.

"David, he needs to clean it to get off all the bad germs," I explained with words I thought David would relate to.

With sniffles, he slowly held his injured hand up again. The paramedic cleansed the finger gently with disinfectant-soaked gauze. David watched and winced.

"David, how old are you?" Kevin asked as he did his task.

David glanced at me for assurance, then answered, "Four . . ."

"And?" I prompted softly in his ear.

"And a half," he finished.

"Do you go to nursery school, David?"

"No."

"How about day care?"

"No."

David, as usual, wasn't volunteering any information. I whispered a cue in his ear: "Pre . . ."

He turned to me for an instant before facing the paramedic again. "I go to preschool."

"Preschool, huh?" The paramedic's eyes glanced up at David's face, then back at his finger. "What's the name of your school?"

David eyed me for another cue. . . . "My—"

"My Own Montessori."

The conversation halted when, after carefully examining the finger, Kevin raised his eyes to his partner. "Here, take a look."

"Geez, looks like the tip of it is gone."

Could I have been wrong? I peeked over David's shoulder; the finger still looked the same to me.

David start crying again.

"Where did it get caught?" the bearded one asked.

"Near the pulley," I answered, trying to make myself heard above David's squalls.

He knelt down to look. He stroked his bearded chin; I could see he had no clue as to what he was looking at. I couldn't explain it myself. It was only later, when things calmed down, that I made the connection between the displaced drive belt and David's injury— piecing together how his finger got pinched between the moving drive belt and the metal pulley of the motor and how, in David's effort to get it loose, he pulled the belt off the track.

"He'll probably need stitches," the bearded one said as he stood up.

But there was no skin there to stitch!

"Let's get him to the hospital."

"No," I protested immediately. "I'll take him to his doctor."

"We can't let you do that."

"Why not?"

"He needs immediate attention."

"I'll get there in ten minutes," I lied.

The two paramedics gave each other wary glances, indicating they had no intention of letting us go anywhere. The blond one spoke. "We need to fill out some paperwork. Why don't I go get it and David could come out to get his finger bandaged?"

Instinctively, my arm tightened around David's waist, although he made no move to get up. In fact, he scooted farther back into my lap.

"We'll go with you." I started to move.

"No, you stay here." His placating tone sounded very suspicious.

I didn't listen. They wanted to take my child away from me. My years of experience as a helpless child with intimidated parents in the medical world had clued me in. I wasn't naive. We were *all* going out-side!

When their tactic of trying to separate us didn't work, the para-medics pressured me again as they towered over me in the corner parking lot. "We need to take him to the hospital."

"And what about me?" I questioned defiantly. "How will I get there?"

A look at me and then at each other told me they hadn't thought about that. The bearded one suggested, "We could call a paddy wagon for her."

"For her" I assumed meant they would still take David in the ambulance. I couldn't let that happen. "No!"

If David had been profusely bleeding, his arm dangling with an obvious break, or had he been unconscious, I would have immediate-ly sent him off with them. But my son had squarely planted himself on my lap; even his tears had ebbed. I had no idea what he made of all this chaos, but I knew that if I let them take him now, David's trust in me would begin to waver. I remembered so long ago, myself as a three-year-old, crying so hysterically while my mother—coaxed by hospital staff—walked down the dim corridor and disappeared. She came back for visiting day two days later and to take me home on weekends during my three-week hospital stay, but the seed of mis-trust had already been sown—a seed that has haunted me all my life.

A small crowd had followed us outside. The two paramedics had turned slightly from me to have a téte-a-téte. They spoke in low voices, but as a practiced eavesdropper my whole life long, I adeptly filtered out the noisy traffic and the murmurs of onlookers to catch their words. "We'll have to call the police," the blond said to the nodding beard.

Like a bad dream, this was getting more and more out of control. Nobody stopped to think. I knew my credibility was nonexistent. I had to get them to call somebody, somebody who could get them to see me as something other than a raving cripple. But who? I ran down a list in my head: Neil, in this case, was not a likely choice. I wasn't sure whether Janet would be in her office or out selling real estate. Amy had another client immediately after David—her answering machine would be on. Kim, the only late afternoon teacher at David's preschool, had six kids to take care of.

"Look, call my doctor," I desperately implored, getting them to at least look at me again. "Please, don't call the police. . . . Call my doctor."

The repairman, who had fixed my drive belt, knelt on the other side of me. When I turned my head, his face seemed less than three inches from mine. He spoke in a tone as if he were admonishing a child. "You don't understand, he needs to go to the hospital."

"No, you don't understand!" I answered back in a voice from deep inside me, articulated with strength and clarity I never knew I had. "He's not going anywhere without me!"

Surprisingly, the man, as well as the rest of the small group that had gathered around us, seemed to retreat somewhat from the force of my words.

I strained my head, searching the crowd for sympathetic eyes. The paramedics stood over me. They still weren't listening. They made some effort to coax David out of my lap. He remained amazingly steadfast. *Did he comprehend some of what was going on or did his instinct warn him?* Whatever it was, his resistance assured me he wasn't about to let himself be removed from my arms.

I made eye contact with the girl in the uniform again, who was looking somewhat forlorn at the trouble I was having, and, for the second time, she came to my rescue. Borrowing a small pad from the repairman and a pen from the bearded paramedic who was busily informing his partner (above my head) that he had just radioed the police, she wrote down the number I gave her and our last name.

Then she disappeared. I prayed she would get the call through before the police arrived (having a vision of my arrest). I also prayed that Ellie or Judy, who answered the phones at the doctor's office, would still be there (I was losing track of time).

A few minutes later, the girl reappeared into the small muddled crowd and announced, "The doctor would like to speak to one of the paramedics!"

Suddenly, a hush settled over the crowd, as if everyone had been slapped into sense. The bearded paramedic went to take the phone call. The crowd dispersed, leaving the other paramedic to squat down to my eye level and finally speak to me as a human being. I wondered if they had been so amazed that I had the intelligence to remember a phone number that it shocked them into attention.

"We'll do whatever the doctor says," the paramedic now assured. "If he wants us to take you to his office, we'll do it—even though we're really not supposed to. Although he may want you to go to the hospital."

"That's fine," I said, relieved that I had finally broken through his preconception of me. "We'll go wherever he thinks we should go. Right, David?"

David turned to me first and then nodded to the paramedic. He had calmed down soon after everyone left. Even his dry sobs began to ebb. I kissed his round, damp, tear-stained cheek.

I was almost certain that we would end up being sent to the hospital if the other paramedic had described David's finger as he saw it. I intended to pursue an agreeable course of action. "How will we get there?"

His answer surprised me. He had actually thought it out. "We could lift David and you onto the stretcher and put your chair up front next to the driver's seat."

I felt an obligation to warn him that my wheelchair weighed three hundred pounds without me. That wasn't a problem, he assured me. *What a difference a minute could make!*

Indeed, the bearded paramedic returned with the news I had expected. He spoke to me. "The doctor said you probably should go to the hospital because David will most likely need stitches and X rays."

"Okay," I nodded, giving David a reassuring squeeze. "We're ready whenever you are."

First the bearded paramedic had to explain to the policeman who just arrived in his squad car that his services weren't required.

With one paramedic on my right and the other on my left, they lifted us on to the stretcher and wheeled us to the back of the red and white ambulance.

"Wow, David, this is your first ride in an ambulance," I said as they were loading us on.

"And hopefully your last!" the blond paramedic added, echoing my unspoken sentiment.

Our eyes caught one another's. We smiled to acknowledge our similar thinking. I never would have suspected that, propped up on a stretcher in an ambulance with my four-and-a-half-year-old son resting contently on top of me, I could feel so very much in control.

I provided Kevin, the blond paramedic who rode with us in the back of the ambulance, with all the necessary information so that his company could bill us its standard fee of $300 for a ten-block ride that I never requested. We were all so calm now. I spoke so clearly; he understood me so well. David's head gently rolled from side to side against my chest as the ambulance proceeded on its way.

"Do you have any more children?" he asked after he finished filling out the form.

I chuckled to myself. First people think it's unlikely for me to have even one. Then they think I'm crazy enough to have more. "No," I answered. "One's quite enough!"

"It must be hard," he commented, looking at me with his blue eyes full of sympathy.

I've heard that observation so many times and have not really known how to respond. The comment, I've always felt, reflects the assumptions of a person's own shortcomings. How could someone like me meet the demands of an active child? How could a child not take advantage of such obvious physical limitations of his parents? People seem to get so caught up in what they can see that they ignore that which is invisible to them, the most important part of raising a child—the relationship between him and his parents. Suddenly, I knew how to answer that question.

I looked straight into his eyes and said, "The hardest thing is having other people assume that I'm not capable of being a parent."

The sympathy in his face disappeared. "I'm sorry for what happened back there. Very sorry."

As if to make up for it even more, when we arrived at Children's Hospital, Kevin announced my maternal ability to every staff member we passed on our way to an emergency cubicle where David and I spent the greater portion of the next three hours.

By the time I had gotten back into my wheelchair, David, sitting beside me on an orange chair (which matched the trim on the walls and door) and swinging his legs back and forth while he held his bandaged finger up in the air, caught his second wind. He obligingly answered the head nurse when she asked him his full name.

"I have two," he told her.

She rolled her eyes: *Oh, great, a crippled mother and an out-to-lunch kid!* "Oh yeah?"

"Yeah. One is David Jacobson and the other is Dave the Great."

She couldn't help laughing. Subsequently, every time she passed by our room with a different staff member, she'd poke her head in and ask David to repeat his two names. He delightedly complied.

With help from a volunteer, I used an out-of-reach wall phone to call my neighbor, Deborah, who lived down the street from us. It was a little after five and I doubted whether my lackadaisical housekeeper, Brenda (*"but she's been with us for two years,"* Neil staunchly defended), had yet arrived at my house. I gave my neighbor Neil's work and beeper number so she could try to reach him and asked her to send one of her three kids down to my house in a little while to tell Brenda to answer the phone when it rang.

David and I were soon sent up to X ray. The pictures showed no broken bones. Afterward, we went back to the cubicle and waited for treatment. A few staff trickled in and out, a couple of doctors and nurse's aides. They looked at David's raw finger. He'd scream if he thought anyone was going to touch it.

A resident ordered it to be soaked in an antiseptic solution in a shallow metal dish. David refused. Indifferent, and even hostile, to my little boy's fear of the pain, the doctor threatened to have David held down. David, of course, screamed even more. *Where'd they get him?* I wondered at this man devoid of all compassion. Luckily, one of the aides, a Dave the Great fan, appeared with a deeper dish for David to soak his finger in.

Another resident wrapped the finger in a medicinally treated strip and then a gauze bandage. She gave David an injection and wrote a prescription for an antibiotic that I had time to get filled the next day.

"It comes in capsules," she said as she handed me the paper.

"Capsules?" I echoed, raising my eyebrows.

She nodded back innocently. "Yes, just open it up and pour it into a glass of juice."

I wasn't about to spend the next ten days futzing with capsules, but I took the prescription without another word—I was too tired. I had no intention of filling it. I would get a liquid or chewable antibiotic tomorrow when I took David to Dr. Berberich. I wanted my own doctor to check the finger. I also wanted to gloat: *Not one stitch.*

It was almost seven o'clock when we left. The nurse wanted to call a van service but I assured her we would be okay. I could travel the ten blocks in less than fifteen minutes and it was still daylight. Besides, she would never have gotten a van to come on such short notice—they booked rides days in advance—and even if she did, I'd probably have a good long wait before they picked us up. If I had wanted to wait, I could have waited for Neil, whom I expected to be arriving at our house at any moment.

David and I rolled down two blocks on 51st street and crossed over onto a concrete island to avoid a broken sidewalk. The sun had just set, leaving a graying sky and shimmering streetlights. I saw our blue van driving toward the hospital, but we were out of Neil's sight.

"There goes Daddy," I told David, almost with a chuckle. "He missed all the fun!"

Epilogue
The Three of Us

November, 1992

It isn't often, I suppose, that a dream becomes a reality. And to a world that views disability, at the very least, as an unfortunate circumstance, Neil and I seem the two most unlikely people to have our dreams come true. Certainly, we would both say that this one in particular came true beyond our wildest imagination, for David is a child with a spirit that we would have never dreamed existed.

Neil adores David and, after almost six years, I'm still very much in love with him. Our love for him, however, is not shortsighted. Like a child in any family, at times, he tries our patience, exasperates us, and makes us angry.

David's love for us is under no illusion, either. He'll tell you his parents are in wheelchairs and "their hands aren't steady." He'll ask me why I sometimes drool and say he doesn't like it. "Neither do I," I'll agree. "Then, Mommy," he'll say, "just remind me and I'll give you a tissue."

If only we could all see life out of David's remarkable blue eyes—those eyes that first held mine with a steady gaze that pierced my heart and sewed our lives together with everlasting thread. The thread has been woven into a thick and strong yarn, as steadfast as the root of a hundred-year-old oak tree, our bond as deep.

The three of us have risks and struggles, more tears and more laughter, to face in the years ahead. Other questions will come up for all of us as we weather the willful breezes of childhood, the tornadoes of adolescence, and the undercurrents of young adulthood. But for me, the most important question had been asked and answered the very first instant David's eyes met mine, the moment when I knew that David belonged with us, and Neil and I belonged with David. No matter how calm or stormy our years ahead, the three of us will journey through them together.

213

Denise Sherer Jacobson's goal as a writer is to weave her uncommon experience with common ones, inviting readers to share and celebrate the parts of themselves that are like her, and to respect, understand, and honor the parts of her that are different. Whether she writes of growing up in the 50s and 60s, of Judaism, having cerebral palsy, or motherhood, Sherer Jacobson helps people to shed their prejudices and create a clear, easy path towards insight, compassion and community.

Ms. Sherer Jacobson's work has appeared in the anthologies *Prejudice : Stories About Hate, Ignorance, Revelation, and Transformation* and *The Adoption Reader: Birth Mothers, Adoptive Mothers, and Adoptive Daughters Tell Their Stories* as well as numerous newspapers and literary magazines. She was born and raised in the Bronx and makes her home in the San Francisco Bay Area with her husband, Neil, their son, David, and their sixteen-year-old kitten, Aries.